COMMANDO
TO
CAPTAIN-GENERALL

To Paul,
With very best wishes,

COMMANDO

TO

CAPTAIN-GENERALL

The Life of Brigadier Peter Young

by

Alison Michelli

Aul Michelli (Capt)

Pen & Sword
MILITARY

First published in Great Britain in 2007 by
Pen & Sword Military
an imprint of
Pen & Sword Books Ltd
47 Church Street
Barnsley
South Yorkshire
S70 2AS

ISBN 978184415651 1

A CIP catalogue record for this book is
available from the British Library

Typeset in Sabon by
Phoenix Typesetting, Auldgirth, Dumfriesshire

Printed and bound in England by
CPI UK

Pen & Sword Books Ltd incorporates the Imprints of Pen & Sword
Aviation, Pen & Sword Maritime, Pen & Sword Military, Wharncliffe
Local History, Pen & Sword Select, Pen & Sword Military Classics and
Leo Cooper.

For a complete list of Pen & Sword titles please contact
PEN & SWORD BOOKS LIMITED
47 Church Street, Barnsley, South Yorkshire, S70 2AS, England
E-mail: enquiries@pen-and-sword.co.uk
Website: www.pen-and-sword.co.uk

For Neil who may never know how important
his being there really is.

Contents

Preface

For King or for the Commonwealth –
No matter which they say,
The first dry rattle of new-drawn steel
Changes the world today!
                    Rudyard Kipling, *Edgehill Fight*

As a child Peter had met Rudyard Kipling: 'one,' he wrote, 'who really understood Old England'. What would Peter, that un-reconstructed Royalist – or indeed Kipling – make of the re-enactment scene today?

There is no doubt that, albeit unwittingly, the huge numbers of people who are now involved in re-enactment owe their hobby to a few over enthusiastic war gamers who met at the Mitre Hotel nearly 40 years ago and founded the Sealed Knot. There is, equally, no doubt that what those early pioneers intended was very far from what actually transpired. Never has the expression 'go with the flow' been so appropriate (although at times Peter might rather have felt that he was 'rolling with the punches'). In some ways Peter's private army created itself, for it very quickly took on its own impetus and rolled inexorably forward. A lesser man might have attempted to wrest control back again; Peter's genius was to let it go and see what happened.

Some years ago I was taking part in that spectacular pageant known as 'History in Action', run at that time by English Heritage at Kirby Hall. At the end of the final day, all the participants – over 2,000 of them – lined up and paraded in front of a delighted crowd who cheered each contingent as it marched across the field. Once out of sight of the public, an extraordinary thing took place. As each unit reached the end of the parade line, it began to form a path through which the succeeding formations passed before itself becoming part of the line. As the weary performers entered this path they were applauded by those already there, and at the end, when all 2,000 or so men and women had walked this path of praise, those who had begun the line themselves led the march off through the lines and received, in their turn, the approbation of their peers.

I was profoundly moved. For it struck me as I walked across the parade ground that without Peter Young this would not be happening. Intentionally or not, he had created the appetite for re-enactment societies and this was surely its apotheosis. What, I wondered, would he have thought if he could have seen this? I remember rather hoping that he was looking down at us and enjoying the spectacle, a historical time line that began with the Romans and ended with some Cold War East German border guards, closely preceded by some Second World War Dutch bicycle troops. Every person in that parade felt so drawn to some particular period of history that they were prepared to go to considerable trouble and expense to kit themselves out in the costume of the period and to give up large amounts of spare time in order to convey to a fascinated public the minutiae of daily life in those bygone days.

This is not what Peter had in mind when he created the Sealed Knot. This is something even more powerful than the 'private army' he had, tongue-in-cheek, envisaged. He once said to me that if he had known what he was going to create, he rather thought he might have thought twice about going ahead with it. 'The tail,' he told me, 'is wagging the dog with a vengeance!'

Certainly, the Sealed Knot grew quickly into something far bigger than he had planned, which indicates that he had tapped into some deeply felt need in large numbers of people. Having allowed the organisation to pick up its own momentum to see where it would go he could scarcely have imagined that, thirty-five years after its founding, it would be only one of very many historical re-enactment societies.

Curiously, this remains his most visible legacy to us, but it is not the only one, I fancy, that he would want us to remember him by. What is most extraordinary about Peter is that he is greater than the sum of his parts: the soldier with superb tactical acumen and the gift of supreme leadership qualities demonstrated time and again, not only during the Second World War but in a very different theatre and at a very different time in Jordan; the academic who constructed his own department of War Studies at Sandhurst which outlived him and continues to provide a steady stream of first-rate military historians; the war gamer who decided that the sand table was too small and who wanted to see for himself what musket drill looked like. All these facets of his character, each one a lifetime's achievement in itself, go to make up a man whose life is so hard to encompass. In the end, like his great hero Prince Rupert, he found he needed a field larger than a piece of paper, and a sword instead of a pen. There is only one word which comes close to explaining the effect of his personality on everyone he met: charisma. Like the grin of the Cheshire Cat, it is what is left when the body has faded away.

There was a great deal more to Peter Young – soldier, historian, writer and bon viveur – than is clear from this final, almost accidental, offering to the cultural life of the nation. I hope that this will become evident in the ensuing chapters.

Acknowledgements

Of all the stories I have started, finished or dreamed about writing, Peter Young's life loomed largest. It has been the most marvellous adventure, made all the more exciting by the many people who have walked with me down the sometimes twisting road of his life, and who have helped immeasurably with information, wisdom and insights.

In no particular order I must mention specially:

The late Marilyn Caron Delion, Peter's step-daughter, was unfailingly helpful, kind and patient, and wonderfully generous with her time, recollections and material.

Olive Christopher, widow of Peter's wartime batman, Sergeant Bob Christopher, has been equally supportive; she allowed me access to her late husband's unpublished memoir which included many insights into Commando life. In addition, her anecdotes and huge treasure trove of photographs have been an inspiration and I am greatly indebted to her.

Peter's wartime colleagues were a delight and a ready source of stories; I am indebted to them all: John de Lash, 'Ossie' Osborne, Ted Piggott, Keith Ponsford, the late Douglas Johnston, and members of the Southwark Commando Association who welcomed me at their meetings; Stan 'Scotty' Scott, Fred Walker, Bill Britnell, Roy Cadman, John White, Doug Roderick and Harry Winch among others.

Peter's academic colleagues were no less helpful; thanks are due to Dr John Adair, Dr Christopher Duffy, Professor Richard Holmes, Sir John Keegan, Professor Ian Roy and the late Dr David Chandler.

With regard to the birth of the Sealed Knot I am very grateful to the late Dr Alastair Bantock and Stephen Beck, to Andy Gillitt, Peter Bloomfield and Ralph Willatt for all their insights into the beginnings of 'The Knot'.

Others have very kindly racked their brains on my behalf, amongst whom I must acknowledge Joseph Devines jr, author of a study of the battle of Vaagso, John Robson and Charles Stacey.

There is a huge amount of unpublished material in the Peter Young archive at the National Army Museum. I am extremely grateful to the staff at the Templer Study Centre for all their help during my researches in this treasure trove; their help made my task considerably easier.

I am indebted to Richard Pantall, at one time Peter's Orderly Room Clerk, who typed up Peter's own fascinating – and unpublished – account of 3 Commando's Mediterranean campaign in 1943. He passed this invaluable volume to David Chandler who, in turn, passed it to me.

I have received great editorial support, and owe a debt of thanks to Henry Wilson and Bobby Gainher who have steered me through the pitfalls of the publishing world so that the end result is, I hope, a testimony to their help; as ever, any errors in the final work will be mine!

My friends and family have been superb and I hope they will think that the end result is worth the trips to London and the anguished cries of guilt when the word rate dropped off. John Stallard and Chris Brewer have been a help and support throughout; without John's encouragement I might never have started at all so I am truly grateful for his faith in my ability to get the words down! Finally, of course, my love and thanks to Neil and Matthew (not forgetting the dogs); without them none of it would be worth the candle.

Publisher's Note – The Spelling of 'Captain Generall'

When the Sealed Knot was formed, it was decided to adopt the style and spelling of earlier ranks and appointments dating back to the Civil War. Peter Young, as the first Commander-in-Chief, thus became Captain Generall, roughly equivalent to a modern Army Commander. Despite the obvious risk of being accused of inaccurate proofreading, the Publishers have agreed to retain the archaic spelling.

Introduction

It is October. In a field beside the road which runs between Radway
and Kineton a group of uniformed people are gathered for a drum-
head service. This is the commemoration of the battle of Edgehill,
fought on 23 (Old Style) October 1643, the first major encounter
between the forces of King and Parliament in the English Civil War.
Standing a little apart is a portly figure clad in 'civilian' clothes,
sporting lace collar, wide-brimmed hat and bucket boots. He is white-
haired and genial. Those who approach him do so with deference and
he welcomes them heartily. Then begins the service and, in the full-
ness of time, the genial figure steps forward to give the address. Behind
gold-rimmed spectacles which glint in the autumn sunshine his eyes
are steely grey. They are eyes which have reviewed a thousand troops,
weighed a thousand men in the balance of wit and courage, eyes which
rarely miss anything. When he speaks his voice is melodious and
carrying, his delivery confident. He is at ease in his environment. The
Sealed Knot is performing its annual homage to the fallen in the
battle. And the speaker is Peter Young.

He was known by a variety of names: Bungy, Brig, PY, Captain
Generall – even Sir, on occasion. Those closest to him always called
him Bear. Retired soldier with a distinguished military career behind
him, few of those with whom he came into contact in his later years
had any idea of his extraordinary rise from Second Lieutenant to
Brigadier in the six years of the Second World War. Or, indeed, that
out of 4 million combatants he was the most decorated soldier of the
war, one of only twenty-three men to be awarded three Military
Crosses in addition to his Distinguished Service Order. Most were
aware of his academic achievements, and those who asked for help
with their own researches received unstinting and generous support.

1

Peter Young was the soldier scholar who unwittingly discovered that a truly astonishing number of otherwise normal people enjoy spending their weekends dressed in historical costume, re-enacting battles and camping in muddy fields. Nobody, it is fair to say, was more surprised than he was. The Sealed Knot was the original re-enactment society. The dozens of re-enactment societies of every historical period which now entertain us all over the country are the unexpected result of a publicity stunt concocted to publicise Peter's book *Edgehill 1642: the Campaign and Battle*, published in 1967.

He remained, however, first and foremost, a soldier. This is perfectly illustrated by the sermon which he gave on Remembrance Sunday 1977, a copy of which is in his papers in the National Army Museum. It is worth reproducing here because so much of it underscores his own values and beliefs. The object of this book is to try and provide the background and fill in the detail of the man himself.

He took as his text St Matthew, Chapter 8, Verse 9: 'I am a man under authority, having soldiers under me: and I say to this man, Go, at he goeth; and to another, Come, and he cometh; and to my servant, Do this, and he doeth it.'

And this is what he had to say:

This is Remembrance Sunday. You might think, because it falls in November, with its fogs, and its chill and its leafless trees that it is a Sunday for Mourning. But to Remember the Dead is not necessarily to mourn, far less pity them. When I was young this Sunday, or rather the eleventh of November, used to be called Armistice Day. Because at 1100 hours on the eleventh day of the eleventh month of 1918, the Armistice began, which put an end to four years of fighting on the Western Front in France and Flanders. It was in 1919 that for the first time the Nation as a whole began to remember the fallen with a two minutes' silence at 11 o'clock, which was taken very seriously. In my young days, woe betide anyone who so much as flickered an eyelid during that sacred pause. Times have changed since those days. We are in my view a far more frivolous lot than we were fifty or sixty years ago in the days when cinema was in its infancy, the wireless was listened to through earphones, TV was fifteen years in the future, and the fields were ploughed by Shire horses. In those days people were educated, by and large, by the written word and – you may be surprised to hear – the standard of literacy of

2

education in this country was rather higher than it is today. An unlettered soldier was the exception in 1940. In 1947 it was a shock to find that as many as 1per cent of the men in an infantry brigade could not write.

Well, from 1919 to 1977, then, we have made a practice of honouring the dead – the British dead (or do we sometimes think of our Allies too? – and even our enemies) – who fell in the two great wars of this century. We do not, generally speaking, spare a thought for those who fell in earlier wars, for the men of Ladysmith, or Omdurman or Tel-el-Kebir. Far less for those who fell not half a mile from this church in the Civil Wars, or those of Crecy and Agincourt who, like Chaucer's Knight 'fought in Flanders and Artois and Picardie' – he knew his Western Front – who tried (rather a good idea I've always thought) to take over France in the days of Edward III and Henry V. Of course, it was very naughty of us. I mean that's exactly what we had against Hitler and the Kaiser, they were trying to do a bit of what you might call empire building at the expense of Russia, France and poor little Belgium.

One good thing we can say about those of our kith and kin who fought in World War I and World War II: they had no ulterior motive. These were not offensive wars. We fought to defend weaker nations against unscrupulous aggression. This made it easier. In what way? Well, in CONSCIENCE. Thou shalt not kill we were told almost in our cradles. When I write sermons – not very often and this is probably my last – I find it useful to have *The Concise Oxford Dictionary of Quotations* by me. I looked it up and this is what I found, not under 'Old Testament' but under 'Arthur Hugh Clough – 1819-1861'. 'Thou shalt not kill, but needs't not strive officiously to keep alive.' I suppose that might be just about the British serviceman's attitude to the painful duties and decisions that come his way on active service. No doubt St Matthew's centurion had the same idea.

I add to my dictionary any nice quotes that come my way. Here's one about the Spanish Armada – and what could our ancestors, however pious they might have been feeling, have done save beat that off? Here's what the Mayor of Queensborough – wherever that may be – said to Queen Elizabeth I when the crisis was safely over and half the galleons safely sunk: 'When the Spaniards meddled with Your Majesty they took the wrong sow by the ear.' It was a pretty compliment, and somehow it summed up the British soldier's attitude to war. You don't seek it but if it comes you do your stuff – your Duty. The French take it more flamboyantly.

Long ago, 25th July 1799 to be exact, there was a rough fight at Aboukir between young General Bonaparte and the Turks. Colonel Fugieres, an old soldier, led his regiment with true gallic panache but he got shot through the arm, banged on the head, and then had the wounded arm carried off by a cannon ball. Not unnaturally he thought he was dying. As Bonaparte bent over him he said, 'My General. Perhaps one day you will envy me my fate. I die on the field of honour.' In fact he lived for another fourteen years – they were tough in those days. But it doesn't alter the fact that he had the right idea. Why mourn a man who falls doing his Duty? The centurion, old heathen though he was, would not have sought pity if he had fallen for his war god.

Remember the fallen: Yes.

Grieve for them: No.

Mourn them: No.

Don't forget those who are still dying daily in Ulster.

And don't forget the Allies, far less the enemies – 'as we forgive them that trespass against us'. As Clarendon, the great Royalist historian of the Civil Wars, wrote: 'I am careful to do justice to every man who has fallen in this quarrel, on which side so ever'.

I will quote one more saying. It is from Sir Arthur Bryant, one of the great British historians of our time. 'The key to a nation's future is in her past. A nation that loses it has no future'.

A congregation of this sort is composed in the nature of things of people who have served in the past, and no longer have the physical power to do very much in any present or future crisis, and of young people who will not perhaps reach the height of their powers for ten or twenty or thirty years. To those who have served in times past, however well, however inadequately – for not all soldiers do well – it will be sufficient if the Remembrance of their service, and I suppose I may as well say sacrifice, should serve, not exactly as inspiration, but as a sort of hint to do as well, or better, when your crisis comes, as come it surely will.

For Duty is the surest foundation of religion. The centurion knew that.

This then is the day when we remember those, with pride

rather than grief, friends, relations, comrades among them, but millions unknown, who died doing their Duty.

He was sixty-two years old when he spoke those words to the congregation of St Mary the Virgin, Ripple, words which carry so much of his own experience and philosophy of life, as soldier and historian. The wit is there, but so is the message. It is uncompromising and, surprisingly, founded in his Christian faith. Like many who have been bellicose in their youth, Peter had a strong belief instilled in him during childhood and which stayed with him all his life. It underpinned his life's work and informed his actions. Ultimately, it was his Maker he wished to face with a clear conscience.

Chapter One

Beginnings

In the summer of 1915 the war to end all wars was about to enter its second year. The Gallipoli campaign was unfolding in the Dardanelles. On the Western Front there was a lull following the Battle of Vimy Ridge. In London it was beginning to be realized that the coming war would be longer than any of the over-confident predictions of the previous year – it wouldn't be over by that Christmas, and probably not the next one either.

In the previous summer, with the coming war looming, Dallas Hales Wilkie Young, aged thirty-five, had married Irene Barbara Lushington Mellor in Kensington, where they were to set up home. Barbara – as she was known – was, at twenty-five, somewhat younger than her husband who was Clerk at the Admiralty Supreme Court of Judicators. The arrival in Fulham of the Youngs' first-born on 28 July 1915 was cause for joy in the midst of crisis. The child, a boy, was named Peter.

The daughter of a clergyman, William James Mellor, and his second wife, Leila Annie Lushington, Barbara had spent much of her early life at Rodmersham in Surrey, where her father was vicar at St Nicholas' Church. Here, he restored the church and built the vicarage, indicating that he enjoyed an income which enabled him to carry out improvements to his living. The entire church bears witness to his relatives: the lych-gate was erected in memory of Barbara's grandmother, Anne Wildman Lushington (née Bushe), and the side chapel altar in memory of her uncle. This display of late Victorian patrician pride was certainly communicated to young Barbara. Her son was later to say, 'My mother often used to tell me that her family was much better than my father's.'

Certainly her great-great-great-grandfather, George Harris, an officer in the 5th of Foot, became Lord Harris of Seringapatam after a distinguished military career which saw service in America – he had bought a captaincy and commanded the Grenadier Company which fought at Bunker Hill – the West Indies, Ireland and India. Wellington wrote of him: 'It is a fact not sufficiently known that General Harris himself conducted the details of the victorious army which he commanded in Mysore.'

Dallas, born in Thanet, had been raised for his first six years at 239 Brompton Road, known as Hyndford House after Lord Hyndford who had caused the property to be built. Thereafter the family moved to Church Street, Chelsea. His father, Sidney, had married his first cousin once removed, Caroline Hales Wilkie. The Youngs had shipping interests in the form of Curling Young and Company, Shipbuilders of Limehouse, a firm which had acquired the name on the marriage of Sidney's grandfather, William, to Ann Spencer Curling. William, a Vice Admiral who had also seen service in the American War of Independence as a Lieutenant RN, had become Inspecting Agent for transport on the River Thames, as a result of which he met his future wife. The family was descended, it was believed, from one Sir John Young Bt. of Leny, Perthshire who, as Chamberlain to Mary Queen of Scots, conducted the young Queen from France to Scotland in 1561.

The Hales and the Wilkies, whose names Dallas was given, were maternal antecedents. The male line of the Wilkie family died out when none of Caroline Hales Wilkie's brothers produced heirs. Dallas had two older brothers, William Hales Wilkie Young and Horace Edward Wilkie Young. William had no issue, although in 1924 he married Amy Hathorn, and Horace had one son, Peregrine, killed at the Battle of El Alamein without issue. When Peter, too, died without issue, the male line of this branch of the family came to an end.

It is on both sides a distinguished pedigree and one to which Peter devoted some research. Though not aristocratic, it has its share of upright characters who made their mark on the times in which they lived and helped to create the social and economic environment into which Peter was born in 1915, and which was to be so radically altered in his lifetime – upheavals in which he, in his turn, would play his part.

In 1919, Barbara had another baby, this time a girl whom they called Pamela. Although she was four years younger than her brother, they were to be close throughout Peter's life.

At some time after the end of the war, the Youngs moved out of town to Deards Elm, Knebworth, Hertfordshire. In 1924 Dallas's oldest brother, Will, became engaged to Amy Helen Hathorn whose father, Kenneth, was Judge of the Supreme Court of South Natal (Natal Provincial Division) in South Africa. Will, who was commissioned into the Leicestershire (late 17th) Regiment of Foot, the Tigers, served in South Africa throughout his career, retiring eventually in Rosetta, Natal. Shortly after their engagement, Amy and her father made a visit to England and extracts from her letters to her fiancé in South Africa give a glimpse of what life was like for Dallas, Barbara, Peter and Pamela at that time:

Dallas rang up the next morning [11 July 1924]. We couldn't arrange to see him that day or yesterday because he was so very busy but we asked him and Barbara to come to lunch to-day, and he turned up this morning, on his way to Buckingham Palace, to say they could come. He is good looking and charming to meet. He was most immaculately dressed in a morning coat and beautiful grey trousers. All for the King. He went to get an M.B.E. for war service. He brought it with him at lunch time and we looked at it. I like him very much. Both he and Barbara are ready to be good and kind to us. She is pretty and I liked her. She is sensible and looks young. I'm sure she's not 30. She doesn't look more than 28. [She was actually 35.] I think she makes Dallas happy and she likes you. Talked of you in rather an amused and friendly way. She says their boy Peter thinks there is no one like you and he wants to be a soldier too, and as soon as he is big enough, he wants to come and see you at your farm. She brought the little girl (to lunch) Pamela, a beautiful child with golden hair and pink cheeks.

The following extract describes Amy's impressions of the Youngs' house:

Thursday evening, 16.7.24
Dallas and his wife asked my father and me to go down to Knebworth last Sunday. My father didn't go . . . , but I went. Nobody could have been kinder and better to me than they were. They both met me at the station, and as soon as we got into the house they asked me to stay for the night. Barbara said she could lend me everything, even a toothbrush and would

8

drive me up to town in the morning as she had to go up to lunch with someone. So I rang up my father and told him, and I stayed. We sat and talked all the morning and half the afternoon . . . and in the evening we talked again, mostly about you. I did so enjoy having someone to talk to who knows you.

Their house, Deard's Elm, is charming. Very small and compact with all kinds of labour-saving devices. Yet they have four bedrooms. Their furniture is beautiful and Barbara seems a most capable and clever housewife. Dallas minds the garden. He grows vegetables and flowers and cuts the lawn, all himself, and he has some ducks and fowls, and I was pleased to find the fowls are Speckled Sussex, like yours . . .

I slept in Peter's room. There was a map of Africa on the wall and a bunch of snake skins that you had sent him, and there was a cupboard that used to be in your bedroom at your father's house.

Peter first appears on 27 August 1924 when he was just nine years old:

Last Friday afternoon Dallas and Barbara came and we had dinner and went to 'The Great Adventure'. They stayed here [St. James's Court]. One can get rooms for guests. On Saturday morning Barbara fetched Peter from her mother's where he had stayed the night and he and she and Dallas and I went to Canterbury. We lunched at the Rose and Crown and then Barbara and Peter went walking in the town ending up at the Cathedral while Dallas and I went to see Mrs Christopher Wilkie, and after that we met the others and came home, and went to another theatre that night. Dallas and Barbara went home on Sunday morning.

On 10 September she writes: 'The two children [Peter and Pam] have just come in with a basket of blackberries, their fingers and palms are purple with the juice and they are most frightfully pleased with themselves.'

Blackberrying was a favourite occupation for the next extract reads:

I think the whole family uses Dallas to do jobs . . . So often I have been told 'Dallas knows' or 'Dallas will do it' and I've used him myself thinking at first he only attended to your affairs, but he does everybody's . . . I must stop now and go with Barbara to look for the children. They had gone off blackberrying again . . . Pam and Peter send you their love. Peter remembers you, he says. He remembers someone very tall talking to his father. He hopes to come and see you some day . . . Barbara says if you stop giving jobs to Dallas you will take away some of his interests in life. He certainly does them very willingly and kindly.

It is hard from these fleeting mentions to gain a clear picture of what Peter was like. He was part of a happy and close-knit family and enjoyed a typical middle-class childhood. Even at that age he had expressed interest in a military career – his uncle Will was a soldier and Peter kept some of the military papers relating to his career in the 17th and 8th Regiments, and to his later career in South Africa. His other uncle, Horace, who died the year before Peter was born, was employed in the Levant Consular Service.

After prep school, Peter was sent to Monmouth College where his contemporaries, he was later to boast, included the actor Richard Pearson. He was academically bright and a good sportsman, his preferred sports being hockey and cricket.

When considering much later the leaders he had encountered he wrote:

At school I came under the influence of a first class headmaster, C.F. Scott, who had very marked powers of command – real bite – but was also a man of culture who stimulated my interest in, for example, the Elizabethan Theatre. I was head of his house for a year and learned, by experiment, that I could get results just as much by talking to the boys as by caning them. I tried the two methods, quite deliberately, in alternate terms. I don't suppose I was much liked! The heavy-handed term was the second – and upon reflection – by far the least effective.

At Monmouth, too, he later claimed to have first formed the idea of a military career, inspired, he said, by the statue of Henry V in the main square. He began by joining the Officers' Training Corps (OTC) from which he gained his Certificate 'A', Infantry syllabus, as a member of the Junior Division Officers' Training Corps of the Monmouth School contingent. The date was 8 November 1932 and he was seventeen. This qualification entitled him to a commission in the Supplementary Reserve.

During the summer holidays he went to the Naval and Training Ships Leave Camp at Norman's Bay. This was run by the Reverend C.W. Hutchinson, an old family friend who was vicar of St John's, Waterloo. Later, recalling this man's influence on him he wrote:

> He [Hutchinson] . . . was a great character and a great leader. It was he that prepared me for Confirmation (which for good or ill did not in fact have much influence on me).
>
> In the wide sense of leadership – as opposed to purely religious influence – I believe, thinking back, that the influence of this sincere and human being had a lasting, though subconscious influence on me.

From Monmouth he went up to Trinity College, Oxford, to read Modern History with Military History as a special subject.

> At Oxford we led each other and I made a small group of friends at Trinity . . . My military history tutors, Sir Ernest Swinton [at the beginning of the First World War, Colonel Swinton, who was then the official journalist to the British Army, mooted the idea of the caterpillar-tracked armoured combat vehicle which ultimately became the tank] and C.T. Atkinson, taught me a very great deal, some of it about leadership, and we remained friends until they died. They were among the few lecturers in Oxford in those days who seemed to take a personal interest in the people they taught. Swinton actually asked his audience their names! Unheard of!

It was while he was up at Oxford that he began to study what was to become his lifelong passion – the English Civil War. He was always a Royalist, and made no apologies for the fact that he believed that, however bad the King, it was treason to take up arms against him. Sadly for him, the examiners at Oxford did not share his fascination with that period of history, and failed to set any questions about it for his finals in 1937, and since he had studied little else, the result was that he gained only a Third.

During his undergraduate years he was also introduced to another consuming interest: war gaming. His first mentor was Captain J.C. Sachs, based in Bushey, whose particular speciality was the First

World War. One must conclude from this that his battles were more in the nature of miniature exercises since he developed a very elaborate set of rules to enable players to reproduce the unusually static operations of the time. Peter quickly developed an interest in eighteenth-century warfare, encompassing the years between 1702 and 1815 (which more or less spanned the life of the Brown Bess musket) and this period remained an abiding interest, although he would campaign in any war if asked. It was possibly Dr P.B. Cornwall who introduced him to this era for he was an exponent of Napoleonic warfare. War gaming certainly reinforced his interest in military history, and in particular the more technical aspects of the physical and logistical limitations of warfare in times past; whether it had any bearing on his decision to become a career soldier is harder to gauge. At all events, given his disappointing degree, his career options were not rosy.

He had had a vague idea at some stage – and it was never much more than that – that he might want to teach, but his degree was not good enough to pursue that line, and in any case his eye had been caught by the situation on the continent. Shortly after he came down from Oxford, on 26 August 1937, he was commissioned as a University Candidate Second Lieutenant (77254) in the Territorial Army – Unattached List. By February 1939, he had joined the 2nd Battalion the Bedfordshire and Hertfordshire Regiment which was then at Gravesend. The die was cast.

Chapter Two

Dunkirk Campaign

Given his subsequent career, it is ironic that Peter did not attend the Royal Military Academy, Sandhurst. As the war clouds gathered, it became inevitable that he would convert from a Territorial to a Regular Commission, partly because he was already committed to a military life, and partly because he felt it was better to be in the system as a volunteer rather than being conscripted.

Probably because his cousin, Major Christopher Keenlyside, was in the Royal West Kent Regiment, his initial military service was on attachment at their depot at Maidstone. From there he moved on to the 1st Battalion the Royal West Kents at Shorncliffe where he did summer camp. Although he ultimately joined the Bedfordshire and Hertfordshire Regiment he retained many friendships in the Royal West Kents and even contributed articles to their journals.

His Regular Commission dates from 28 January 1939 (with seniority from 26 August 1937). He admitted later that he had been concerned about whether he would pass the eye test on his medical, but got round the problem by memorising the line of letters which he read first with his good eye because he was – he said – practically blind in the other one.

On 10 February 1939 he joined his unit, the 2nd Battalion of the Bedfordshire and Hertfordshire Regiment, as a Second Lieutenant commanding 7 Platoon of A Company. (The Bedfordshire and Hertfordshire Regiment was colloquially known as the Nuts and Bolts, a soubriquet Peter detested.) The Battalion was stationed at Milton Barracks, Gravesend. An interesting footnote attesting to the impact he made on his battalion came from a former NCO who worked in the Orderly Room at that time and who wrote much later that 'at the time I knew him he was very friendly with another young subaltern, Brian Pincombe. They were respectfully known to us as "The Scatter Brain Twins" – absolutely fearless and always up to some trick or other.' Which goes to prove that even Peter Young had to learn his craft from the bottom up.

He was at Gravesend when war broke out on 3 September 1939, an event which he thought lacked the drama he felt was its due, for Neville Chamberlain spoke 'rather in sorrow than in anger – no heart-stirring call to action. Somehow, this did not seem the way to declare war; how differently these things had been done in the past, in 1914, or in the old Boer War days.' Despite the anticlimax, things began to happen, although many of them were not entirely to Peter's liking, mostly because they seemed to involve the calling to the colours of 'reluctant' reservists. He also noted, with disapproval, the arrival of – as he inimitably put it – 'lieutenants of highly unsatisfactory seniority'.

His battalion was part of 10 Infantry Brigade which also consisted of:

2nd Battalion Duke of Cornwall's Light Infantry (DCLI)
1st Battalion Royal West Kent Regiment (RWK)
10 Anti-tank Company

The brigade formed part of the 4th Division in II Corps.

At that time, his own battalion was commanded by Lieutenant Colonel J.S. Davenport MC, but he was succeeded by Lieutenant Colonel J.C.A. Birch, whom Peter summed up thus: '[He] was very popular. He was a good trainer and tactician, but "gun-shy". I didn't much like him, but on reflection think he was really rather good to me.'

From the first, he assessed the officers around him and was ruthless in dismissing those he felt were inferior. Many of the regular soldiers he joined in early 1939 were veterans of the First World War; his company commander, Major Geoffrey Anstee MC, had fought on the Somme. (Anstee's comment, on hearing that war had been declared, was: 'Now we can get back to normal.') Peter considered some of them to be past their best. Lieutenant Colonel Anstruther, commander of 1RWK, fell into this category. Peter wrote in his journal: 'Anstruther was sick on mobilisation and so Barker [Commander, 10 Infantry Brigade] managed to get rid of him. He was an excellent pianist, and had probably been some use as a soldier in World War I, but he was a hopeless CO.'

Shortly after his arrival, Peter noticed the medal ribbons on Anstee's chest, of which the Military Cross was the most prominent. He had to ask Brian Pincombe what it was. The story was clearly repeated for not long before his death he wrote to Ted Piggott, one of the Commandos with whom he kept in touch, assuring him that it was true. It is a glimpse of his scant knowledge at that time of the life he had chosen and how limited his ambitions were when he began.

One of the tasks which the Army had to carry out from time to time was evaluation of new equipment. Peter was involved in the trial of a new light machine gun called the Bren. The existing LMGs, the Madsen and the Vickers Berthier, both suffered from stoppages; the Bren, it was hoped, would perform more consistently. He wrote of it:

I felt quite bucked to have the chance to be acquainted with what was rumoured to be the wonder weapon. My contribution to its future was tiny, but I was proud of my two penny worth. The Vickers Berthier had a curved top mounted magazine and was prone to stoppages at the beginning of its cycle – my sergeant had seen this in India before the war – an over-full magazine was thought to be a fault. The new Bren performed beautifully but after several magazines there were stoppages – I suggested that the 30 round magazine should have 28 cartridges so that the magazine should have less strain put upon it. It solved the problem and it was written into operating procedures.

From Gravesend, the battalion joined the rest of the brigade at Aldershot, from where they left for France in October 1939. Arriving at Cherbourg, they moved to Malicorne-sur-Sarthe, north-east of Angers, where they spent about a week. The brigade then moved to Carvin, a few miles south of Lille, and finally to Lys-lez-Lannoy which lies north-east of Lille, yards from the Belgian frontier.

From the time of the outbreak of war he kept a more or less continuous war journal, a practice he encouraged others to follow. His war diary of the time shows that when his battalion was not on patrol he spent much of his time drinking and playing poker. Life was, by all accounts, convivial if at times uncomfortable. In fact, when the brigade arrived on station there was little enemy activity and the first few months, though cold and wet because it was winter, were not marked by any action.

Before Christmas 1939, Peter was seconded to Captain Inglefield, the Intelligence Officer attached to 10 Anti-tank Company, and he also attended the II Corps Vehicle Maintenance Course at Sainghin-en-Weppes, south-west of Lille. He was soon back with his battalion, though, this time with D Company in which he commanded 16 Platoon. Based in the village of Lys-lez-Lannoy, he was billeted with Madame Durred-Delannoy in January 1940. His journal records that during these slow days he spent a lot of time reading military history, claiming that with few exceptions, it was from the great generals of the past that he learned most, although it is clear that he was still at this stage (and as he admitted) inclined to look on his own immediate commanders for help and inspiration. This was something he would do less and less as he became more experienced and refined his own unique style of command.

While he was a platoon commander in D Company Peter first came under fire. In February, the brigade was moved 200 miles south-east, first to Lorry-les-Metz, and then to an area between Metz and Saarbrucken, east of the Moselle and near the German border – Company Headquarters at Halstroff was less than 5 miles from the frontier. They were not yet in contact with the enemy but the brigade was to be given some battle hardening. A sector of the French front in that area was 'lent' to the British and occupied in turn by various British brigades.

In late February 1940 it was the turn of 10 Infantry Brigade and the Beds and Herts, as senior battalion, were given the first tour in the front line. Peter commanded two platoons of D Company on the left of the line in a wood called Grossenwald, with his left flank anchored by the French. As he took over the position, it came under mortar fire from the Germans, which resulted in four soldiers from the Hampshires, from whom he was taking over, being wounded. It was not a prolonged affair, and, as he describes it, 'When it was over I walked back to Company Headquarters at Halstroff . . . relieved to find that [I] had not been unduly alarmed, and that [I] now had the advantage over [my] men – they still had their baptism of fire to come.'

The battalion spent a week in the line and during that time improved the defences, only occasionally being disturbed by German mortar fire which was returned by French artillery. Peter discovered that they were playing a cat and mouse game – as their own side sent out patrols at night, so did the Germans, infiltrating the large

16

gap in the line between C and D Companies and occupying the wood behind the British position. From there they would throw grenades and fire their weapons, but at midnight, a flare would go up and they would retreat. This experience did much to de-mystify the Germans – they, too, had to learn their trade and they, too, could make mistakes. He was, for instance, grateful that the Germans did not cut their telephone wires as they had no radios in their position.

They stayed in what he referred to as the *'ligne de contact'* for a week before handing over to two platoons of the DCLI, following which Peter returned to Halstroff and slept for twelve hours. Although he had not really enjoyed the experience because he thought that their position had not been good, he was buoyed by the fact that they had taken no casualties and was of the opinion that platoon training had been pretty thorough 'in all the normal operations of war, the platoon in the attack and in defence; the advance to contact and the withdrawal; and patrolling by day and by night'. This somewhat naïve conclusion was rudely shaken when, during the DCLI's tenure of the line, they were subjected to a raid during which two senior NCOs were killed and most of two sections captured. It was a salutary lesson. Raiding, as Peter pointed out, was not part of the British Army's training syllabus.

At the end of March, he returned home on leave, but was back in theatre on 2 April by which time the brigade was back in Lys-lez-Lannoy. In May the Germans invaded the Low Countries and the brigade rapidly found itself fully engaged. Peter's opinion of the Brigade Commander, Brigadier (later Lieutenant General Sir) Evelyn 'Bubbles' Barker MC was typically candid. He was 'very brave . . . He was hard on us in training and very pleasant in the battle.' In his unpublished account of the Dunkirk campaign, written seventeen years later, he wrote: 'Sir Evelyn Barker was the coolest man you could wish to see under fire. He seemed to like it; indeed I feel sure that he did. He liked to observe his officers and men in times of stress, because it helped him to weigh them up. After so many years I am not ashamed to confess that I always felt braver when he was present.' Peter did emulate Barker to a degree for he always focussed on training, and those who fought with him testify to his *sang froid* in battle. He took the view that if soldiers have had adequate training, a commander should not fear for the performance of his troops.

By the time the Germans advanced into Belgium on 10 May 1940, Peter was acting as a liaison officer with 10 Infantry Brigade

17

Headquarters. This kept him on his toes and he was lucky to get three hours' sleep a night. With a hundredweight truck, he visited the various battalions and carried messages between them. When the brigade became engaged, as it very shortly did, he was in a good position to observe the bigger picture.

On the same day that the Germans invaded Belgium and the Netherlands, Winston Churchill became Prime Minister. The fall of Eban Emael enabled the Germans to advance unopposed over the Albert Canal into the Low Countries and the Allies, sizing up events along the front, determined that the German advance through the Ardennes would be slower. Advancing from north-east France into Belgium they fell into the Germans trap, for while Army Group B, under General Bock, dealt summarily with Holland and then advanced into Belgium, General von Rundstedt took Army Group A through the Ardennes and smashed through to the French coast at Boulogne. The Germans thus isolated the British Expeditionary Force (BEF) with a few French troops in Belgium and began to squeeze it into an ever smaller area.

Before von Rundstedt's movements had become clear, and along with the rest of the BEF, 10 Brigade moved north across the Belgian border shortly after the German general advance began. On about 15 May, the brigade moved north via Alost (Aalst), north-west of Brussels, to the villages of Crainham (Kraainem) and Saventhem (Zaventem) where they dug in. This represented a considerable march for the infantry – it is about 40 miles from Lille to Alost, and a further 20 to their final position. The following day, watching the Germans' relentless advance, they moved again, back towards Alost, withdrawing through Brussels, a manoeuvre that took two days and included a night march. On Saturday, 18 May, shortly after they arrived at Alost, they moved again in the afternoon to Avelghem, by way of Oudenaarde (Audenarde), a distance of about 25 miles.

Avelghem is a small town on the River Scheldt (or Escaut, as Peter called it) which was to be the line held by the Allies. 10 Brigade advanced up the west bank and on Sunday, 19 May reconnoitred the area of Mont de l'Enclus which was a prominent feature about a mile from the river bank. Whether or not they occupied it is unclear. At all events, for the following three days, they fought a rearguard action against men from Reichenau's Sixth Army. On the night of 22 May, they withdrew across the Bossuyt Canal, during which a courier contrived to ambush a German staff car which was perhaps the only

18

good news of the action. While the withdrawal took place, Peter remained behind to guide the Bren Carrier Platoon which was covering the retreat. Eventually, they caught up with the column and encountered Bubbles Barker in his car. Sportingly, he offered Peter a lift, but Peter was so tired that he kept dozing off and, as he said, 'Every time I woke up there were long columns of men marching along the sides of the road. They looked dead-beat and I felt ashamed to be travelling in comfort.'

He did not have to feel guilty for long. On 23 May, the brigade established its headquarters in a village called Roncq, north-west of Tourcoing and just over the border in France. By this time the Belgians were on the point of surrender and any forces left in the country would be in danger from the local population as well as the German invaders. Peter went out on patrol with five men the following day, and not far from their lines met a Belgian civilian who told them that there was a party of three Germans at a crossroads about half a mile away. His unpublished account describes what happened:

This seemed a Heaven sent opportunity to get an identification for I had passed the place the previous day and thought I knew exactly where the enemy were. I led the patrol through back gardens to some houses within two hundred yards of the cross-roads. We peered round the corner, but to my chagrin there was nobody in sight. Clearly we had been misinformed – or perhaps the enemy had cleared off. We walked down to the crossroads. Perhaps a hundred yards away to our right there was a low ridge, and I decided to go that far and have a look round before falling back. We strode up the road and had only gone a little way when I saw a man apparently carrying a stick; it was several seconds before it dawned on me that he was a German soldier with a rifle. He ran across the road. I fired my pistol, and the Germans fired their rifles. Three bullets sang past. We ran for the cover of some houses and tried a door. Locked! Round the corner! I snatched a rifle and we fired at the place where we had seen the enemy. They had cleared off.

The three Germans were cyclists acting as an outpost.

The Belgian information had been good, but I had taken it too literally. Instead of sitting actually on the crossroads the Germans were covering them from the ridge beyond. I returned to our lines feeling that I had had the ball at my feet and an open goal and had miss kicked [sic]. I reported back to Brigade Headquarters where Brigadier Barker made one or two candid remarks about my tactical skill.

On 25 May, the brigade remained in Roncq awaiting the German attack. Peter discovered that more German cyclists had advanced to within a few hundred yards of the battalion's Forward Defensive Locations (FDLs) where the sappers had blown a large hole in the road to delay any enemy advance. He was lent a few soldiers by Colonel Birch to go and investigate further:

I visited Bill Peters, who had been my Company Commander in the Saar. Rather to my surprise he said he was going out . . . We set off down a slope into the No Mans Land ahead, where two long rows of houses stretched away towards the enemy [on the edge of Neuville-en-Ferrain on the Franco-Belgian border].
Before long we met and joined forces with Charkham's patrol. They were working through the back gardens of houses on the right of the road. This was slow work and so we began to push on up the main road, but we had not gone far when a burst of machine gun fire shattered the glass of a shop window on the right of the road. There was an explosion, a grenade perhaps, and Bill Peters, who was leading, was hit in the arm though he did not tell us so.
From this time onwards we were more prudent. We worked forward through the gardens of the cottages on the left of the road. After a while we detected a group of German soldiers level with us and not far off; they were standing at the back door of a house evidently in earnest conference. I had armed myself with my driver's rifle.
'Shall I shoot?' I asked Bill Peters.
'Yes, go on.'
Some wire obstructed me as I took aim; it was a rotten shot, and before I could reload the enemy had vanished; no answering shot came back. It dawned on me that the Germans had got the wind up . . . I took up a position in an out-house and kneeling down rested my rifle on the window sill. A German appeared walking cautiously along a road from our left to our right about a hundred yards away. He stooped as he went and he carried his rifle at the trail in his right hand. I fired and he disappeared.
'Where did he go?'

20

'You hit him, Sir,' said one of my escort.

Meanwhile Charkham, Corporal Stancliffe and another man were working forward up a ditch to our right, and still resting my rifle on the window sill I was watching for signs of opposition. Suddenly a German head appeared, practically on my foresight. A man was looking at us from out of the long grass near a hedgerow. I fired, and this time I was sure of my shot. The head dropped from view. A crackle of musketry from Charkham's group accounted for the other members of a machine gun crew, which we had caught in our crossfire.

There was a gap between houses two hundred yards ahead. Suddenly a German section began to run across it, one at a time – about ten of them. They ran the gauntlet, and not all of them made it. There was a pause and then to our astonishment they all ran back, not all in a bunch, but again one at a time. Very foolish. Several were hit and staggered into cover behind a house; one fell right in the middle of the gap. Things were going well. We pushed on and joined Charkham in his ditch. Not thirty yards away lay the crew of the German machine gun. I thought I would get an identification, and walked across to them. I was a few yards from them, when someone fired at me from a garden nearby. I dashed back to cover. We worked forward up the ditch. It was not very deep, but it was better than nothing . . . The enemy were very near, but invisible in houses or gardens. We went into a building, and found it to be a kind of garage. We found ourselves confronted by a hearse – a hint not to tempt Providence. I peered out of the garage and up the main road. There was a group of grey clad figures not far off, grouped round a vehicle or a gun. One of our men had a Bren gun. I borrowed it and shoved its nose quietly round the corner, raking the road from side to side with a long burst. I pressed the trigger until the magazine was empty, swinging the muzzle back and forth across the road. There was a big flash and something hit the pavement ten yards ahead. Some kind of anti-tank gun I thought. I withdrew.

There still remained the question of getting an identification. The dead Germans were lying just outside the hedge round the local cemetery; if we could reach its cover the thing might be possible, even though the bodies were being watched by Germans concealed not far off. A little way to the rear there was a low bank, and under its cover we crept from our ditch to the cemetery. Dodging among the tombstones we came to the corner nearest to the enemy. I lay down on my belly and crawled through the hedge. The nearest German was not two yards away. He had been shot through the jugular vein and looked ghastly. I laid my hands on his equipment and gave a heave. He was very heavy. With the effort of pulling my feet went up in the air. With long scrubbing my gaiters were nearly white. Perhaps some opthalmic [sic] Hun took them for my face. However that may be, I suddenly felt a blow on my left ankle like the lash of a whip as another shot rang out. I gladly abandoned my grisly task and shot back through the hedge. My boot was soon full of blood, and though I did not feel the wound was mortal, I imagined that my ankle was ruined.

After this I was glad to call it a day; reaching D Company's position I met John Harrison, Bill Peters' second-in-command. I sat down, in full view of the enemy as far as one could tell, while he bandaged my ankle with a field dressing. As it turned out there were no bones broken, though bits of the bullet lodged under the ankle bone – nothing to get excited about. I was pleasantly surprised to find that it was not very painful – I suppose because we had been skirmishing about for some hours and our blood was up.

This patrol marked two important rites of passage: for the first time he had inflicted casualties on the enemy; and he received the only wound he was to suffer during his long and busy war.

He seems to have remained with his battalion as they withdrew once again to Kemmel, moving at night via Warheton, Wytschaete and Ploegsteert. At Kemmel, he briefly met his former battalion second-in-command, Geoffrey Anstee, who was now commanding the 5th Northamptonshires. The battalion was struggling to hold the line as he reappeared and announced, 'All will be well. My battalion is behind you.' And indeed it was. On 28 May, they reached Oost Dunquerque where they remained for two days. Here 10 Brigade found their right flank under pressure from a German push out of Nieuwpoort. The Divisional Commander, Dudley Johnson VC, visited them at their headquarters, 'a tall figure, immaculate in Service Dress and glistening riding boots. He listened to my report without a trace of concern and at the end said quietly: "Um. Infiltration. Infiltration." As if the subject was, at worst, distasteful.' That afternoon a company of the East Surreys drove them back with heavy losses. Any hope of holding their ground had vanished when on 27 May Churchill ordered the Royal Navy to evacuate Gort's BEF. Moving under cover of darkness on 31 May, via De Panne (La Panne), the brigade reached Dunkirk on 1 June. Second Lieutenant Peter Young embarked from Dunkirk mole on the *Ben-my-Creech*. His first experience of active warfare, the last he would fight with his own regiment, was over.

Good though they were, we were overrating the Germans. This, at least, I had learned. If you took them by surprise, they would run away; if you opened fire on them, they would take cover; if you shot them, they bled. In a word, they were human. They disliked being bombed and shelled just as much as we did – only in those days they did not get quite so much of it. Their turn was to come.

Chapter Three

'Special Service'

At the outbreak of war, Geoffrey Anstee had fixed Peter with a steely gaze and said, 'In a year's time you will be a company commander.' Peter thought it was far more likely that he would be dead, however,

> I had by this time fallen, half unconsciously, into a habit of believing everything Geoffrey told me, particularly when he appeared to be joking. I therefore had no difficulty in believing that by September 1940 I should be a captain, which, I thought, would be very fine. At the same time it occurred to me that, if that should come to pass, in 1941 I might become a major. The thing had endless possibilities.

His first experience of action had been chaotic and instructive – as war usually is – but he had been fortunate in the men he had fought under. They were virtually all First World War veterans for whom the Dunkirk campaign bore no comparison to their former travails over the same landscape. Their coolness and professionalism made a lasting impression on Peter and he learnt much from their attitudes and behaviour under fire. He learnt quickly; henceforth he would be dispensing wisdom rather than acquiring it. As he put it in a note on leadership which he wrote in 1966:

> One learns from one's CO and the company commanders. The trouble is – even in the best unit – they are a mixed bunch and the poor subaltern has, at a time when his loyalty is un-questioning and his judgement unformed, to sort out his 'heroes' for himself. And, of course, some have bad qualities as well as good. My first CO in the Bedfords [Lieutenant Colonel

J.S. Davenport MC], though in many ways an excellent officer, had rather violent and obvious personal prejudices – fortunately he had a good opinion of me, which was not as far as I can see based on more than a vague and emotional feeling that I was 'the right type' for the regiment. This did me no good as the Adjutant [Captain R.H. Senior, or possibly Captain Denis Rossiter who took over as Adjutant during the Dunkirk campaign], a serious-minded Roundhead, took pains to redress the balance!

Of leaders who had inspired him he wrote: 'It was from my own company commanders, Geoffrey Anstee [Major G.A. Anstee MC] and Bill Peters [Captain G.W.H. Peters MC], and from others of our WWI veterans, Freddie Spicer [Major F.W. Spicer MC], a great tactician and trainer, and Ted Ashby [Major E.E. Ashby], so cool *"au feu"*, that I learned so much of what carried me through the war.'

Peter arrived back in England on 1 June 1940 and 10 Infantry Brigade returned to Yeovil. The battalion in which Peter served was still, at 570, up to fighting strength – a considerable testament to the dexterity of its commander and senior officers.

In London, Churchill wasted no time in trying to recapture the offensive. As the evacuation of Dunkirk drew to a close on 4 June 1940, Dudley Clarke committed to paper an idea he had conceived which would allow the country, stung by its defeat, but far from accepting it, to continue the fight. On 6 June, the CIGS, General Sir John Dill, told Churchill about Clarke's plan, and on 8 June, Clarke was told that his plan was approved. That afternoon, Section MO9 of the War Office came into being and planning for the Commandos began in earnest. Churchill had instructed the War Office to set up a special raiding force to harry the enemy on the Continent, not so much to cause a major disruption to their operations – they were too well established for that – but more to remind them that the Allies had not given up, and, crucially, to provide some good headlines for the British public for whom the war was providing little other than gloomy news. To this end, a letter was despatched to every command outlining the terms for 'special service' as it was called, and asking for recruits. Only the best were to be sent.

This letter arrived at Yeovil at a time when the CO and Adjutant were both on disembarkation leave, and Ted Ashby and Peter were in their respective chairs. The letter outlining the requirements to commanding officers stated that recruits were to be young, absolutely fit, able to drive motor vehicles and not prone to seasickness.

Peter's approach was typical. A draft of men was due to arrive to replace casualties sustained at Dunkirk and Peter, mindful of Anstee's prophecy about becoming a company commander, was concerned lest any of the replacements be senior to him, reducing his chances of getting a company. He resolved, therefore, that if any of the incoming officers were senior to him, he would volunteer for 'special services'. When he discovered in the intake a 48-year-old lieutenant called Herbert, he wrote a letter 'strongly recommending' himself. Ted Ashby signed it and it was duly despatched. (Two weeks after Peter eventually left the battalion, Herbert went into hospital suffering from piles; he never returned.)

The battalion moved to Bognor Regis and settled down to the dull business of guarding the beaches. Life went on and Peter forgot about the application. He was therefore surprised to be summoned into the CO's presence and told to explain why a letter had arrived asking that he be sent up for an interview. Peter told Birch that he had sent the letter off during his absence on leave and he had therefore been unable to ask permission. Given leave to attend, he had to acquire transport to get to Romsey, where he had been summoned. The Adjutant, Bob Senior, was not at first disposed to help him, but relented after a while and offered Peter the use of a motorbike.

Peter's previous experience of this mode of transport had been as a pillion passenger during the Dunkirk battle when he had visited 2DCLI with one of the dispatch riders, one Private Fetter. He found Fetter who gave him a brief introduction into the intricacies of the machine. Having ridden it round a tennis court for ten minutes and mastered starting it, he 'thought I'd better set out before I discovered something disheartening'.

It was a hair-raising journey, during which he destroyed the kick starter and got so desperate he tried to hire a taxi only to find there were none available. He finally reached Mountbatten House, just outside Winchester, 'in a desperate mood and ready to volunteer for anything, particularly if it did not involve motor-bicycles'. Arriving an hour late for his interview, he was fortunate that his interviewer was two hours late.

John Durnford-Slater, who was to become Peter's commanding officer and a firm friend, had been commissioned into the Royal

Artillery in 1929. After six years in India he had returned to England and a life little to his liking, but stayed in the Army because he could see that war was inevitable. Given the job of recruiting for the new force he set to work immediately, trawling the whole of Southern Command for suitable officers. Peter's interview took place as part of that search. His first impression of Durnford-Slater was that he bore a superficial resemblance to Mr Pickwick. Deciding that he was some staff officer from the War Office, Peter fixed him with what he hoped was a steely expression and when asked if he was 'all for this sort of thing', replied with a prompt 'yes'.

Durnford-Slater, for his part, was anxious for the new force to become operational as soon as possible; invasion was feared to be imminent and the new force might have to be deployed within a fortnight of its formation. He therefore interviewed at frantic speed and had selected the thirty-five officers he needed to form the commando within a week of his appointment. Of these, ten were drawn from the regular forces and the rest were reservists or Territorials. Peter clearly fulfilled the criteria Durnford-Slater had set down for admission into the new force. He described Peter thus: 'He was of medium height, very intelligent, very cunning and strong, with a caustic tongue.'

The officers having been appointed, Second Lieutenant Young was sent to H Troop, commanded by Captain Vivian de Crespigny, Royal Army Service Corps (RASC), with Lieutenant John 'Joe' Smale, Lancashire Fusiliers, as second-in-command. These three were sent out to recruit their own men from the ranks of the 4th Division which was now billetted in the Chichester area.

They toured all units and found almost total co-operation – this would not continue, but at that time, commanding officers thought volunteers would only be required for three months, after which they would be returned to their units. Once this policy was rescinded, as it soon was, it became harder to recruit good men; they were often offered only prisoners and slackers, while the genuine volunteers were kept back. Although they took recruits from the Royal Artillery, Royal Engineers and Royal Army Service Corps, it was from the infantry regiments that the backbone of the commando was selected, a lot of whom were reservists. Many had served in India and were steady, experienced soldiers with a thorough knowledge of their craft. It was to their own regiments that the recruiters primarily turned. Of all the regiments that were approached, only one company of the 2nd Battalion Beds and Herts did not co-operate. From the rest, the first cadre of troops was formed and they included, on Joe

Smale's recommendation, a man awaiting court martial whom they nonetheless considered to be worth springing from incarceration in the guard room. Considerations arising from disobedience to the Manual of Military Law and King's Regulations did not stop a soldier from being recruited to the Commandos. They were looking for men who would be raiding behind enemy lines – such individuals might not find the strict rules of regimental life easy to follow.

By the end of their tour round the 4th Division, they had their full complement which included several men from the Beds and Herts: Hopkins, the brothers Fred and Pat Drain, 'Curly' Gimbert and 'Duff" Cooper. From Peter's old CO, Geoffrey Anstee, now commanding the 5th Northamptons, came George Herbert MM, already decorated for gallantry at Oudenarde. These, and the rest, were the backbone of what Peter declared to be the best troop in the commando.

They decided not to take up all the NCO vacancies, preferring to promote their own men in due course. It was a decision which provided them with a raft of NCOs who knew their business from the bottom up and whose total dedication gave the troop an edge which was to stand it in good stead time and again. In later years Peter referred to these early times as 'makee learnee' days. They were all on a steep learning curve. Peter felt that they were all in it together and as they developed their fighting techniques, they would develop the command structure to go with them.

Peter's military record states that he was posted to No. 3 Commando at Larkhill on 3 July 1940. The newly formed unit was sent to train at Plymouth, close to both military and naval training facilities, and far enough west to be out of immediate danger from enemy in-cursions. Arriving there on 7 July, Peter lodged with Smale and de Crespigny in a small house on the edge of town, owned by two elderly sisters. The Troop HQ was in a shop in Plymouth where all personnel assembled daily. No special equipment was issued, and no facilities were made available to the new units; part of the idea was to make them 'live off the land' and to this end, officers were paid an extra 13/4d per day and other ranks 6/8d as a subsistence allowance. Weapons were not stored centrally and each man kept his own until a firefight occurred one evening, after which an armoury guarded by a storeman was set up at the Troop HQ.

The first Commando raid had already taken place on the night of 23/24 June in the area around Boulogne and Le Touquet. It caused considerable surprise, little damage but an encouraging boost to the morale of both participants and public, for whom evidence that the armed forces had not given up the struggle was very well received. Thus heartened, MO9 came up with another plan, this time a raid on Guernsey to be carried out in mid July, codenamed Operation Ambassador. For this operation, Durnford-Slater selected H Troop as part of the 3 Commando raiding force and training began at once for their baptism of fire.

Training, however, was problematic. Since an amphibious operation of this sort had never really been carried out, no one was quite sure what skills to practise. The result was a rather sketchy and half-hearted attempt to rehearse various aspects of the proposed action: pulling (i.e. rowing) a navy cutter one day, carrying out what they imagined their roles would be on the football ground at Raglan Barracks another, and practising on the Tregantle Firing Ranges on another. It was not clear what weapons they would be using – they had been steered towards a pre-war stock of Lee Enfields, brand new and in beautifully oiled condition, somewhere outside Plymouth, but by the time of the raid the men were using the gun of the moment – the Thompson sub-machine (tommy) gun.

Swimming tests were carried out, although these did not, it transpired, fully explore the capabilities of the participants. In the event, the plan was changed so that even these attempts at preparation were to be rendered futile.

Guernsey had been invaded by the Germans on 1 July. On 8 July, a British agent – a local man – landed on the island, contacted the local baker and discovered that the strength of the invading force – based upon its requirement for bread – was 469 men. The idea was to carry out a swift attack, killing or capturing as many invaders as possible; their greatest concentration was in St Peter Port and they had secured the coast by occupying a string of Martello Towers. The invading force had requisitioned all available transport, which meant that they could deploy forces all over the island in a relatively short time. Any surprise operation would therefore need to move fast in order to carry out its objectives before it was discovered.

After being twice postponed, the raid was finally set for the night of 14/15 July and the troop, plus a detachment from Commando HQ, set off from Plymouth for Dartmouth in two Western National buses although Peter travelled with de Crespigny and his batman, McGovern in the Troop Commander's car. The weather was glorious

29

and the two men were fired up by the prospect of action once again, so when they were held up behind a car carrying two men to a cricket match at a leisurely pace they became increasingly impatient. Finally 'after some time and much hooting I suggested firing my pistol into the bank. The result was highly satisfactory, for they shot off with commendable speed – not without backward glances.'

At the Royal Naval College the men were given the run of the gymnasium and they were finally shown their objective in the Physical Training Instructor's (PTI) office. They also learned that while they had been practising for a landing on the north side of the island, the Germans had reinforced a number of their positions in that area, and that the landings would now be taking place on the south-east of the island, on Petit Port Bay.

Their partners in this enterprise were to be 11 Independent Commando, commanded by Major Ronnie Tod. This unit had already been in action in the earlier operation in the Boulogne/Le Touquet area and they were to attack the airport while H Troop carried out diversionary attacks against a machine-gun post at Telegraph Bay and the barracks on the Jerbourg Peninsula.

In fact, it was not until the convoy had embarked and were at sea that final dispositions were made and Peter found out that he was to guard the beach. He was not pleased and said so. Durnford-Slater mollified him by saying that if all was quiet, Peter might come up and see what was going on.

The convoy was made up of two 1918-vintage destroyers, HMS *Scimitar* and HMS *Saladin*, and five RAF crash-boats. The crash-boats were intended to land the troops and travelled empty; one of them developed engine trouble during the crossing and had to be sunk. At about midnight, the convoy stopped and transferred the Commandos into the four remaining crash-boats. The destroyers had orders to wait two hours, after which they would turn for home. In fact, the raiding party very nearly missed its target – in the case of the boats carrying 11 Independent Commando, one missed Guernsey entirely and landed on Sark, while the other foundered on rocks so that the main thrust of the raid never took place.

The inexplicable failure of the Royal Navy to navigate between Dartmouth and Guernsey was due to the fact that the ships had been degaussed to avoid attracting mines. Unfortunately people were not yet aware that the degaussing process also causes the ship's compass to go haywire so that if John Durnford-Slater, who happened to be on the bridge at the time, had not pointed to a passing island and asked if that might be their destination, none of the raiding party would have attained their objective.

Peter thought that the launches were incredibly noisy and he felt sure that the element of surprise was compromised. The men who were operating the crash-boats were sticking to their standard operating procedures and calling out course changes between boat commander and helm at the tops of their voices, despite the fact that their passengers were whispering. The crash-boats hit the beach safely, though rather farther out to sea than their occupants might have hoped – these were not landing craft and they drew several feet of water. By the time that the men finally reached dry land they were all sodden, their woollen battledresses seemed to weigh a ton and they squelched their way up the steep concrete steps in a 250-foot cliff to begin their diversionary action. Peter had felt it necessary to carry a veritable stores depot with him:

> As I struggled ashore water poured from every part of my equipment; we wore battledress, steel helmets, canvas shoes and army gaiters. In an old style officer's haversack I had three Mills grenades, a drum magazine for the tommy-gun and a clasp-knife. In my breast pockets were more magazines of the clip type. My armament included a .38 pistol and I also had some five feet of cord with which I intended to secure my numerous prisoners; maps, saws, compasses and other impedimenta were sewn into various secret parts of my costume. For some obscure reason I was carrying an additional fifty rounds of .303 ammunition – we took our soldiering seriously in 1940!

During this exposed and noisy part of the operation, the welcome sound of an Anson overhead gave the men cover; the aircraft's pass down the Jerbourg Peninsula gave morale a boost as the men set forth to secure their objectives.

Peter felt that he was better employed off the beach than on it, despite his orders. As they reached the top of the cliff they set off for the Doyle Monument and almost at once heard a burst of fire. Everyone froze. Peter, not quite at the top of the cliff, had wondered what would happen if they were attacked during the ascent of the cliff as it would have been impossible to deploy. Happily, the culprit turned out to be Smale who had tripped over his tommy gun, and even more happily, the noise of firing had not elicited any hostile reaction.

31

The rest of the raid was more fiasco than fight. The barracks which were supposed to be there were unoccupied, the one old man whom they found to question knew nothing and was secured by being locked in a lavatory, and the machine-gun nest they were to capture was empty. However, a road block was successfully set up by Smale's men who then stood around uncertain what to do next until footsteps were heard on the road ahead. Corporal 'Curly' Gimbert burst out and thrust his bayonet at the approaching troops. It was John Durnford-Slater and his party returning from their abortive reconnaissance. Fortunately, they remembered the password, 'Desmond'.

They now had only fifteen minutes to get back to the rendezvous point on the beach. The party formed up at the foot of the Doyle Monument and began to double down the cliff to the beach. Peter was the penultimate man down, followed by Durnford-Slater waving his torch in one hand to signal the crash-boats and carrying a cocked pistol in the other. As they reached the bottom, Durnford-Slater lost his footing and fell, firing his pistol in the process. Although he did not hit anyone this did finally elicit a response from the Germans and for the first time, tracer fire was seen across Saints Bay. A searchlight was briefly switched on, but it did not locate the crash-boats or the men.

Re-embarking proved fraught because the crash-boats would not come inshore and a dinghy was used to ferry men and weapons to the boats. On the third trip, the dinghy hit a submerged boulder and sank so the remaining men were ordered to abandon their equipment and swim for it. It now became clear that some of the men had been less than truthful about their ability to swim. Three of them had to be left on the beach, to be captured by the Germans three days later. A year later, Peter received a letter from Private Frederick Drain confirming that the missing men were with him in a prisoner-of-war camp.

Once embarked, the men faced the prospect of a long, exposed journey back to England in the crash-boats. The destroyers should have turned back by now, the two-hour window having long elapsed. When one of the crash-boats broke down the other took it under tow. With dawn approaching it looked as if they were sitting ducks. In a final throw of the dice, Durnford-Slater flashed a torch out to sea and, to his amazement, received an answering signal. HMS *Scimitar* was still on station, having at great risk to herself decided to make one last pass at the rendezvous point. Peter spent the return journey drying off in the engine room.

The lesson which the abortive operation on Guernsey taught the participants in no uncertain terms was that if these raids were to rely on the combined operations of the Army and the Navy, it was necessary to implement a battlefield philosophy predicated on the two services being able to dovetail their methods of warfare and – crucially – their ability to communicate with each other. Interoperability and command, control and communications are modern military buzz words; the Commandos were at the cutting edge of the development of these ideas.

Chapter Four

Troop Command

The summer of 1940 was glorious, but Britain was fighting for her life. While No. 3 Commando learned the lessons of the debacle on Guernsey and began to set up training procedures that would benefit them in their new role, the rest of the country was poised on a knife edge, awaiting the onslaught of Operation Sea Lion. Practising seaborne landings along the coasts of Devon and Dorset caused panic on the beaches on more than one occasion.

Peter, celebrating his twenty-fifth birthday, enjoyed that summer – both work and play. His sister, Pam, came down to stay with him, and Vivian de Crespigny took them both to Polperro for the day where they were able to bathe and enjoy the wonderful weather.

Training principally involved becoming adept at naval skills and by August, Durnford-Slater's men were able to handle a naval cutter in all weathers with all the acumen of sailors in the Royal Navy. There was also more conventional land-based training: live-firing and troop exercises, and weapon training. So arduous were some of these activities that Durnford-Slater had medics on hand to check over the men at the end of the period. Those who were unfit or otherwise infirm were returned to their units, so that their strength was somewhat reduced. Peter thrived.

Admiral of the Fleet Sir Roger Keyes, now sixty-eight and a veteran of Gallipoli, was appointed Chief of Combined Operations, but he was a long way from the sharp end and the Commandos were finding life difficult. This was principally because their army colleagues did not like the preferential treatment they seemed to be getting and became obstructive at regional headquarters. The army hierarchy resented the perceived lack of discipline in a Commando unit, which did not have to live in barracks, and where at first there was not even a requirement to attend parades (although these were gradually reintroduced as the men liked them and missed them – H Troop paraded regularly outside the old butcher's shop on Embankment Road in Plymouth before starting daily training).

Whilst the staff of GOC Plymouth were resisting requests for an allocation of a training area, the naval authorities were delighted to support the Commandos' attempt to become adept at beachcraft and seaborne landings, lending skilled seamanship instructors to advance their technical skills. By the end of August, the troops were able to put on a display to show Keyes exactly what they had been up to. Impressed by how keen and fit all ranks were, he promised that the men of No. 3 Commando would be the first to be employed in active operations. In fact, he went further; on visiting No. 8 Commando a few days later, he informed their commanding officer, Bob Laycock, that he ought to be using the same training methods as No. 3 Commando.

At the beginning of September, with the threat of invasion at its height, the Commandos and Independent Companies were temporarily added to the troops already being employed in the 'primary duty of defence' of the country. In practice, this meant that the commando came under the operational command of GOC Home Forces, and, more immediately, under the Commander of South-Western Area for the defence of Plymouth. They had perforce to divert their energy from training for their own brand of operation to a purely defensive role in the event of invasion. For several weeks the commando spent their time rehearsing in the region of Tamerton Foliot.

On the same day that the commando temporarily lost its independence, 16 September, Peter was promoted to Captain and took over command of H Troop from de Crespigny. Anstee's prophecy was beginning to come true.

He now had a cadre of newly arrived subalterns to train. Peter was shocked to discover that one of them, Dick Wills – far from being a callow youth on whom he could imprint his own ideas and leadership – was in fact a Cambridge graduate several years older than he was. When Wills overslept and missed a scheduled patrol in one of the minesweepers based in Plymouth, Peter prepared a 'Never in all my service' rocket, but Wills's crestfallen countenance made him burst out laughing and the speech was never delivered. It was the start of a friendship that would last throughout the war.

Keyes had ambitious plans to use Commando forces to occupy

Atlantic objectives, such as the Azores, and to capture the island of Pantelleria, which lies in the Mediterranean between the toe of Italy and Tunisia.

In order to concentrate Commando training and remove from it the distraction of supporting the Home Defence Forces, the commando was moved in early October 1940 to the Combined Operations base on the shores of Loch Fyne in Inverary, where a half-finished camp consisting of Nissen huts had been earmarked for their use. Given the approaching Scottish winter, it was as well that the huts themselves were complete, even if the plumbing was not. Here the men had their first sight of a proper assault landing craft. They made a dramatic entrance, advancing on the beach at their top speed of 6 knots, a large wave obscuring their square bows which rode low in the water. There was no superstructure which made them difficult to spot when out at sea. Within half an hour of their arrival training on embarkation and disembarkation drills had begun.

At the outset, a Commando troop consisted of 3 officers and 47 men, but due to the capacity of the landing craft this was altered to 3 officers and 62 men, which gave a neat ratio of two landing craft per troop. Training on these landing craft was a top priority: Durnford-Slater insisted on twenty or thirty practice landings every morning and the competition to achieve the best time was intense. Under the strict eye of the Adjutant, Charlie Head, the men were driven to new heights. In the end, F Troop, under Algy Forrester, held the record – disembarkation with all weapons and running 25 yards up the beach in ten seconds. Peter's H troop held the record for the reverse operation, in fourteen seconds.

The training regime was not confined to amphibious activities. The challenging Scottish terrain also served to weed out those who had thus far survived the rigours of the training programme in Plymouth. Both Durnford-Slater and Peter were surprised at the number of men who succumbed to the punishing regime. Having begun the day on landing craft, they moved on to drill, marching, shooting and training on the hills, which Peter particularly enjoyed planning. In addition, they covered obstacle courses and close combat, taught by two ex-Shanghai policemen whose novel methods, including the use of wrestling, knives and pistols, were not part of the average infantryman's arsenal.

The attack on the Azores was finally called off and No. 3 Commando was moved to the seaside. Largs, in Ayrshire, was to Glaswegians what Southend was to Londoners: a place to get away

36

from the city. Large numbers of people visited during the summer months and the town was well equipped with accommodation of all sorts in which to billet the new influx of soldiers. Peter lived at the Royal Hotel and by all accounts the hospitality was excellent. They continued their training at the back of the town where the terrain was ideal, being rough moorland.

Peter was a hard taskmaster – when Corporal Duff Cooper's section was wiped out by an umpire early on in one exercise the men repaired to the local tavern where Peter eventually found them. 'What the bloody hell is going on here?' he is reported to have demanded. 'Dead men are no good to me!'

His standards were exacting – if he thought that an exercise could be carried out faster he would make the men march, then double, then march again, all the while singing their favourite tune 'Mother Reilly's daughter'. While this was going on, he would run up and down the column to make sure they were all singing. His batman at that time remembered that Peter was constantly out on the 'wet hills' behind Largs, and that his boots were always very muddy.

At about this time, the War Office decided to rename the Commandos and to call them Special Service Battalions. As this would have meant the British acquiring their very own SS troops, Durnford-Slater resolutely and angrily refused to use the title. After a few weeks he won the day and the Special Service Battalions once more became Commandos. In the meantime, Peter's (undated) posting to Largs appeared in his records as being to 'No. 4 SS Bn'. On 10 November 1940 his record reads: 'Reposted No. 3 Commando', clearly a paper move.

In December, the raid on Pantelleria was rehearsed, the troops were embarked on three fast merchantmen, *Glen Roy*, *Glen Erne* and *Glen Gyle*, and taken from Gourock to Lamlash Bay on the Isle of Arran to prepare for departure. Once again, Peter did not let up on his training regime.

If Peter's temper was not precisely volcanic, his men certainly knew when he was displeased. He had a way of smiling which put the fear of God into those who knew him well. He spared no one the rigours of his training regime – to an increasingly large extent he was running the training of the whole of No. 3 Commando – and had no compunction about returning men to their units if they were not able to keep up. He did, however, reward endeavour and his men responded to that, anxious on the one hand not to incur his displeasure and on the other to make their troop the best there was.

During the waiting and final training for this operation, Nos 3 and 8 Commando had an unfortunate misadventure. There was to be a full-scale rehearsal of the landings near Brodick, witnessed by Keyes and other VIPs from the beach. The fate of the operation rested on the performance of the commando on that exercise. It was due to begin at 0200 hours and Durnford-Slater requested a wake-up call at 0100 hours. It never came. He awoke at 0145 hours to find the ship dark and quiet. By the time he had aroused his exhausted officers, they were already late for zero hour. The landing craft pushed off ten minutes late and their progress to the shore was watched by two-thirds of the men who had arrived on deck, bleary eyed and half dressed but too late to embark; the landings were a trickle where they should have been a flood. Mortified, Durnford-Slater apologized to Keyes for letting him down. Keyes, who had a reputation as something of a martinet, gave a wise response.

'You've had your lesson,' he said. 'Now this will never happen to you operationally where it could truly mean disaster.'

Whether or not this debacle affected the decision, Pantelleria was called off. The men departed on Christmas leave having been enjoined by Keyes to keep their 'spearhead bright'. This, Peter noted, was easier said than done. Both the raids for which they had spent the summer training had been cancelled, and now the Commandos were to be split up, with Nos 7, 8 and 11 Commandos, plus A Troop from 3 Commando – Layforce – departing for the Middle East under the command of Lieutenant Colonel Robert Laycock.

Morale was low and some men threatened to return to their units. Durnford-Slater gathered the men together below decks on the *Glen Roy*, which should have been taking them on their first mission, and, as Peter said, 'gave them the speech of his life; he went round each troop in turn, picking on some characteristic of its men and drawing roars of delight from his audience'. Of H Troop he said: '[They] are the old soldiers, just like the men I used to have in India before the war. I'm very fond of H Troop.'

H Troop, however, was not long to survive. On return from Christmas leave, the number of troops was reduced from ten to six and they were given numbers rather than letters for identification. Accordingly, H Troop became 6 Troop, a much better arrangement that suited Peter particularly well. 6 Troop was nearly up to strength so it did not need to merge with another troop as most of the others did.

At this auspicious moment, another operation was announced. Operation Claymore was designed to send the Germans a message: although the British Army might not be on mainland Europe, they were nonetheless a force to be reckoned with.

The more modest objectives of the raid on the Lofoten Islands were to destroy fish oil installations and shipping, and to bring back prisoners as well as volunteers. It was a perfect job for the Commandos and, if successful, could have far-reaching effects; the islands provided 50 per cent of the herring and cod oils which were refined in occupied Norway.

This obscure group of islands lies within the Arctic Circle about 850 miles from Scapa Flow. For the purposes of the operation the four major ports were allotted to the two commandos which were to carry out the raid: Stamsund and Henningsvaer to No. 3, and Svolvaer and Brettesnes, to No. 4. The nearest German garrisons were 100 miles to the north-east at Narvik, or 60 miles to the south, at Bodø; the climate meant that no airfield north of Trondheim, 300 miles to the south, could be used unless the aircraft was fitted with skis. Intelligence indicated that German shipping in the area was infrequent, with only one mail ship making a daily round. It was believed that there were small parties of about twenty Germans on each of the islands but there were none at Stamsund or Svolvaer. U-boats had been seen in Narvik in January, but the threat from warships in the area was considered to be neglible.

All in all, the planners considered that a raid carried out by 3 Commando and 4 Commando, with a combined strength of about 500, would deliver a short, sharp shock to the Germans in general, and the Quislings in particular.

The weeks between the Commandos' return from Christmas leave and their embarkation were filled with more training as the men accustomed themselves to the prospect of an ice-bound landing in sub-zero temperatures – whereas before Christmas they had been hoping for more balmy conditions. Peter also used this training to ensure that the men did not think too much about the operations for which they had prepared throughout the summer and autumn of the previous year.

Despite the prospect of another show the men were fatalistic, expecting that it too would be cancelled and worse, that the commando might be disbanded. Peter dealt with the situation by contriving ever more ingenious exercises to test the men's battle-craft and stamina. Not only did their ever-improving performance give them confidence in their own abilities under fire, but they were being welded into an unbeatably strong team, both independent and interdependent. Much later, Peter wrote to John Adair on the subject of military leadership: 'I believe that a good infantry unit is one that is fit and hard, is superlatively good with its weapons, and widely trained in tactics. The CO may sleep when he has taught all his followers all that he knows himself and is confident that they will act as he would wish when he is not there and hasn't been for 6 months.'

Peter certainly aspired to be a commander in that mould, differing from his contemporaries, not in the desire to be at the head of the best unit in the Army, but in the way he set about trying to ensure his men were the best they could be. He was an innovative trainer and a gifted tactician. This happy conjunction of abilities enabled him to excel at the tricky task of bringing his troops to battle readiness at a time when morale was low and the future uncertain.

On Friday, 21 February the troops embarked once again at Gourock, but this time proceeded to Scapa Flow which they reached the following afternoon. Anchored between HMS *Nelson* and HMS *King George V*, the *Princess Emma* (4 Commando) and the *Princess Beatrix* (3 Commando) were the hub of activity as they finalised the plans and operation orders for their first real trial by fire. Durnford-Slater had issued detailed instructions and final training was conducted with personnel with whom they would need to operate: landing craft crews, sappers and Norwegians who would be accompanying the raiding force, among whom was Martin Linge, a leader in the Norwegian resistance. Peter's troop, forty strong, was to be in one of the leading landing craft, acting as scout, and Durnford-Slater elected to ride with them. They staggered the landings to try and ensure that the whole raiding force did not come under fire at the same time.

On 1 March the signal arrived giving the order to proceed. The force was commanded by the Commander-in-Chief Home Fleet and consisted of HMS *Nelson*, *King George V*, *Nigeria*, *Dido*, five destroyers and the submarine *Sunfish*, as well as the *Princess Emma* and *Princess Beatrix*, Dutch cross-Channel ferries which had been converted to carry landing craft, but which were not designed to operate in deep waters. They arrived at Skaalefjord in the Faroes nineteen hours later, pursuing an elliptical course to keep out of range of German air cover. After a five-hour pause to allow the destroyers to refuel, the fleet moved on into the Arctic Circle and were in the vicinity of the Lofotens by the early morning of 4 March. It had been an uncomfortable crossing, during which it had become clear that those who had claimed to be immune to seasickness had not been entirely truthful.

They sailed into Westfjord on the morning of 4 March, and by 0400 hrs the navigational lights of the waters round the Lofotens were clearly visible. It was still dark, but the weather was unseasonably warm. So far everything had gone according to plan; even the *Sunfish* was on station to guide the force to its final destination. The landing craft proceeded ashore at a steady speed despite the boat commanders' apprehension that they would be spotted and attacked before they could land.

From the Largs Hill Hotel four days later, Peter wrote an account to his mother of what happened next. It gives a clear idea of how he himself viewed recent events.

I suppose now you will want some account of our raid on the Lofoten Islands . . . We had a big naval escort.

My troop was in the first boat to land at Stamsund. A destroyer [HMS *Legion*] led us in, firing a few bursts to turn back the fishing boats, which, it being dawn, [landings began at 0600 hrs] were leaving the harbour in great numbers. We had the White Ensign hoisted in our bows, and when they saw it all the Norwegian fishermen cheered and ran up their flag from half-mast to their mastheads. We shouted 'Ver ar Teesker? [sic] 'Where are the Germans?' and were told there weren't any. We scrambled onto the pier with the aid of our scaling ladders and made our way through the streets to our various objectives. Wills took the Telegraph Station and Telephone Exchange, which was all one building. No message had been sent out about our arrival. I took over the Post Office, 2 Germans were arrested at an hotel, civilians. One was a friend of the Gauleiter of Kenigsberg, the other his secretary. The big noise was there to start a cod oil factory, purely for the benefit of the German Govt. (but he owned 23 out of 25 shares!).

I took charge of Mr Johansen, who is the wealthiest man in the place, the Post Office was apparently run for his own profit. I took him for a walk while my men sacked the place. There were 3 Officers and 36 of [6] Troop in this operation. I

41

had 3 Norwegians, one a Capt. [Martin Linge] who speaks good English, attached to me. We were pretty busy with police work, keeping the Norwegians from the demolitions. We also rolled many barrels of oil into the fjord and shot holes in them!

They gave gloves to many of our soldiers – one woman gave me a grey pair, I gave her four squares of a bar of chocolate I was consuming. One soldier actually got a pair of shoes. We brought 106 Norwegian volunteers back from Stamsund. One appeared with his army tunic and greatcoat and his rifle, which he had kept hidden in his house . . . death penalty if he had been found out. Some few had suitcases, but most came as they were in their thick fishing clothes.

At Svolvaer a German lieutenant, who was on leave, was taken prisoner, he didn't mind much.

The best of the whole business was that the Bosche were apparently building some kind of air base and W/T Stn. [Wireless Transmitter Station] at Svolvaer. 197 prisoners were taken without opposition, though a Troop Commander [Captain Cooke] of No 4 shot himself with his pistol which was in a trouser pocket and went off by accident. 98 civilians [including] 8 women were brought away as volunteers from Svolvaer. The destroyers brought off more. The only fighting was when an armed trawler [the *Krebs*] attacked the *Somali* with the Brig. [Haydon] on board. The trawler was eventually sunk with 7 Bosche killed.

The capture of the Post Office was not without its lighter side. Bill Bradley, one of Peter's subalterns, was left to secure it once they knew that no warning message had been sent. A copy of the chit he left there is in Peter's papers:

This is to certify that His Majesty's Forces have visited STAMSUND POST OFFICE, and removed any such Mails, Monies etc as may be useful in terminating the War.

Any such claims against His Brittanic Majesty's Government should be tendered when Hitler meets his deserts [sic] when the War is over.

Given under my hand,
4/3/41
E.W. Bradley, Lieut.

Not to be outdone by this, Dick Wills, who secured the Telephone Exchange and Telegraph Office within minutes of the landing, broadcast his presence there by sending the following telegram to A. Hitler, Berlin:

YOU SAID IN YOUR LAST SPEECH GERMAN TROOPS WOULD MEET THE ENGLISH WHEREVER THEY LANDED STOP WHERE ARE YOUR TROOPS? (signed) WILLS 2-LIEUT.'

Peter's orders had been to secure the landing place and its approaches, control communications, protect the landing craft after disembarkation and cover the withdrawal. The lack of enemy resistance rendered much of this mission unnecessary and the rest was executed with almost disappointing ease. The hardest part of the raid came at the end when, at about 1045 hrs, 6 Troop was ordered back to the quay to organise re-embarkation. The extremely friendly Norwegians were by now thronging the dock in holiday spirit, making orderly withdrawal very difficult and marching anywhere impossible.

The Quislings who were rounded up during the raid were not taken prisoner, having been identified by business rivals who had an interest in exaggerating their treachery. Before Durnford-Slater left he had them drawn up in a single rank and delivered a homily to them. Peter described Durnford-Slater's delivery as follows:

He always spoke in a rather breathless, high-pitched voice. Now, speaking with great rapidity, he said: 'Yeah, well, I don't want to hear any more of this bloody Quisling business. It's no bloody good, I'm telling you. If I hear there's been any more of it, I'll be back again and next time I'll take the whole bloody lot of you. Now clear off!'

Their limited command of English left them wondering what, among other things, Quisling business (which Durnford-Slater uttered as if it were one word) might mean.

By 1105 hrs, the last Commando had re-embarked without mishap and two hours later the ships turned for home. After so many false starts, the success of the raid provided a boost to the men's morale, but the lack of resistance had been, to use Peter's own word, 'unsatisfactory'. As yet untried under fire, the men had nonetheless achieved all their objectives and proved to the Germans that they could get under their skin. It was promising, but it was only a beginning.

Chapter Five

Vaagso

Writing to his mother, Peter gives a glimpse of how he thought his war was going:

> By the way I am now seventh senior officer in this Unit, which I joined as a Second Lieutenant in June. I have been to Metz, Lille, Brussels, Guernsey, Largs, Plymouth, Carvin, Glasgow, Edinburgh, Roubaix [he does not mention Dunkirk!] none of which I had ever seen before. In the four years before, I saw only Oxford and Oxshott [the family home] and though I adore both, I tended to be narrow minded. I have done different things, I have had command of two different Infantry Platoons and one in an A/T C [Anti-tank Company]. I have been Liaison Officer, Asst Adjt [Assistant Adjutant] and commanded a section and then a Troop in a Commando. All these changes have made the War one of the happiest times of my life – which of course is shocking.

This paragraph manages at once to convey excitement, pride and a certain naïve pleasure in his accomplishments. The mention of his seniority within the commando shows that his ambition to forge up the promotion ladder was undimmed. His extravagant attachment to Oxford and Oxshott would have mollified his mother – he knew that she was concerned, as any mother would be, about the dangers of his present employment, but in the end he is unable to disguise the fact that he was thoroughly enjoying himself.

This letter was written in haste, but it shows a terse command of language, desirable in military writing, that conveys much in few words. He kept detailed records of his exploits for he was ambitious enough to foresee the need to write memoirs once he achieved his twin wartime objectives of reaching the rank of Brigadier and winning the Victoria Cross.

He spent the remainder of the year at Largs, with occasional forays into other Scottish training territory. He soon acquired a new member of the troop from the Beds and Herts in the form of Private Freddie Craft who joined the commando in March 1941. He was to become his batman and, later, driver before being killed at Agnone in 1943. By coincidence, Craft attended the same school in Maple Cross as Robert Christopher who was to succeed him as Peter's batman. In Christopher's unpublished memoirs he expressed surprise that Craft became a batman: 'He was always so untidy at school.'

It was a frustrating time during which operations came and went without coming to fruition. Peter remained focussed on training, something he enjoyed, and Durnford-Slater was pleased to make use of his talent:

> Peter Young continued to study his troop attack and I often went and worked with his troop. Their technique had come on a lot since the Plymouth days and I found work in one of his movement groups the hardest exercise I have ever taken.
>
> Another of Peter Young's activities was the training of potential NCOs. I frequently took him off all other duties for this purpose, giving him a squad of about twenty-five promising men. They would do an intensive three-week course, after which Peter could tell me with almost unfailing accuracy which men would make good NCOs and which would be just ordinary, good, private soldiers.

This ability to judge people so accurately required a shrewdness which was evident to everybody who ever met him. Many never realized that the deceptively mild questions being asked and the apparently casual glance accompanying the smile were weapons of extraordinary power.

The true nature of the relationship between Peter and his commanding officer is hard to determine. Durnford-Slater was a Gunner with little or no infantry background. He therefore relied on Peter from an early stage to provide tactical direction and Peter always fully supported his CO on the grounds that part of his job consisted of making his own superiors look good. Peter's personal views about Durnford-Slater's tactical acumen remained somewhat vague, although he once said that he thought Durnford-Slater was lazy. If true, it suited Peter to provide the impetus he felt was lacking in order to raise his own profile within the military hierarchy. There was a contrast in the two men's style for, despite indications to the contrary, Peter was a fairly cautious soldier, preferring to sit still and weigh up a situation rather than rushing in at once – whereas Durnford-Slater favoured a more robust approach once the planning was over. John de Lash, who admittedly did not like Durnford-Slater, felt that he leant on Peter, and that it was Charlie Head with whom Durnford-Slater formed a closer friendship.

Whilst relations with his CO were cordial, Peter felt that he was the superior infantry officer, and his drive to develop training and tactics was his way of making his mark on the commando. He was not alone in this drive to be 'first among equals' – it was a competitive environment and there were other officers who felt equally well qualified to excel; relations amongst the troop commanders reflected this. There was a certain waspishness which characterized their relationships which arose more from the competitive instinct than any real dislike of the personalities involved. Peter, at all events, identified and exploited his own opportunities for advancement which he rapidly made as his own.

Gruelling exercises and NCO training were alleviated by periods of leave. Durnford-Slater recognized that there was only so much training which could usefully be carried out and some time needed to be spent keeping the troops motivated, happy and in peak condition. He therefore saw to it that the troops were regularly sent off on leave, even when unauthorized by Brigadier Haydon, the commander of the Commando Brigade. These leave periods were usually very short so that troops could not travel far. The change, however, was as good as a rest, and 3 Commando maintained a commendable level of fitness and preparedness despite a succession of cancelled operations which tried both their patience and their enthusiasm.

On 27 October 1941, Sir Roger Keyes was succeeded as Director of Combined Operations by Commodore the Lord Louis Mountbatten. Though a highly respected veteran, Keyes was accorded no more resources by the War Office than those deemed necessary to keep the Commandos operational. Such resources were not enough to enable them to mount the hit-and-run seaborne attacks for which they had been formed. Failing these, and in order to try and provide them with

47

some operational reason for their existence, Keyes had tried to mount much larger expeditions which were unsuitable for the Commandos. It was this impasse which had caused the lull in operations after the Lofoten Islands raid and was now threatening their very existence.

The appointment of Mountbatten was the inspiration of Winston Churchill who, almost alone, continued to believe in the potential of this new form of warfare. It was an inspired choice. From the Commandos' point of view their new Director was everything their previous one had not been. Keyes was highly respected but he had gained his experience in the First World War. Mountbatten, at forty-one, was a destroyer captain with a distinguished war record, and of the same generation as the men he was now to lead.

The operation which materialized soon after his appointment was an attack on more Norwegian islands, Vaagso and Maaloy, which lie midway between Bergen and Alesund. The objective for the raid was more ambitious than that on the Lofotens. German troops from the 181st Division were known to be stationed there, and the attack was an attempt to induce the German high command to increase troop numbers in the area, forcing a reduction elsewhere, in particular Africa and Russia. The tactical aims were to destroy the garrison, the fish-oil factories and any shipping, as well as to capture Quislings and bring home anyone who wished to volunteer for the Free Norwegian Forces. A success would be excellent public relations at a time when the British public had little to be cheerful about.

Mountbatten was anxious for his first operation to be a success and when the plan was outlined to him he asked Durnford-Slater whether it might not be better to attack an easier target. Ever pugnacious, Durnford-Slater assured him that with the aid of ship-board ordnance there would be no problem with shore-based resistance.

Durnford-Slater gathered his troop commanders at his headquarters in Largs, Broomfield House, and briefed them on this new adventure. It was early December 1942. 3 Commando were to take the lead, reinforced by two troops of 2 Commando – a total of eight troops, divided into five forces of varying strengths. Peter was disappointed to discover that 6 Troop was under the command of Major 'Mad' Jack Churchill, Durnford-Slater's deputy, who was to lead the attack on Maaloy rather than Vaagso. He thought he would not, therefore, be in the thick of the fight.

The force embarked at Gourock on 13 December in two Belgian cross-channel steamers, *Prince Charles* and *Prince Leopold*, converted to carry assault landing craft. The force assembled at Scapa Flow where the final exercises and briefings took place. Joint command was shared between Rear Admiral Burrough RN and Brigadier Charles Haydon DSO, leaving Durnford-Slater to handle the tactical elements. The destroyers HMS *Chiddingfold*, *Offa*, *Onslow* and *Oribi* provided a screen for the ships carrying the troops. These were followed by HMS *Kenya* which carried the force commanders. The submarine HMS *Tuna* had gone on ahead to signal to the force the narrow entrance to the Vaagsfjord.

The force left Scapa bound for the Shetland Isles at 2115 hrs on 24 December and had a rough passage with gale-force winds producing tumultuous seas. Despite this, the men were heard singing Vera Lynn's song 'Yours' during the crossing. On arrival at Sollum Voe at 1300 hrs on Christmas Day the creaks, groans and crashes heard during the passage were investigated and 14 feet of water was found in the forward area of the *Prince Charles*, along with considerable damage to the superstructure; it took the pumps of HMS *Chiddingfold* several hours to rectify the problem on Christmas afternoon. An extra day was required to carry out repairs which immediately gave rise to talk that the whole operation was being postponed or cancelled, so when the wind started dropping towards the evening of the following day, there was a sense of relief all round. They put to sea again at 1600 hrs on Boxing Day and the weather continued to improve over the final leg of the journey.

During the crossing the final briefings were given. The men had been thoroughly prepared ashore using aerial photographs and a model of the area. Peter remembered feeling the need to impress on 6 Troop that they must take prisoners, mindful of possible resentment over their treatment at Dunkirk. A group of officers and sergeants fell to discussing the operation and most were of Durnford-Slater's opinion that the battery on Maaloy would offer the stiffest opposition. Peter held the minority view that the hardest task would be in the town of Sor Vaagso itself. He felt – correctly, as it turned out – that the layout of the town, a long, thin development with a fjord on one side and a steep hillside on the other, would mean that troops advancing, effectively in file, up the only main street could be separated by the defenders and that control, and possibly impetus, would be impossible to maintain.

Early the following morning Peter got up and, fully accoutred, went on deck. It was still dark and very cold but all the troops had been issued either with a leather jerkin or a roll-neck sweater. Restless, he toured the mess decks to make sure that all the equipment was ready, although he knew there was nothing he could do about it if he found any deficiencies. After breakfast at 0500 hrs the men assembled on the boat deck. Although first light was at 0850 hrs, dawn was beginning to lighten the sky. Incredibly, *Tuna* was sighted within one minute of the rendezvous time (0700 hrs) which was heartening to everybody as there could not now be any doubt about their position. Peter took this considerable feat of navigation for granted: 'I had a touching faith in the navigational abilities of the Royal Navy – fortified by an intimate acquaintance with the career of Captain Hornblower – and did not for one moment imagine that they could not find their way anywhere, by day or night, with perfect ease.'

Vaagsfjord was in effect a coastal waterway that allowed German shipping complete protection from both the enemy and the elements as it plied up and down the Norwegian coastline. The interdiction of this route was part of the plan, and as the small British force steamed into the peaceful German-controlled seaway there was a collective intake of breath to see what would happen. The channel lights were functioning at Hordenoes and Bergsholmene which indicated that no one had been alerted to their presence. As planned, the *Prince Charles* and *Prince Leopold* pulled into a bay and transferred the men into their landing craft. As the landing craft hit the water, *Kenya* opened fire on Maaloy Island. It was 0842 hrs.

The exercise of command and control in this action was new because it relied on combined operation from both the Army and the Navy. The net set up from the command ship (HMS *Kenya*) and Durnford-Slater's headquarters position ashore was crucial for it enabled Haydon's staff to co-ordinate troop movements and reinforcements.

At 0857 hrs Durnford-Slater – whose first time in battle this was – fired ten red Very lights to signal the end of the bombardment and the start of a bombing run. His group, consisting of 1, 2, 3 and 4 Troops, were to land in Sor Vaagso itself. On cue, the Hampdens arrived and dropped their phosphorous smoke bombs to shield the men during landing. The Germans scored a hit when anti-aircraft fire got one of the Hampdens which ditched its bombs into and around one of the incoming landing craft, causing several casualties. The medical officer, Sam Corry, was on hand to take charge of the casualties, and once the landing craft had been evacuated and pushed back out to sea the remaining forces continued with the landing.

Meanwhile, Churchill's men landed in perfect formation on Maaloy. Peter described it: 'Jack Churchill took up his bagpipes and began to play ['The March of the Cameron Men'] . . . standing the while, fully exposed, in the front of the craft and gazing calmly ahead. The men liked that.' Peter's men remembered that he similarly led from the front and spurned taking cover even under fire. As the landing was completed, eerily unopposed, Churchill calmly summoned his batman to exchange his pipes for his claymore.

Peter went ashore on rocky, dead ground. He sprinted up the cliff and waited for his troop to join him, deploy in formation and fix bayonets before advancing in formation, as Durnfold-Slater observed from the other side of the Sound: 'Nos 5 and 6 Troops, only fifty yards from the beach when the naval barrage lifted, were up the slopes of the island like a flash. I saw them advancing through the smoke in perfect extended order.'

It was not until Peter's troop had taken one of the German gun positions that any enemy activity was forthcoming. A grenade exploded at the same time as a German soldier appeared, running towards them. Taking cover inside the gun emplacement and resting his rifle on the wall, Peter shot the man, observing to Sergeant Vincent that if he was killed that day, at least he would take one of them with him.

There was no further sign of the expected counter-attack, so Peter pushed on to take the fight to the enemy. They systematically went through the hut encampment searching and destroying buildings as they went, but found nobody there. One of his section commanders, George Herbert, appeared with about fifteen prisoners, one of whom was the military commander, Hauptmann Butziger, who had been taking cover in a shelter below the hill on which the camp stood.

Sending them back to the beach, Peter continued to clear the huts, accompanied only by Lance Corporal Rocky Harper. At the battery office, which was already on fire, they discovered two further Germans who were less co-operative; one of them snatched at Peter's fixed bayonet. Surprised, Peter drew back thinking that the man would surrender, but instead he ran, sensing Peter's hesitation. A moment later, Peter fired from the hip and hit his man.

All effective resistance was now at an end. Peter set the demolition party to work and returned to the burning battery office to remove any papers that might prove useful. This done, they left it to burn to the ground.

51

At 0920 hrs, Churchill signalled that Maaloy was secure and was shortly afterwards instructed to send troops to destroy the factory at Mortenes. For this task he selected 5 Troop, leaving Peter and his men at a loose end. From all that could be seen, the attack on Sor Vaagso was going well – there was little in the way of a firefight. Peter searched the remainder of the island but found nothing beyond three more German bodies and a Christmas tree. It was 1012 hrs.

The operation on Sor Vaagso now ran into severe opposition and half Peter's men were ordered to join Durnford-Slater's group as reinforcements. Peter requested permission to go himself and, summoning the nearest sections, Herbert's and Connolly's – about eighteen men in all – he boarded one of the assault craft. Although he would have preferred to take a larger force, the men on Maaloy were scattered and time was short.

Jack Ramsden, one of the official photographers, recalled: 'I . . . heard an officer say: "Well boys, I don't know what we're going into, but it looks pretty sticky. Remember what your job is and your drill and we'll pull through."' The officer could only have been Peter and he remembered thinking that he had no clear idea of what was going on, or what to expect, because no one had any information.

Assessing the situation as best he could, he decided not to land at the original disembarkation point since the action seemed to have moved north from that, so he asked the boat officer to land them further up the coast where khaki uniforms could be seen advancing up the town. To his surprise he was met on landing by Charlie Head who shook him warmly by the hand, and by several other colleagues. Komrower's men greeted the newcomers with: 'Good old 6 Troop!' Peter realized that things were, indeed, pretty sticky. Normally the men of 4 Troop had not got a good word to say about those from 6 Troop.

On hearing of Peter's arrival, Durnford-Slater found him with George Herbert lobbing grenades through every window and door they could. 'They appeared,' he wrote in his memoirs, 'to be enjoying themselves.'

While Peter's men took cover in the cemetery, Durnford-Slater took him forward to reconnoitre as he brought him up to date. It had been a hard and expensive fight. The commanders of the two assault troops, Algy Forrester and Johnny Giles, had both been killed, as had Martin Linge. Together with the wounded, this had made a signifi-cant dent in the strength of the attack which was running out of steam. The Germans were unexpectedly reinforced by about fifty men who had been sent north on Christmas leave; they were from a good, battle-hardened unit and had ensured that the attack in the town had stalled. Durnford-Slater was anxious to get some forward momentum once more and, along with Peter's reinforcements, he had also called up 2 Troop from Halnoesvik.

While Peter listened, he carried out a swift appreciation of the scene: the layout of the town favoured the defenders with the main street more or less unassailable and well covered by enemy snipers. To the west, there was a steep snow-covered hillside, and to the east lay the fjord. The best way to press forward was, he thought, by going towards the seafront and using the warehouses down there as cover. He made this suggestion to Durnford-Slater and the plan was agreed. Denis O'Flaherty, with 2 Troop, was put under Peter's command.

He returned to brief his men and found that they had been resupplied with ammunition. In order to reach the dockside warehouses they ran in single file across the square where he had been briefed and, from the cover of a warehouse doorway, O'Flaherty pointed out known German positions. Leaving a Bren gunner in an upper window to cover their advance, the party moved on to the next building, a small shed about 20 yards away. As they reached the nearest doorway a group of Germans ran into the building. As Peter approached shouting, '*Hände hoch*!' he was joined by Trooper Sherington who crouched in the doorway and emptied his tommy gun into the building. This had the desired effect, and three Germans and a Norwegian surrendered.

To the north of the shed lay a wood pile stacked in an L-shape to create a small, sheltered area which Peter described as a breastwork. There was only one narrow entrance and most of the troop had crowded into this small space. A sniper opened fire, resulting in two casualties, one of them fatal. While Peter sent the walking wounded back to the landing site with the prisoners, Durnford-Slater arrived and decided that it was time to move.

About 60 yards away there was a large warehouse which seemed to offer the best place to regroup. Peter led off, hampered by the slippery conditions and a haversack full of grenades. He was making satisfactory progress until a German soldier appeared in a doorway about 30 feet away and threw a stick grenade at him. Reacting instinctively, he swerved to avoid it, firing from his hip as he went. A second grenade followed, landing in almost the same spot, but Peter evaded them both and reached the warehouse safely.

As the rest of the party joined him a stick grenade was thrown from

53

the building and landed just 8 feet away. 'We looked at it, fascinated, for a second or two,' he wrote later, 'wondering how much damage it was going to do to our legs, but it did not go off.' People were talking inside and they lobbed a dozen or so Mills grenades through the warehouse door before entering the building. In front of them was a small hallway with a wooden staircase leading to the right and a doorway straight ahead, affording plenty of cover for the occupants – as Peter swiftly found out. Silhouetted against the light in the doorway he was fired upon from the right, but was not hit and immediately withdrew, firing back as he did so.

Outflanking this building would be difficult as one end of it was on the water and the other on the main street. Posting guards at every possible point of egress, Peter and O'Flaherty reconnoitred to see how best to proceed. Even as they did so, Durnford-Slater reappeared once more, urging them on.

Peter decided to set fire to it, but just as George Herbert threw a bucket of petrol into the building and lit it, O'Flaherty decided on another course of action and, accompanied by Trooper Sherington, ran through the doorway. Peter felt bound to follow them in. He had reached the bottom of the stairs when two shots rang out and both men fell. Peter fired towards the source of the gunfire before he withdrew, miraculously without being hit, wondering how best to extract his wounded comrades. Before he could take any action they appeared at the doorway. Sherington had been hit in the leg and O'Flaherty in the face, the bullet having entered his eye and left through his throat. As Peter organized their evacuation the fire caught and in moments the wooden warehouse was ablaze. His men rescued three horses from stables in another part of the building and eventually two Germans were killed trying to escape from the inferno. When, later, Peter and his men withdrew back down the street, the heat from the fire was so intense that they had to cross to the other side of the road.

He pushed on up the town towards the Firda Factory, the final rendezvous point, with about a dozen men. They left the dock area and moved up the main street where there were a number of German dead. At the Hagen Hotel, also on fire, they moved off the main street and made their way along the hillside behind the houses on the left of the road. Although they were in the open, no one fired on them but progress was nerve-racking for they did not know where the enemy might be and the few Norwegians they encountered were too frightened to help.

Towards the top of the town, Peter decided to move back into the dock area to the right of the main street, although the buildings ran down to the water which made progress more difficult. He had noticed a motor car nearby which indicated that one of the houses might be the German commander's billet. When Durnford-Slater appeared once again at his elbow they searched the suspicious house and discovered a German officer, apparently in a bad way, in one of the bedrooms. Prisoners subsequently identified him as Major Schroeder of 111/Infanterie Regiment 742, the garrison commander, wounded during the initial bombardment and left to die.

They advanced slowly. Peter and his men lobbed grenades through windows and fired on any positions where they thought Germans might be concealed. He was not amused to discover that one of his sections had been taken by another troop commander to recover the dead and wounded to the landing point, however Durnford-Slater replaced this missing section with a scratch team of his own and together they continued the advance. Just south of the Firda Factory they encountered a stream running from the hillside into the fjord. This afforded some natural cover and Peter deployed his men in the stream bed to cover Durnford-Slater's advance. Durnford-Slater, pistol in hand, marched through the stream and continued up the main street at a smart pace, flanked by his runners.

There was a strange pause until George Herbert gesticulated urgently although there was nothing to be seen, much less to fire at. Then there was an explosion and Peter saw Durnford-Slater flying through the air. Some shots followed and two members of the Colonel's section were seen limping back towards Peter, who went forward at once to where Durnford-Slater had last been seen. The two runners were badly wounded; the explosion had been a stick grenade thrown by a German in one of the houses nearby. Durnford-Slater's spectacular aerial manoeuvre had saved his life – he had dived for a doorway and escaped with grazed knuckles. Sergeant Mills, who had been in Durnford-Slater's party, completed the action when the German sailor who had thrown the grenade emerged from a side street intending to surrender, but when he saw the look in Mills's eyes he faltered.

'Nein, nein,' he said desperately.

'Ja, ja,' Mills responded implacably, and shot him.

With trademark sangfroid, Durnford-Slater took in the scene and remarked, 'Yeah, well, Mills, you shouldn't ha' done that.'

Shortly afterwards, they reached the Firda Factory. Durnford-Slater organized the demolition of the buildings, and placed Peter and his troop in a substantial house on the right side of the main street in case the Germans tried to counter-attack before the demolitions were complete. He then fell back to his headquarters near the landing site to make his report to the flag ship. It was then about 1145 hrs. Peter's part in the action in Sor Vaagso had taken about an hour and a half; he was under orders to fall back no later than 1310 hrs.

Apart from the acquisition of a prisoner who became unreasonably incensed when Peter asked him if he was Prussian – he claimed to be Pomeranian – and the start of a belated, sporadic air attack by German Heinkel 111s, the action was over. Just over an hour after he had taken up his position, the whole area was quiet and the demolition party had pulled out. It was time to go.

An hour is time enough for the blood to cool. They were all hungry and thirsty and aware that they had to move back through the main street of the town where there were still snipers. It would, Peter thought, be a pity if the men were shot up at this late stage. At the German headquarters, the Ulvesund Hotel, he acquired a memento of the day, an epaulette with yellow piping from a dead German signaller. At the site where the force's 3-inch mortar had been positioned, they recovered a number of unexploded mortar bombs which had been left behind during the withdrawal, but they did not see anybody from their own side until they reached the quayside where the Adjutant, Captain Alan Smallman, and RSM Beesley were marshalling men into boats for re-embarkation.

One final piece of demolition remained to be done and Durnford-Slater had ordered that it be left until the rearguard had passed through. The sergeant in charge of the demolition lit the fuze and sounded the warning blast on his whistle that was the signal to take cover. The factory collapsed gently onto the shuddering earth and the job was complete. Final evacuation proceeded without incident although a number of Norwegians – men, women and children – now swelled the ranks of the returning troops.

Peter returned to the *Prince Leopold* to find 6 Troop already embarked. He reported:

During the voyage back, I had very little sleep because I helped to interrogate the prisoners who were all stripped and searched before questioning. We kept them shut up in the lavatories . . . If they talked they were given a hot drink and a sandwich of

56

bread and bully; if they did not talk they got nothing to eat. One prisoner invoked the Geneva Convention. He was asked why, if he believed in Geneva, was he in Norway.

Tactically, Operation Archery, as the raid on Vaagso was called, was a success. As their real baptism of fire, 3 Commando's first action was all that Mountbatten could have hoped for and the publicity was just what Churchill needed.

In the cold light of day, however, lessons had been learnt, and they had not been without cost. Although it can have given him no pleasure, given the casualties that had arisen from the action in the town, Peter must have taken some satisfaction from knowing that his instincts before the action had been right: all the difficulties of operating in such a restricted area had caused the attackers problems. He wrote afterwards of the situation which confronted them in Sor Vaagso:

[The German] snipers had the main road 'taped'. Any move-ment of our people in the open was overlooked from the houses or from the ridge above. It was the kind of situation which normally called for a deliberate attack supported by heavy guns, tanks, flame throwers and mortars. In this raid there was no time for such tactics. This meant that the troops' section commanders must go in front and take what was coming to them. Leading from behind was not feasible. There is nothing especially heroic about this. It is part of an officer's job, but in our case it was perhaps more dangerous than usual because we were quite unpractised in the art of street fighting. True, we had done something of the sort in a street in Largs, but you cannot simulate the conditions of war in a built-up area where houses and back gardens are all inhabited . . . It is not surprising that men were used up rapidly under such conditions and John [Durnford-Slater] soon had to call for reinforcements.

Peter did not neglect his men's welfare either. His personal account of the action, written on HMS *Leopold* and dated 28/12/[19]41 also contains some useful lessons learnt about what rations he felt should be taken on such operations. The Operation Order stated that water bottles were to be carried, but not filled. Peter commented that 'my own view is that they should have been filled', and the subsequent Operation Order for the Dieppe raid does state that water bottles should be filled. Haversacks were optional for Operation Archery, and no emergency rations were issued 'which,' Peter opines, 'I thought was a mistake'; no sandwiches were taken, and only two containers of cocoa per troop were carried. Although no rum ration was issued before the operation Peter discovered that many of the men had saved previous grog issues in their 'empty' water bottles. As all officers come to understand, their men acquire talents from which they could learn, and Peter was quick to do so.

None of the participants in any of the raids carried out by the Commandos ever forgot the distinct scent of each battle. This, 3 Commando's baptism of fire, in the most literal sense, proved to Peter one vital thing: he could fight the fear and do all that his training required of him – and more. He felt justified in his authority now and, above all, he had confidence in his own ability to perform well under pressure. Provided he survived, the only way now was up.

Chapter Six

1942 – Operation Flodden

Peter was awarded the Military Cross for the action at Vaagso. He had told anybody who asked that his two wartime ambitions were to win a Victoria Cross and to reach the rank of Brigadier. Before long, he was responding to letters of congratulation on his promotion to Major.

The uncertainty which had characterized the previous year for the Commandos had vanished; those who had become disillusioned and returned to their regiments now saw the star of the new force begin its inexorable rise. After Vaagso came St Nazaire, the greatest of all the Commando raids. This new form of warfare had finally made its mark on the notoriously conservative military establishment, and its inclusion in operational planning became routine. At the end of February 1942 the Commando Depot was established at Achnacarry, which lies about 8 miles north of Fort William, between the ends of Loch Arka and Loch Lochy. Here volunteers were put through their initial Commando training, and unit commanders came to inspect the intakes and take on replacements.

After a period of leave, when participants in the raid were encouraged to spread the word of their exploits, 3 Commando returned to Largs and continued training. The officers had been sent on a recruiting drive to replace the losses sustained at Vaagso (17 killed and 53 wounded) – Durnford-Slater gave them extra leave to visit units with a view to poaching suitable men. When Peter had done the rounds originally he had had no problem in obtaining volunteers. Now that the Commandos were here to stay, hard-pressed regimental commanders baulked at letting their men go and potential volunteers were actively discouraged from putting themselves forward. Those who did so found themselves summoned to their interview by Peter calling out, 'Come in if you're good looking.' The exchange was usually brief for Peter knew what he wanted and his gimlet eye missed very little. Returned to full strength, 3 Commando resumed training with renewed vigour.

For Peter, however, there were some more momentous changes. In March, along with his promotion to Major, came his appointment as GSO2 Combined Operations HQ in London where, located at 1A Richmond Terrace, he helped to plan the St Nazaire raid. Wartime life in London was a mixture of anxiety and elation – the hours were long, but the social life was exciting and by all accounts, Peter had an eye for the ladies, although there is no evidence that he developed any lasting relationships. He was also able to spend time with his family all of whom, except for his father who still worked for the Admiralty Courts, were now in uniform. Barbara was involved in ARP ambulance work and Pamela served in the WRNS.

However, Peter missed life with the Commandos and after the St Nazaire raid he asked to be returned to No 3. His army record states that he relinquished his appointment on 26 April 1942, and was re-posted to 3 Commando on 18 May on appointment as second-in-command. He returned to Largs where things were also changing – after so long in Scotland, 3 Commando were to move back down south.

Before they left a new volunteer joined the unit: Sergeant Robert Christopher of the 2nd Beds and Herts volunteered for special service. He later wrote:

> I was going to join No 3 Commando who were then stationed in Largs in Scotland, but first I was to be interview[ed] by Lt-Col Robert Senior the Bn. Commanding Officer, he told me I was going to join a very good friend of his a Major Peter Young who was then second in command of No 3 Commando, and that if I came back to the 2nd Herts in disgrace not to expect any mercy from him.

Christopher ultimately became Peter's batman and the friendship that was forged lasted for the rest of their lives.

As Peter left London planning began for the biggest Commando operation undertaken during the Second World War, a major raid on Dieppe, selected because it was not a site under consideration as an invasion port for the Second Front – at that juncture in its very early planning stages – and also because it was within fighter range. The part to be played by the Commandos was originally assigned to airborne units due to the difficulties of beach landings, but co-ordinating two airborne landings and a frontal assault from the sea was felt to be too complicated. The major objectives were to capture the port and to force the Luftwaffe into an air battle with the RAF. There was a feeling that the Germans should not be allowed merely to sit on the northern coast of France indefinitely with no response from across the Channel – it was two years since the evacuation from Dunkirk and some show of strength was called for.

Now based in and around Seaford and Alfriston, Peter took on the mantle of second-in-command and settled into doing what he did best during the long periods in between raids, overseeing the training of the commando which Durnford-Slater left almost entirely to him. There were problems. In Scotland the only troops in the area had been 3 Commando, who had had complete freedom of movement during training exercises and a reasonably free hand about using live rounds; now they were surrounded by other units, which restricted their activities. On the plus side, they were regularly visited by the Luftwaffe, which gave proceedings 'the necessary warlike atmos-phere'.

There were only six officers left of the original intake of twenty-seven. Besides Durnford-Slater and Peter, the others were Charlie Head, Joe Smale, Bill Bradley and John Pooley. Peter did not mourn most of the departures. 3 Commando had a successful policy of 'growing their own' officers and NCOs, so that their hierarchy was steeped in the training regime of the unit and encouraged to jettison baggage from previous, regular, operations.

3 Commando's part in the Dieppe raid, Operation Flodden, was rehearsed by day and night at Gurnard Ledge on the Isle of Wight. One of the obstacles they had to overcome were the chalk cliffs which rose up at the back of the landing beaches; this meant that the Commando's speciality of cliff climbing, hitherto a party trick to impress visiting brass, became a central part of the whole operation.

According to Durnford-Slater's official account, rehearsals were completed by 10 August and from then until embarkation on 18 August (a month later than originally planned) unit arrangements were completed and supplies checked and issued. This was a huge undertaking, an assault on three fronts using 3 Commando to the east, 4 Commando to the west and the 2nd Canadian Division to the front. 3 Commando's position in the order of battle had been dictated by the terrain. Free French and, for the first time, US Rangers, were also represented. (During training Peter was presented with a Garand rifle which he came to prefer over all others.)

Operational security was always an issue and few people knew where the attack was to take place. There was a flutter of alarm, therefore, when two days before the raid the word 'Dieppe' appeared as the answer to a crossword clue in the *Daily Telegraph*. This, coupled with an unfortunate incident during the planning of the operation when an officer was overheard in a train saying that he hoped the Dieppe 'thing' would come off, made everyone nervous.

The Canadian troops were stationed, like 3 Commando, in and around Seaford, and had been there when the commando had arrived from Largs. The Canadians regarded this new influx of troops as a threat, particularly when the two groups began competing for the attentions of the local female population and some ugly incidents ensued. Matters were brought to a head by Peter, after an evening when some Commandos came off worst in an altercation. Told of the Canadian victory, he remarked that it would not be good for morale to leave matters thus. Summoning one of the best unit boxers, he suggested that he might care to even the score on their next foray into town. Although all the participants were nominally confined to barracks he ensured that a group of men found themselves in the company of some combative Canadians and in the ensuing melee, his volunteer duly floored his opponent. After that, the units were the best of friends.

On an official level, Peter accompanied Durnford-Slater on a visit to the Canadian headquarters, where relations were cordial. The Canadians were anxious to find out as much as they could about how the Vaagso raid had unfolded and they were grateful for any information the two men could provide.

The 1st US Rangers, among the first American troops to fight in Europe, had been trained at Achnacarry, and were anxious to take part in their first engagement. Twenty officers and men joined 3 Commando at Seaford, under the command of Captain Roy Murray. Split between the troops of 3 Commando they were accepted at once.

Both Commando groups had as their objectives coastal batteries, consisting of 5.9-inch guns, which had to be deflected or silenced to allow the main assault to get ashore. 4 Commando, split into two groups commanded respectively by Derek Mills-Roberts and Lord Lovat, was to land west of Dieppe to silence the batteries there. 3 Commando's objective was located 3 miles east of Dieppe, just outside the village of Berneval le Grand. With the main party, Durnford-Slater was to land in the village itself, in an area designated Yellow 1, while Peter's party was to come ashore at Yellow 2 to the west near Belleville-sur-Mer with 3 and 4 Troops and a 3-inch mortar section. They were to rendezvous and proceed to attack Goebbels battery which was located just north of Berneval at the top of a 300-foot cliff. The Operation Order states: 'The Coast Defence Batteries at BERNEVAL will be captured and destroyed as rapidly as possible. (NOTE: Should the capture and destruction of these Batteries prove an impossible or lengthy task, they must be engaged at the earliest possible moment so as to prevent them from bringing accurate fire to bear on the ships of the main force.)' Presciently, Durnford-Slater added the note as an afterthought in case the force which made it ashore was insufficient to carry out the main task.

Aerial reconnaissance showed that the Germans were continually strengthening their defences in the Dieppe area. The Luftwaffe was also flying reconnaissance missions and the LCP flotilla in Newhaven, secreted under canvas, had been photographed so often that there could be no doubt that the Germans were suspicious that something was afoot.

The Dieppe raid is now known principally for the fact that it was a failure. Durnford-Slater's official account states that the troops from 3 Commando embarked at Newhaven between 1830 and 2000 hrs, and that the flotilla, known as Group 5 and consisting of twenty Eurekas (Landing Craft Personnel, or LCPs, which each carried eighteen men and their equipment), sailed at 2030 hrs on 18 August. Other troops sailed from Southampton, Portsmouth and Shoreham. Eurekas were not designed to take troops any distance, being wooden, flat-bottomed transports for ferrying men and matériel ashore from ships. Headed by a steam gunboat (SGB), in which Durnford-Slater travelled, the Eurekas followed in four waves, five abreast; Peter was in the starboard craft of the first wave, commanded by Lieutenant Buckee RNVR. It was an uneventful crossing, although cramped and uncomfortable; three LCPs broke down en route and had to drop out. At about midnight the men in Peter's boat resolved to take some sustenance in the form of cans of self-heating soup. The technology did not rise to the occasion, however and they were tepid. Until 0350 hrs – an hour before the landings were to begin – all was quiet. Most of the men in Peter's craft were trying to sleep when light and fire erupted all around them. Star shells illuminated the scene as German gunners aboard E-boats opened up on the exposed and vulnerable flotilla. Pandemonium ensued. Peter described that moment as 'by far the most unpleasant of my life'.

A short but devastating encounter took place. In fact, they had run into a German escort accompanying a routine convoy moving from Boulogne down the Channel. It was coincidence that it came across the attackers and, although British radar had picked up its presence, a breakdown in communications meant that the information never reached the raiding force. The destroyers which had started out providing cover for the little force were nowhere to be seen – they had forged ahead and become separated from their slower charges. The SGB held its course and drew much of the enemy fire which to some degree protected the LCPs in its wake. Within a short time, however, the gunboat was put out of action and slewed off course leaving the LCPs unprotected.

Peter made his way to the bows where Buckee was located. With the resignation peculiar to those who have experienced combat he reasoned that he had already survived Guernsey, the Lofotens and Vaagso, so had had a good run for his money and it would now be as risky to retreat as to advance. Buoyed up by a certain bloody-mindedness they proceeded south towards the designated landing point. This required the LCP to make straight for the German gunboats and go through them, on the face of it a suicidal move. Miraculously, although the LCP was hit countless times, the men aboard were unhurt and eventually they moved out of range of the enemy. They had been out of sight of land and it was still dark when the battle began. Now dawn was breaking and the coastline was appearing before them, with the lights of Dieppe off to their right. They were alone. Of the twenty boats which left Newhaven only five made the landing, of which just one was part of Peter's force. Instead of two troops and a mortar section to carry out his objectives, he had nineteen assorted men.

During the run-in to the beach, Peter put a loaded clip into his Garand, but now, as dawn broke and under intense fire, his un-familiarity with it did not seem to be such a good idea. The performance of familiar tasks in a fraught situation often calms the nerves, and the fact that this small, but vital, activity was new and strange served only to emphasize the peril they were in. The men Peter commanded all say he never showed any fear – the Dieppe raid was a turning point in Peter's development as a soldier. Here was a situation where the battle plan had been destroyed even before deployment. How he dealt with the developing scenario hardened his inner steel.

Having positively identified their landing site, Buckee told Peter he had instructions to land even if there was only one LCP. Peter admitted that he had had the same orders, although privately he was wondering what he could do with the small force he now had at his disposal. Fearing machine guns located in the gully, Peter asked Buckee to run in about 50 yards to the west of it. Buckee beached the LCP and they agreed that he would remain there unless he came under heavy fire, in which case he would move to Yellow 2, where all the troops were due to re-embark after the action. If Buckee was not there when they returned, Peter resolved to go on into Dieppe and join up with the Canadians.

Although they landed five minutes ahead of schedule, it was under these inauspicious circumstances that Peter launched his first attack as a commander. It was not impossible that more LCPs containing his men would make it through the German boats, but he could not hang about on the beach on the off chance they might make it. He did not hesitate once they were ashore, making directly for the shelter of the cliffs. The gully they were due to climb had been thoroughly blocked with barbed wire, but to Peter's annoyance they had no equipment to deal with it. As a result, he wrote in his post-operation report on the operation: 'We had no bangalore torpedoes in our boat, and no wire cutters. The latter would have been comparatively ineffective, but it is recommended that on future raids every boat should carry at least two bangalore torpedoes if there is any chance of meeting wire on the beach.'

Despite the intensive reconnaissance carried out by the Luftwaffe over Newhaven, and even with a firefight out to sea, the trenches which had been dug on the beach were unoccupied and the lighthouse at Dieppe harbour was visible offshore. Neither of these circumstances supports the idea that the Germans were prepared for the landings.

There was no time to dwell on the situation and Peter tried to climb up the left-hand side of the gully, which appeared to be the easier option. Loaded down with equipment, and with a rifle on his shoulder, he lost his balance and fell back down, at which point Lieutenant John Selwyn suggested that they return to their boats. In doing so, he inadvertently saved the day for Peter had been thinking the same thing. The presence of doubt in the mind of a junior officer aroused his innate bloody-mindedness – 'one of the less charming facets of my character' – and he responded to Selwyn's suggestion by turning to the other side of the gully. When his rifle slipped off his shoulder and unbalanced him, he nearly performed an encore of his earlier failure, but managed to retain his balance and get to the top using the barbed wire as a sort of rope ladder. He cut his hands, but not badly enough to hinder him. When he walked round to the front of a notice which was posted facing the beach he read the words 'Achtung Minen'. Their failure to set any off was the first piece of luck that day.

The rest of the men followed him up the gully in the same fashion. Stanley Scott, who was on this raid, noted that overcoming barbed-wire obstacles was an important part of their training. Commandos learned to jump barbed-wire fences by using the top strand as a sort of springboard to get them clear. The barbed wire in the gully at Berneval and the pegs used to secure it actually helped them because it gave them so many footholds.

It took an hour to get all the men to the top of the cliff, which seemed interminable. They could not, however, haul up the 3-inch mortar, probably no bad thing since it would have hampered them given their small numbers. During this phase, they were able to observe a number of landing craft going ashore at Yellow 1, so were able to estimate the amount of support they might receive when they got to Berneval. It did not seem to amount to much and the small party was not happy as it began to make its way towards the village. Faced with sinking morale, Peter called them together under cover of a small wood and delivered a pep talk which he later described as being of the 'Once more into the breach variety'. He was aware that he was not very convincing, probably because he was not convinced himself and in fact the speech seems to have had more of the St Crispin's Day about it since he recalls telling the assembled company that if they could achieve anything it would be something to tell their children about. The force thus exhorted was divided into three groups under Selwyn, Captain 'Buck' Ruxton and himself, and moved off. They went inland towards the road running parallel to the coast, and towards Berneval, Ruxton's section acting as advance guard while the rest covered them. They met no resistance, although they did witness an attack by six Hurricanes on the village which produced a volley of ineffective fire from an ack-ack gun. A fleeing

French teenager was terrified when some of Peter's men grabbed him off his bicycle and questioned him about the situation in the village. He assured them that there were 200 Germans there and that all he wanted to do was escape the fighting. When he was allowed to go on his way the lad was so relieved that he kissed Peter on the cheek before pedalling onwards.

The coastal battery fired its first round as they reached the village. They paused only to cut some telephone wires, leaving a woman calmly milking a cow in a nearby field, and doubled up the main street towards the church, where they were to due to rendezvous with the party from Yellow 1. Thoroughly roused by the air attack, the inhabitants were on the streets by now and the local fire brigade was in attendance as one of the houses was on fire. Peter was disturbed to learn that no one had seen any sign of the force from Yellow 1, nor, ominously, was there any sound of gunfire coming from the direction of their intended advance. Everybody he spoke to, though distracted and anxious to keep out of the firing line, seemed friendly.

As they reached the church a German machine gun opened fire on them from about 60 yards ahead. As they engaged the enemy Ruxton fired on a couple of German soldiers who ran across the road to take up positions behind a hedge. The Germans returned fire, but did not hit their man who continued to fire at them with his tommy gun. He was joined by Selwyn, Lance Corporal Abbott, the Bren gunner, and Lance Corporal Bennett with the 2-inch mortar, which was positioned behind the church, shortly followed by another group which moved into the churchyard to increase the pressure on the Germans. Peter considered this situation risky, the two sides being effectively pinned down and his own men exposed. He regarded it as something of a miracle that no one was wounded during this exchange and concluded that it must have been because the Germans were firing high – at one point they hit the roof of the church and some of the tiles fell off onto Abbott.

As Peter cast about to find some way of breaking the stalemate he was encouraged to see that the onset of a battle, together with a little brisk exercise, had greatly improved the men's morale. They were not now considering the odds but just doing what he had trained them to do.

It occurred to him that they were next to the church tower, which would have a commanding view of the German positions. If they could get the Bren gunner and some snipers to the top of it they would be able to pick off their opponents, while the rest of them held the surrounding area until the party from Yellow 1 came up. With this in mind he reformed the men behind the church and went to recce the steeple, but the plan came to nought as there was no access to it. (He later learned that the steps began 10 feet above the ground, requiring the use of a ladder which the sexton had had the foresight to hide.) In any case, the view at the top was obscured by a row of trees.

Fire from the enemy battery was now increasing, and – rendezvous with Yellow 1 or not – it was their main priority. Disengaging from the machine-gun post, they moved north towards the coast again. At the edge of the village there was an orchard through which they began to advance. The earlier firefight had alerted the Germans to their presence, however, and they were sniped at continuously. Once again they were lucky not to take any casualties, but Peter decided to try another line of attack. To the west of the orchard lay a cornfield. Being August, it was at its fullest height and afforded better cover than the fruit trees. Signalling to the men to regroup once more at the edge of the village, he gave another pep talk, rather different in content to his earlier one.

'We are going to advance through the cornfield because it is much safer than the orchard. You know nine inches of earth stops a bullet. Well, fifteen feet of standing corn will do the same thing.'

The men accepted this assertion without demur and prepared to move into the field. In later years, Peter recounted this incident with glee. He knew that if they were not to become bogged down without achieving anything he would have to do something unconventional. He prized his ability to remain cool under fire, a trait he exhibited throughout his career. At the same time his men recognized and admired his talent for focussed thought and tactical awareness when under pressure, and they also knew that he was well able to out-perform them in physical terms as they had seen him do so many times during training.

They were fired on again from the edge of the orchard as they moved towards the cornfield, but took no casualties. Peter sent Selwyn first, then Ruxton, while he provided covering fire towards the left-hand gun. As they entered the cover of the corn, they got close enough to the left-hand gun to discover that it was a dummy – a fortunate revelation since their ammunition supply was limited and wasting any more of it could have been critical.

Once in the corn, Peter formed the men in extended order with a second line positioned so that it fired between the gaps in the first.

This enabled them to pour continuous and steady fire into the defenders around the main battery position. Meanwhile, the guns continued to fire sporadic ranging shots, confused either by the amount of smoke which, thanks to the attentions of the RAF, had enveloped the position as well as the whole area off Dieppe, or by a lack of communication due to the telephone wires having been cut.

They kept up a steady rate of fire into the battery, moving around to provide as difficult a target as possible. With only nineteen men it was impossible to do more, but Peter was determined to keep the enemy's heads down and his angle of approach meant that any bullets fired at No. 4 gun would whistle over the heads of No. 1 gunners as well. They persevered until, at about 0800 hrs, there was an enormous explosion about 150 yards ahead of them and a shell screamed over their heads: one of the guns had turned its fire on them.

It was a deafening experience and caused one of the men to exclaim angrily, 'Sir! We're being mortared!' It gave them all an unpleasant shock until they realized that the shell was still in the air somewhere well to the south of them. Being coastal battery guns, they were unable to depress their barrels sufficiently to bring them to bear on so close a target, although this did not stop the German gunners firing another four rounds over the cornfield to equally little effect.

Peter's men responded by firing a volley in the direction of the gunfire, even though they knew it was unlikely they would hit anyone. By now, however, they were starting to run low in ammunition, having come ashore with only 100 rounds per man. Peter therefore exhorted the men to fire slowly and steadily, which kept the enemy's heads down and distracted them from their primary task. In fact, the battery continued to fire slow ranging shots, effectively at random, throughout the attack. It did not get off a salvo which meant that its effectiveness was minimized, whether by the Commandos' harassing fire, or through a lack of communication. Coastal defence guns should be able to get off a couple of rounds a minute, but the whole battery managed no more than thirty during the whole of the time that it was under attack. They were in the cornfield for about an hour and a half, after which the shortage of ammunition became critical. There was an increasing likelihood that the Germans would regroup sufficiently to launch a counter-attack which could include armour. Understandably, Peter had no wish to encounter tanks in an open field.

Sending Selwyn ahead to form a small bridgehead round the beach, he told him to send up three white Very lights if the landing craft was still there. Meanwhile, the remainder of the force also began to move back to the landing point, leaving Peter, Ruxton, Craft, Clarke and Abbott – who had been winged in the ear during the fighting and was so far the only casualty – to turn their attention to an observation post which had been firing unsuccessfully on the waiting LCP. Ruxton fired a burst with the Bren gun which got their attention and attracted reciprocal fire, however, just as the engagement was getting under way Clarke saw three white Very lights. It was time to go.

Under cover of a small valley, the party withdrew, followed by a group of German riflemen, and harried by a lone sniper who was positioned on the Dieppe side of the gully.

Selwyn and his party embarked, covered by the remaining force on the cliff. The Germans who had followed the withdrawal of the rear party were now only 300 yards away and were beginning to make their presence felt, to the discomfort of the sailors who were helping Selwyn's men aboard. Once the Commandos were safely in the boat, they lost no time in bringing the Lewis guns on the LCP to bear on the cliff and the enemy suffered some losses. As Peter, with the final few, got to the water and began to wade out to the boat, it began to move off. Lifelines were thrown to the men in the water and they were dragged out about 300 yards before finally being hauled aboard. During this time the Germans did some damage and one of the sailors was wounded, however the smoke canister in the stern was also hit which fortuitously screened their final withdrawal.

As they withdrew, another LCP, incapacitated by engine trouble and therefore unable to take part in the landings, was finally sunk by German fire. One of the men who ended up in the water was 'Joe' Smale, who watched as Peter's LCP moved out to sea. Hoping to attract their attention, Smale waved, but they were too far away; he was eventually captured and spent the rest of the war in a POW camp. He later recalled feeling the water vibrate with the force of the explosions of the shells being fired on Peter's retreating boat.

Further out to sea, the LCP encountered a motor launch and transferred her passengers into it, so that the men had a rather more comfortable return trip. Buoyed by a potent mixture of whisky, cocoa and rum, they were able to take a sanguine view of an unsuccessful attack by a Junkers 87 (Stuka), and by the time they got back to Newhaven towards lunchtime they were feeling very relaxed.

There was no news of the rest of the commando, however, so after lunch Peter went up to London to report back to COHQ where news was anxiously awaited. Having been on the planning staff, Peter knew that any information he could provide would be welcomed, and indeed he was accorded interviews both with Lord Mountbatten and General Haydon. Summoned to the post-action conference which was to be held the following day, Peter asked permission to be allowed to wear his somewhat war-torn battledress. Mountbatten, he recalled, assented with the words: 'What the hell, there is a war on.'

Thence he returned to the family home in Oxshott and slept in his own bed that night.

There is a scene in the film *Dr Zhivago* where a group of White Russian soldiers launch an attack through a cornfield and are cut down mercilessly. In after years, Peter watched that film and confessed that it gave him nightmares because it reminded him forcibly of the cornfield in Dieppe and what could have happened. It was clear that, by normal military standards, the Commando officers and NCOs were taking far bigger risks, not only with their own lives, but with the lives of the men in their charge. Dieppe represented another stride forward in Peter's understanding of how thin the line is between acceptable and unacceptable risk. Often it is based, as war so often is, on nothing more than luck. Soldiers are superstitious for a reason. Lucky commanders brought them back alive, and Peter – in addition to the other formidable talents he possessed – was one such.

In the ensuing days and weeks, he learnt the fate of the rest of the operation. In particular, he discovered the reason why there had been no rendezvous with the force from Yellow 1: the entire party had encountered opposition immediately after landing and had been pinned down in the gully just off the beach. Under fire from well-positioned machine-gun nests, and attacked by German dive-bombers, the men were all wounded before they were finally captured. Only one man made it back to the LCPs and England.

The attack by the Canadians was repulsed with 68 per cent casualties, by any calculation an unacceptably high loss rate. Only the attack by 4 Commando at Varengeville to the west of Dieppe was successful, achieving all their objectives against some stiff opposition. Peter learnt the detail of it shortly afterwards from one of the participants, Derek Mills-Roberts, with whom he had been sent to Inverary as an instructor to help train the United States 168 Combat Team in combined operations. Mills-Roberts, of similar seniority to Peter, had been commissioned from the TA into the Irish Guards; their paths would continue to cross throughout the war and beyond.

*   *   *

Peter's attachment with the Americans, who would shortly be taking part in the North African landings, was a success even though his training methods came as something of a shock to National Guardsmen from Iowa. As he put it: 'The men had a rooted objection to performing any evolution at the double and thought us [Mills-Roberts and himself] distinctly eccentric in trying to make them do so.' Peter was a key player in turning these raw recruits into soldiers. Training had become his forte – instead of teaching history, an ambition which must by now have seemed rooted somewhere in the distant past, he was, in effect, teaching war, and he loved it.

The raid on Dieppe was intended to be, as Peter put it, a 'reconnaissance in force'. Although the Allies sustained heavy losses, the attack was not without value. From their point of view it was forcibly and finally borne in upon them that such seaborne assaults should not be undertaken without a preliminary air bombardment to soften up the target. The reason given for not doing so was that such a prelude would warn the defenders of an impending assault. Given the novelty of the Commandos' tactics and their unexpected approach from the sea, Peter contended that this was not a likely outcome, and that the confusion which would have been caused by an air assault would have outweighed any forewarning which it might have given. Having repulsed an attack by six battalions of men with only one battalion holding the port of Dieppe, the Germans, for their part, felt that their successful defence justified their coastal strategy, and they continued to occupy the Channel ports and defend the coastline in the same way, failing to realize that the Allied response to the operation would be to modify their own plans.

What Dieppe actually taught the Allies, though admittedly at great cost, was that it would be virtually impossible to capture a port during an invasion and that as port facilities were vital, they would have to be transported across the Channel. Accordingly, the Allied assault on D-Day was accompanied by Mulberry harbours which enabled men and materiel to be landed in support of the established beachhead.

As Peter put it: 'In war the right things often happen for the wrong reason.'

Chapter Seven

North Africa

Peter was awarded the Distinguished Service Order for his part in the Dieppe raid. Shortly after he returned from his time with the Americans, 3 Commando moved to Weymouth where it set about rebuilding its depleted ranks – mostly with policemen – and welding the new force into a tough fighting unit. Durnford-Slater believed that this was the best intake that 3 Commando ever had and Peter certainly agreed that policemen were excellent Commando material, being tough and disciplined before they arrived at Achnacarry to submit themselves to the rigours of the Commando depot.

The move was effected with typical lack of orthodoxy. There was a parade at Seaford on the day of the move where the Adjutant announced that there would be a parade at 0900 hrs the following morning in Weymouth square. The men had to make their own way there and find their own billets.

An attack on the Cherbourg peninsula was now planned which would capitalize on the lessons learned at Dieppe, in particular the effectiveness of air attack. In preparation, the men rehearsed in the Portland area, but in the event the attack was cancelled. Peter's recollection of his time in Weymouth is uneventful; although he enjoyed the quality of the billets there, and was able to use the countryside to weld the men into a fit and efficient fighting force, he noted that it was too built up to be much use for live firing. They also used the town to practise street fighting, and Bob Christopher recalled that Peter would set up three-day exercises to keep the men on their toes, during which he would lob Bakelite grenades at the men when they least expected it. They made a lot more noise than they did damage, and had the required effect of making the troops more alert and vigilant. They slept out on the Downs during exercises – after the training that most of them had received at Achnacarry, this was tame stuff, but they were not allowed sleeping bags, carrying only a groundsheet and a blanket. The former could be made into a dog tent as it had holes for tent poles, although these had to be found in the vicinity of the camp; as in all their training, the Commandos were encouraged to improvise.

There was a lively social scene, and although officers and men did fraternize this was limited in case trouble erupted and officers became embroiled in the fracas. Peter's whole focus was soldiering and he does not seem to have spent much of his off-duty time social-ising, although he did visit a medium with Christopher. Her advice is lost to us now, apart from a warning to Christopher that he should always keep on Peter's left during an attack, counsel he followed to his subsequent advantage. When Peter did join the men for a drink he was very approachable and some of them even dared to call him by his first name, although once back on duty the formal-ities were always observed. It is always a mark of affection when soldiers give their officers nicknames. In Peter's case, he became known as 'Bungy', for which Peter produced his own explanation: 'I think Bungy must have been a diminutive of Bung to rhyme with Young, and probably dated from my time as OC H (6) Tp 3 Cdo.' (He did not appreciate being called Bunny which some hapless people occasionally called him by mistake, having misheard his nick-name.)

Men as resourceful as those accepted for Commando training would not confine their energies simply to learning soldiering, and there were occasions when some of the men took on extra-curricular activities which landed them in trouble. Two such were Pat Drain and Doug Roderick who acquired a greyhound called 'Como'. In time, Como was promoted to Sergeant and made the regimental mascot, however when meat started disappearing from the local butcher, the dog came under suspicion. Brought before Peter, Como promptly relieved himself on his boots whereupon he lost his temper and put the dog on a charge. The following day Peter demoted him to Corporal, but lacking evidence of guilt regarding the meat theft, gave him the benefit of the doubt. As Drain and Roderick prepared to march out, Peter said casually that he was partial to a bit of lamb. Lamb he therefore got, though, as Roderick was at pains to point out, the teeth marks had been cut out.

*   *   *

74

The success of Layforce in the Middle East and the rising fortunes of the Long Range Desert Group (LRDG) caused the Ministry to turn its mind towards using 3 Commando in Mediterranean operations. At the end of January 1943 the men were paraded and informed that they were leaving Weymouth for foreign climes. It was a bit of shock for Christopher who had planned to marry his childhood sweetheart, Olive, at the end of February. Fortunately, the banns had been called early and he was able to tie the knot on 11 February, embarking on HMS *Letitia* in Glasgow five days later.

Meanwhile, 3 Commando bade a formal and more or less dignified farewell to Weymouth by holding a church parade. The men were permitted a last night of celebration on condition that anyone who showed any sign of having overindulged on the day of departure would be returned to his unit. Durnford-Slater was exacting in his standards of turnout and discipline and liked to leave his hosts with a good impression. The men paraded at the station at 2300 hrs with, as Peter put it, 'everybody present, even if some were dragged there and propped up in the ranks'. One man was found out and RTU'd on the spot while the rest poured themselves onto the train and left for Scotland.

Their first destination was Gibraltar but the presence of enemy shipping en route required a wide detour into the Atlantic where the sea conditions were uninviting. Seasickness was the inevitable result and the troop decks were consequently unpleasant.

To while away the tedium of the voyage, the men continued to do what training they could and a boxing tournament produced a new talent, Corporal Dennis, one of the new intake of policemen. He packed a terrific punch although he was slow on his feet. Peter took due note.

Once through the Straits of Gibraltar the ship put into Oran to disembark some troops destined for the Africa Theatre. The men regarded it as an opportunity to stretch their legs, have a swim and meet some of the local inhabitants. It seemed a very exotic location. Apart from travel associated with their wartime exploits, all so far associated with Northern Europe, most of them had never been abroad before.

Durnford-Slater and Head went on by plane to Gibraltar, leaving Peter in charge of the rest of the unit for the final, short leg of the journey. 3 Commando were to relieve 9 Commando on the Rock, using it as a base from which to launch seaborne raids into Spain. Durnford-Slater thought this was a fine idea, feeling that such raids could be accomplished with relative ease, despite the positioning of Spanish guns on the coast, which meant that they would have to leave and return under fire.

Peter and the main body arrived in Gibraltar on 12 March, having been at sea for just over three weeks. Durnford-Slater ensured that 3 Commando made an impressive entrance: 'Everybody on the Rock was pleased to see us, and they were rather astonished to see the turnout and saluting of our men.'

Durnford-Slater may have influenced Peter's later views on this matter. 'I like good drill and turnout,' he wrote to John Adair in 1966, 'but mainly because these keep the generals off a CO's back. Image and all that.' He knew that regular parades kept the troops steady. There came a point where parades almost ceased to happen, but the men requested that they be held because they liked the discipline they imposed. Peter was a stickler about how his men saluted – Ted Piggott recalls having to walk round Peter saluting for an hour while Peter sat on a rock correcting his technique.

In the event, 3 Commando did not stay long in Gibraltar although they did make an impact. The officers reconnoitred across the border into Spain by land and air, as much to annoy the Spanish authorities as anything. This method of planning an attack was new and refreshing after having to rely on intelligence reports and photographs. Even the stereoscopic photos which the commando had first used during the planning of the Dieppe raid, though a great improvement on ordinary photographs, were no substitute for the real thing.

Together with planning and training for raids 3 Commando spent their time ensuring that the garrison was made aware of their presence. In the six weeks they spent there, 3 Commando reached the finals of the Governor's Football Cup – thanks in great measure to Christopher's goal scoring – and lifted five boxing trophies against a garrison of more than 15,000 men, Corporals Dennis and Dowling being the major winners. And they continued to train. The Rock was ideal for honing climbing skills, but was not without its hazards. Sergeant Jock Allen received the George Medal after rescuing a junior officer from the rock face after he had suffered a fall several hundred feet up.

When the order to move suddenly came, the men had only a day to prepare. They embarked on 10 April on the *Princess Emma*, minus the padre who contrived somehow to miss the news that they were on the move, despite attending parade that morning. They disembarked at Oran on 14 April. It was a dispiriting arrival, for no one was there to meet them or tell them where they were to be billeted. Durnford-Slater eventually ascertained that they were destined for Fort de l'Eau, about 10 miles west of Oran. It was an inauspicious start to this new phase in 3 Commando's career; Durnford-Slater found at least one of the British officers at the Allied headquarters in Algiers to be 'a classic example of the pompous, obstructionist type often met with in the early stages of the war' which cannot have inspired much confidence or hope. The headquarters housed both the British and American staff, however, and their relationship with the Americans was cordial.

Peter and Durnford-Slater visited Eisenhower's planning headquarters which lay in a village about 3 miles south of Algiers and it was here that the plans for their next operation, the invasion of Sicily, were first discussed. They were to be briefed by a colonel who had been seconded to the staff from London to help plan the operation. He had been held up elsewhere when the two men were shown into his office, where they found the plans for the Sicily operation open on his desk. This was an egregious lapse in operational security, particularly as the people at the headquarters assumed that the visitors were already aware of the plan of attack.

Both Peter and Durnford-Slater were dismayed by what they saw. Durnford-Slater says that Peter's first reaction was to exclaim, 'This is one of the worst plans I have ever seen!' It required the commando to carry out a number of small, dispersed attacks on the south and east coasts of the island where the terrain is unsuitable for large forces to land. Their opposition consisted of a couple of crack German divisions and a number of Italian troops, all configured to be mobile and able to respond to a threat from any direction. Faced with the prospect of a major debacle, Durnford-Slater returned to the camp at Fort de l'Eau with Peter and they devised a training regime to deal with the situation as it stood.

Peter organized a three-day exercise in the Atlas Mountains to ensure that the men were fit for an operation of limited duration but extreme physical hardship – if the men could keep up a punishing pace over a three-day period they could certainly maintain an effective attack over a shorter time.

Peter's bodyguard now began to emerge. It is difficult to define this group for it consisted of officers and men and bore no relation to the normal structure of the unit. Its members were fiercely loyal to Peter and entry into its ranks was much sought after. Durnford-Slater can hardly have failed to be aware of the group which formed around his second-in-command, and although Peter never challenged his authority, it must have been galling for the Commanding Officer to observe such a circle emerging. Among those admitted into this band were Bob Christopher, Freddie Craft and John de Lash. Lash felt that Christopher was the most important of them, and Christopher modestly described his own position thus: 'I was more or less drafted into Major Young's little army, probably after some kind words from my friend Freddie Craft.'

In wartime there is a particular strength in the relationships which spring up. John Kenneally VC, of the Irish Guards, wrote with first-hand knowledge: 'Without being over sentimental, men can love each other. It is borne of mutual suffering, hardships shared, dangers encountered . . . It's entirely masculine, even more than brotherly love, and it's called comradeship.'

Peter knew he had an attractive personality, that ineffable quality called charisma, and he enjoyed exercising his powerful charm over people. He was interested in leadership and knew by now it was something at which he excelled, although in his case it represented something more which found expression in fierce loyalty amongst his adherents. Such groups coalesced around him from time to time for the rest of his life.

3 Commando were now ordered to Egypt. The only regret they had in leaving was that they had to abandon a boxing match between the all-victorious Corporal Dennis and an American heavyweight from the garrison in Algiers. Boxing was an accomplishment in which 3 Commando seemed to be invincible.

Most of the force travelled by train, but Peter took the transport by road. The vehicles were all new and the trip was therefore accomplished at a leisurely pace, taking about two weeks. Christopher remembered:

It fell to Major Young to take [the transport] to Alexandria, some 2,000 miles away. He decided to keep to the coast road; this was a marvellous trip which took in all the major towns on the north African coast and passing through all the desert battle fields still littered with tanks and lorries from both Montgomery's and Rommel's armies. Freddie Craft had taken to driving the Jeep carrying Peter and I [sic], and decided he would

78

rather be his driver than his batman. He asked Major Young about this, who readily agreed and then asked me to take Freddie's place, which I was only too happy to do. I had great respect for him, and I had an inkling that he thought a lot of me.

They entered Egypt from British North Africa Forces command on 8 May 1943. Although it seemed longer, they had been in Algiers for only a matter of days. In Alexandria Peter's party was reunited with the rest of 3 Commando and they regrouped before moving on to Suez to continue training for the Sicilian operation. This had now been modified and their objective was a battery near Syracuse which they were to capture before the main landings. At this stage the exact location of the operation was unknown, although it was generally rumoured to be somewhere in the region of Greece and the Dodecanese (Peter was convinced that the actual target was Rhodes).

3 Commando were brigaded with General Dempsey's XIII Corps as part of Eighth Army; they were to support the main infantry assault on the south-eastern coast near Cassibile, south of Syracuse. One of the objectives was to capture airfields, denying the Germans a base and providing a refuelling stop for Allied aircraft.

Accompanying most of XIII Corps, 3 Commando moved to the plain of Ataka, between the Gulf of Suez and the hills which rose about 3 miles inland, to rehearse the detail of the operation. They were there for most of June and trained meticulously, learning both their own and each other's part of the plan so that every detail was covered and reinforced.

The terrain was unlike anything they expected to encounter on the raid and the objectives were therefore marked out using stones to indicate tracks and walls. It was far from ideal, particularly as the Germans could not fail to notice the concentration of troops in the area. Peter thought that the Luftwaffe did not attack them there because they would have a better opportunity elsewhere, especially when the flotilla was at sea.

Two things permeated this period: sickness and dust. Dysentery and malaria were common and the dust and sand got into everything, aided by a wind which rose most days during the morning and did not die down until about 1700 hrs when the men could go for a refreshing swim. Most of the training was begun at first light so that they were not working through the heat of the desert day. Typically, reveille was at 0430 and parade at 0500 hrs.

Peter kept a detailed journal of this period in which he records both operational matters and his own private thoughts. Thus on 15 June:

We bought some films and had ices in SUEZ [he was a keen photographer]. Then the Officers had their hair cut and a shampoo. The barber, with ready wit, let the water flow down my neck and trickle round my crutch . . . He was very ashamed . . . We bathed at 'Le Cabanon' and so home. The dust storm was much worse last night and there are some small rents in our tent now.

Walter Skrine and I had last night a long discussion . . . We seem to agree. He is a bachelor, aged about 37, with over 15 years' service R.A.

I sleep in the open (these three or four nights).

By now much of the planning was complete. In addition to studying a model of the area, they had managed to get hold of stereo-scopic reconnaissance photographs which provided remarkably accurate 3-D views. Skrine noted on 16 June: 'Obtained a set of stereo pair photo's [sic], the first that have come our way. This is partly because CO of 3 Commando [i.e. Durnford-Slater] discourages amateur interpreters who multiply beach defences to an alarming extent', to which Peter has added '(A lesson of VAAGSO)'.

The Assault Landing Craft loads had been determined: Peter was to go in D3 with thirty-six men including Skrine, Christopher and Craft.

At 1200 hrs on 15 June a CO's conference was held in the Orderly Room during which all operational aspects of the 'scheme' – as Peter referred to it – were examined. Peter's notes include observations from various participants; all the officers, less the sick, attended. The entries concerning the execution of the operational stage show how much they were building on the experiences gained during previous operations:

1 This is where the Officers earn their pay. Algy Forrester's performance at VAAGSO, by going like hell down the main street, 'really won that battle'. You can't just say, 'Just nip along there. I'll be along in a minute.'
2 Boat discipline. Load in daylight. You are in charge in all respects.

3   Be ready to bump into an enemy at sea; we could have done a hell of a lot of firing on the last show [DIEPPE].
4   Never be satisfied until mags are refilled. (4 Troop)
5   All Officers must think at least two stages up in rank. (At VAAGSO, Sgt. [Jimmy] White, D.C.M., from Cpl became Troop Commander.)
6   The morale side is directly concerned with the officer's side. None of the 'men are too tired to do any more'; usually means 'The officer is too tired'.
7   Fullest detailing of posts, piquets and guards. 1 Troop's demonstration.
8   Keep getting information back.
9   Every Officer is to be able to speak on wireless. Budd [the Signals Officer] to have a set near mess.
10 Right or wrong. One real chance – take it in both hands. One moment is the right one. When in doubt go in. (Lash)
11 Discipline. Take every opportunity to wash etc.
12 If there are bars in the ship there is not time for boozing. Plenty of sleep is what's needed. Have what's going if it's there. Have two or three drinks. No parties.
13 Be correct to Civilians and P.W.s. Proper requisitions for horse and cart etc. 'If he's a farmer he's probably a decent chap and he can get it back later.'
14 Officers and N.C.O.s notebook and pencil. Verbal orders of some 'complexity' may be issued.
15 Fire control most important. (6 Troop – Fraser)
16 Life on ship. Officers to spend plenty of time down on mess decks. Briefing, semaphore, talks, lectures – Wonderful material – we can walk both these two jobs – all depends on Officers.
17 CASUALTIES. At the climax we may have to disregard them. There were unnecessary casualties at VAAGSO and DIEPPE. (Pevey and Cave)

On the following day, 16 June, Peter went into Cairo with Durnford-Slater and Skrine to try and glean more intelligence. While they were at Heliopolis studying the model, Peter states that he 'fell ill of a fever' although that did not stop him having breakfast at the Turf Club and lunch at the Gezira Club.

Christopher's twenty-fifth birthday was on 18 June, the anniversary of the Battle of Waterloo. Peter gave him £1.

Two days later, on 20 June, Peter's group moved with, as he put it, 'indecent speed' on to HMT *Dunera*, a ship built just before the war began and therefore offering up-to-the-minute standards of comfort: 'Indian stewards were still serving in the officers' dining saloon.' Without the wind, sand and flies of the desert, life was more bearable and the food was, in Christopher's words, 100 per cent better. One troop of Peter's group could not be accommodated on board *Dunera*, so they were embarked on the *Prinz Albert* with Durnford-Slater. Once on board, they continued to carry out rehearsals, adding boat and embarkation drills to their repertoire, to the particular benefit of the men who had not been on an amphibious operation before. Because the *Prinz Albert* had been used at Vaagso, the landing craft crew were better prepared than those on the *Dunera* for whom this was new. When the flotilla sailed the men were drilled in LCA embarkation at night, although without an actual boat launch.

Peter shared a cabin with Colonel Cator MC, commander of the Raiding Forces MEF, a function which gave him oversight of the commando. This evidently created friction for the delineation between the roles was not clear cut; Skrine thought that 'Col. Cator . . . has worked out a job for himself to "co-ordinate" action of us [sic] . . . In fact he will be merely a hindrance to Peter Young, as he has his own ideas of how the Group should be handled. He appears to have very little practical knowledge of Combined Operations.'

Peter certainly thought that this was Cator's plan and strongly resented his attempts to interfere. During one of the practice landings at which General Dempsey was present:

Suddenly Col Cator said he thought it would be best if he 'co-ordinated' the activities of 'B' Group 3 Commando and 'C' Coy Seaforths. Col Ainslie and Col Durnford-Slater agreed to this without thought or consultation and indeed with what seemed to me to be unflattering alacrity. Col Durnford-Slater went so far as to say – would not this be a great help to me? I refused to commit myself, merely replying, 'It is obviously an advantage to have unified command.' The situation as it presented itself to me . . . was briefly that the Forces attacking Beach 44 came from two Units (Commando and Seaforth) and were commanded by a third formation – Raiding Force.

This merely made my HQ redundant.

No sooner were we back in the car, than Col Cator began to

co-ordinate our training, arranging, despite my protest which he suppressed with some asperity, an exercise for the next day.

In the afternoon when the Colonel was lying on his camp-bed enjoying his siesta, and swatting flies, I bearded him once more and told him I was far from happy about my position under Colonel Cator. He said that if he were in my position he would be very happy to be relieved of the necessity of keeping in touch with the Seaforths, with XIII Corps and, of course, with himself. Indeed he didn't see how I could possibly do all that myself.

I said I had an officer . . . who had nothing else to do but that, and I felt perfectly capable of handling that side of the business. He said that he had had the most explicit assurance from Colonel Cator that he would not interfere with my command. To which I replied that his first action had been to order an exercise for Waylen and myself, which was convenient to neither. The Colonel replied that he thought we ought to have said if we didn't want that exercise.

To this I answered that I had protested at the time and got my head bitten off for my pains. This remark annoyed the Col . . . and he heaved himself up on his elbow and said, with a puzzled look on his face, 'I think you are making a lot of difficulties about this.' 'That is not my reputation,' I said as coldly as possible, and proceeded that he had only to command and I would do exactly what he wished in the matter, but that it was no good concealing from him what I felt. With this he became calm and could only agree . . . This is, as far as I can remember, the only time since I have been in the Commando that I have nearly quarrelled with Colonel Durnford-Slater, whom I have always held most respectfully, and who has usually agreed with what I had to say, while so often disregarding my advice.

On 22 June Dempsey arrived to watch 3 Commando rehearsing at Abadiya Point. Peter did not like what he saw, for he felt that the false beaches that surrounded the landings made the whole thing look 'farcical'. Dempsey, however, was impressed and spoke to the men warmly, welcoming them to XIII Corps and explaining a little of what they were to do. Once the speech was over, he adjourned to his staff car and asked Peter to explain his plan to him. Peter had prepared a detailed set of notes with which to brief the General, much of which consisted of his own views on command and control, and all of which was designed to reinforce his own position with regard to Cator's role in the operation. He did not want the Colonel to go ashore with the assault force.

Eventually their relationship became more cordial. On 8 July 'I went for my gallop with Colonel Cator this morning [they had taken to running round the decks together] and also fooled about boxing with him, until he dotted me on the nose – it bled.'

On about 25 June, General Dempsey brought Montgomery to visit XIII Corps and this included a demonstration landing by 3 Commando near Abadiya Pier. Peter noted that this was a wet landing achieved by Lieutenant Commander 'Chunky' Hewitt with, as he put it, 'matchless skill . . . only possible because he had the courage to disobey his orders completely!'

On 26 June, Peter went aboard the flagship of the flotilla, HMS *Bulolo*, for a conference with Dempsey. Durnford-Slater was also present, looking, Peter wrote, 'very ill, but denied being so. He looked yellow – literally.' Further discussion about the planned landings took place, this time with the help of some photographs and an Italian stereoscope, during which Dempsey revealed to Peter the exact nature of his mission: 'The General,' he reported, 'said to me very precisely and looking at me closely, "Object to get the 17th Brigade ashore. Object to get the 17th Brigade ashore without casualties." Then he said that if we did it might make all the difference in taking LADBROOKE . . . on D1.' (Ladbrooke was the code name for Syracuse.)

Dempsey's manner impressed Peter who concluded the entry: 'He briefed me as quietly and carefully as a Company Commander should do his subalterns. What a change after Dieppe when the first time we saw Major General H.A.M. Roberts was at the Conference afterwards.'

On 28 June, XIII Corps received a signal from Montgomery which boosted everybody's morale:

Would like to tell you and all Officers and men in XIII Corps how much I enjoyed my visit to you all. I was deeply impressed by the fine bearing and enthusiasm of the Troops and it is quite clear that nothing will stop such soldiers. I look forward with complete confidence to the future whatever may be our task and I wish all your magnificent Officers and men the very best of luck. Please convey my best wishes to Admiral Troubridge and the Officers and men of the Royal Navy with whom you are working. You are indeed lucky in having such fine sailors with whom to co-operate.

There was also time for more personal entries in the journal. On 28 June he wrote to Arthur Komrower, who was still recuperating from wounds received at Vaagso:

> I wrote to A.G. Komrower today, in reply to a meaning letter I received last night, complaining that I was the only one of his friends who had not yet written to him. That I once told him that when people were absent from me, their influence over me waned. I wrote reassuringly, but not answering his complaint directly. Evidently he is afraid of not getting back into the Commando, if he takes too long recovering. An absurd fear.

Komrower can have had little concept of the pressure Peter was under at that time, although he should have understood that, on the verge of going into action again, Peter was not emotionally inclined to extend lifelines when he himself might be dead, wounded or captured in the immediate future. This was certainly on his mind that day because a later entry, relating to the disposition of troops for the follow-up assault to the one they were currently planning, states: '*Prinz Albert* and *Ulster Monarch* are the ships we shall use for our second operation; that is, if we survive the first.'

Interspersed with these observations is a litany of activities associated with unit life: three men were RTU'd, one of whom Peter had tried that morning for failing to comply with a lawful command. On parade he found deficiencies in turnout and dress which displeased him. He could not resist adding that his inspection reminded him of Kutuzov's inspection of a Russian regiment in 1865, as related in *War and Peace*, a copy of which was doing its rounds amongst the officers.

Peter also visited the different units which made up the assault brigade to make sure that everyone understood the plans. The plan as it now stood was that Peter's group, in six LCAs, and totalling about 204 men, would go ashore about half a mile north of the main beach, using a prominent rock called the Scoglio Imbiancato as a landmark. Once off the beach, the group was to divide into three parties in order to attack suspected machine-gun positions and pill boxes close to the beach, and, inland, two strong points which had been identified, one of which was a farm. Trenches had also been identified in a nearby quarry along with more machine-gun posts, and these were to be attacked as well. Success would mean, as Dempsey had indicated during their briefing session on board *Bulolo*, that the main landings could be accomplished with the minimum of interference. The intelligence was reliable, the reconnaissance thorough and the training intense – they had held twelve full-scale rehearsals, having reproduced as exactly as possible the terrain they were to encounter in Sicily.

Late in the evening on 30 June, the pilot embarked on *Dunera* and by the early hours they were moving up the Suez Canal towards Port Said. The operation was under way.

Chapter Eight

Cassibile – Operation Bigot-Husky

The *Dunera* and *Prinz Albert* reached Port Said at 1600 hrs on 1 July where the invasion fleet was gathering. 'It was,' declared Christopher, 'an incredible sight, ships loaded with troops, tanks and trucks all set for the big day.' It was the first time they had been in action since the previous August. Just before they left Ataka, they had been rejoined by two of their number who had been commissioned and had had to attend OCTU in England. One of these, George Herbert, had always impressed Peter and was to become one of his most trusted lieutenants.

Some of the junior officers were inclined to buck his authority, which he would not tolerate; they were impatient of constraint and clearly felt that they could do as well as he did, a sentiment he himself had been feeling not so long before. He had risen from subaltern to Major in the space of three years and the new intake must have had similar ambitions. On 30 June he wrote:

Lieut Ellery is very weak with a form of dysentery . . . Says he can be patched up for the operation. No loss if he is not. He apparently is good enough to approve of me now that I have given up chasing him. I was on his side in an argument versus 'Blimp' Leese regarding conscription after the war, which I declared against, to Leese's horror. 'We regular soldiers have got to stick together, what?' Ellery asked me if there was anything he could do for me while he was sick. I've nothing as he's not X.O . . . He is too soft and vain to make a good Commando Soldier, but he is good on administrative matters and clever.

During an argument at lunch yesterday there was some question of Leese having forgotten an order . . . I said to him rather thoughtlessly (because I really think it), 'You never remember any orders that are not convenient to you.' He said, 'That's not true at all' . . . He is impatient of control and always eager to show his independence, although Walter Skrine tells me that he knows exactly how far he can go with me.

Briefings and visits continued as the fleet gathered. It was a motley collection, including, besides the *Dunera* and *Prinz Albert*, the *Monarch of Bermuda*, a luxury liner carrying the 2nd Royal Scots and the 1st Inniskilling Fusiliers, *The Duchess of Bedford* with the 17 Infantry Brigade HQ and the 2nd Northamptonshires, and the *Sobieski* with the Seaforths.

On board ship parades were apt to be interrupted by boat drills, and boat drills by Air Action Stations, each one requiring the troops to assemble in different parts of the ship. Peter continued to prepare his men for battle. Equipment checks revealed deficiencies to be made good. Complaints about the soldiers' food, so impressive when they had first embarked, began to be so universal that the Orderly Officer put in a formal complaint.

There was, however, a lighter side:

Trooper Gibson made my day for me to-day. I was walking about on the boat deck with Walter Skrine, and happened to look down on to the Promenade Deck, where I saw Gibson . . . cleaning his Tommy-gun. Up comes L/Cpl Grewcock to speak to him, catching sight of me as he comes, and asks Gibson what he's on. Gibson (disgruntled) 'Bungy's got a parade on this morning . . . ' and a long series of moans, causing much mirth to the spectators, so that, suspicious in the end, Gibson looks up and sees me. 'Why didn't you tell me? This would happen to Gibson,' he cries, with mock despair.

Troop dispositions were constantly amended, with the sick and those in hospital or in detention requiring replacement by some means since every individual had a task to do. Peter was relieved to be told that he did not have to find men to look after casualties which would be swept up by the infantry units which followed them ashore. On 3 July he tried to get down to the serious business of completing the Operation Order but was constantly interrupted. Durnford-Slater and Head arrived mid morning with their Operation Order 'which is a work of art (though not necessarily science)'.

That afternoon he went aboard the *Sobieski* to brief the company commanders of the Seaforths and have tea. There was much to arrange to ensure deconfliction; each objective was marked out and grid references were identified to delineate the different areas of operation for the various units. Just before dinner, he was brought a signal from the commander of 17 Infantry Brigade, Brigadier Tarleton, requesting that he report to him at his earliest convenience.

He was able to get across to the *Duchess of Bedford*, Tarleton's ship, after dinner that evening. He took Cator with him and their welcome was distinctly frosty. The security detail at the gangway refused to let the visitors aboard and Tarleton was summoned. Upon arrival he lost no time in giving vent to his ire, beginning with the lateness of the hour and continuing with the accusation that Peter had been 'fixing things with his battalion commanders behind his back. "Is this co-operation? It's a damned bad show . . . I've no confidence in your plan . . . I hear for the first time today that you are going up the railway line. You'll shoot up my reserve battalion. It will be a bloody disaster, I'm telling you now . . . "' And so on. Tarleton was so angry that he uttered the name of the village of Cassibile – still a classified location at that stage – in front of a number of troops who were unaware of their destination. This was a gross breach of security, but when Cator tried to suggest that they go somewhere more private Tarleton refused and continued to rave at Peter.

Peter remained calm during this spectacular public dressing-down, realizing he would get nowhere if he tried to respond:

> He repeatedly blamed me for dealing with his battalions which he had expressly told me to do before. He clamoured for my Operation Order, but he never explained why I had not had his, which after all is the correct procedure . . .
>
> He sneered at me saying, 'No doubt he is a very gallant officer and a very distinguished one.' Implying that because I had a couple of gongs I was necessarily bone-headed and rash . . .
>
> We were very civil throughout. H.J.C. [Cator] woke me in the middle of the night to give me his ideas on how this situation should be handled.

They attended a conference with Dempsey the following morning which went smoothly. After discussions detailing issues surrounding ship losses and their possible impact on the operation, signalling and sapper support they finally broached the subject of relations with 17

Brigade. Dempsey asked if Peter was happy with the plan and Peter replied that he was but that he thought Tarleton was not. He delegated to Cator, probably by prior agreement, the task of relaying their encounter with Tarleton the previous evening. He had not got very far when Dempsey suggested that they should take a walk on deck for a few minutes.

Cator now gave a detailed account of what had happened and described Tarleton as 'overwrought'. Both men agreed that their personal feelings were not the issue and reiterated how impressed they had been by the way in which Dempsey had personally briefed them, to which Dempsey responded that it was, after all, they who had to do the job.

Dempsey went away to determine how to proceed while they 'lounged about on deck' and continued to discuss the situation. When Brigadier Sugden summoned them back to the war room Dempsey told them:

> 'You are going across to the *Duchess of Bedford*. General Birney-Ficklan is writing a message to Brig. Tarleton. The points you want to make clear are: about the FOO [Forward Observation Officer], the Light Signals, and your dispositions on landing; (to Cator) I suggest to you that your Staff Work has not been above reproach in not seeing Brigadier Tarleton before. ([T]o me) You've got the fighting part quite clear. These troubles about Staff Work are a minor matter.' Or words to that effect.

Peter took these words as vindication, but there is also the suggestion of self-justification. He did not understand why a plan, previously discussed with the Corps Commander, could be questioned by the Brigade Commander. It was another step in his military education.

The visit to the *Duchess of Bedford* went well. They were invited to stay for lunch and even when Tarleton was presented with Birney-Ficklan's letter there was no outburst:

> I watched him out of the corner of my eye, expecting him to start reviling us at any moment for denouncing him as we had done. His face as he read looked like that of a man who is drinking his own water. He shut the letter with a snap, and become more civil (if possible) even than before.

He evidently had the impression, none the less, that we had been detained aboard the *Bulolo* to receive a rocket from General Dempsey, which may have sweetened him.

After a sweltering lunch, at which they sat at the Captain's table, they adjourned to the war room for a conference where Peter explained his plan once again and was gratified to note that 'not the least objection was raised to it'. The meeting ended on a convivial note, Peter observing that: 'the role of our R.E.s [Royal Engineers] was altered to suit the Brigadier. In a merry moment that worthy said he would give us a dinner – in LADSBROOK [sic] (Siracusa) – if we did our stuff.'

Back on board the *Dunera* he was plunged into the minutiae of quotidien concerns; there had been some indiscipline during the afternoon's march and there was backbiting amongst the junior officers. Peter decided to give all the officers a talk on discipline and what indiscipline to look for, and repeated the same talk for the benefit of the sergeants.

The production of the Operation Order was paramount: it was typed on the Purser's typewriter on 5 July, the day they sailed, and Peter delivered it in person travelling, with Christopher and Herbert, between the troopships in LCP 131. It was a convivial round: he dined on the *Prinz Albert* – where he left his kitbag and a big black box containing, amongst other things, the completed volume of his diaries – and after a final word with Captain Long's boat load he moved on to the *Duchess of Bedford*, where even Tarleton was on good form.

It was only after they put to sea that the men were told of their destination. It was now clear that the commando's part in the operation was to spearhead a large invasion force; their convoy, MWF36 (Moving West Fast Serial 36), was only one of many which were beginning to converge on Sicily.

On 6 July Peter wrote: 'This night a portent was seen in the sky. A star stood near the Moon . . . It was a very large star. The brightest, it seemed, in the whole firmament. The outline of the full moon could just be discerned, and also a tiny star quite unseen for the splendour of the other. The night was full of stars.'

The following morning:

I attempted to divert him [Skrine, who was ill, possibly seasick as there had been a considerable swell during the previous day] and Ellery at breakfast with my reading of the famous quarrel scene between Brutus and Cassius, in 'Julius Caesar'. A better picture of two second-rate general officers could scarcely be written today . . .

It might be a couple of our Troop Commanders. They are just as illogical as Brigadier Tarleton.

It was a passage he was to return to later in life when it formed part of the paper which, as Brother Amphibian, he gave to the Sette of Odd Volumes in 1968.

He also spent time talking to Christopher who he had previously briefed on the coming operation and was pleased that he seemed thoroughly to understand the plans. He also briefed his 'bodyguard' with, as he wrote, 'a map of AVOZA between the two of them' along with the signals detachment. In official documents these men, Craft and Clarke, were referred to as orderlies or runners. Most of his time was spent making sure everybody understood not only their own part in the landings, but also how their roles interacted with everybody else's. Of some men he despaired, but most seemed to satisfy his exacting requirements.

He discussed the subject with Skrine:

Long talk with Walter on deck, mostly on my ideas on training, which boils down to seeing that as far as possible everyone knows the plan as well as I do. A lot of lip service is paid to this, but it is seldom that the men are tested to see that it is eventually made fact. If the men know exactly what to expect they cannot be surprised.

The convoy formed up with others, including a considerable naval escort; there had been a slight alarm when an Axis aircraft overflew the convoy and flew off in the direction of Crete. There was still the possibility of enemy aircraft based on the island attacking, but thankfully nothing transpired.

On the morning of 9 July, Lance Corporal Clay, one of the medics attached to the unit, strapped Peter's ankles; he also had a 'very Bosche' haircut.

At 1145 hrs, Peter gave an address to the men:

I told them that it was the custom to speak to any group that one happened to command before going into action.

That I wasn't worried about the fighting . . . That I knew they were fairly bloody-minded.

I spoke of Discipline, as I had done to the Officers and Sergeants.

That the sod I was watching for was the runner, who went off to the beach with a message and felt tired, had a smoke and started back 20 minutes later, only to find his officer gone.

The man who was busy watching for the first of his comrades to fall so that he could help him to the rear and stop there for the rest of the battle.

The Corporal who allows his section to be borrowed when he ought to 'maintain the objective'.

The Italian steel helmet hunters who ought to be refilling magazines . . .

I said there would be no Umpires, going round saying, 'You're dead,' and 'You're dead,' and 'You can't get on, you're pinned to the ground.'

I [said it] was time enough for them to consider they were dead when they really were.

. . . In the words of the old song, 'It ain't what you do it's the way that you do it'. Any infantry could do our job. Only we can do it in the time. I said I hope some of them would return as they would be very useful the next time I ran a Cadre Course.

I told them they must get ashore if they had to swim, and if some boats were missing they must go on with the important jobs – Strong Point 1 and the Roofless Buildings as opposed to the artistic jobs of cutting off the Italians so as to put them all in the bag.

'We want a VAAGSO not a DIEPPE.'

The weather had deteriorated and there was a stiff westerly wind blowing, calling into question whether the operation could go ahead. In the end, Admiral Ramsay decided that the sea state was acceptable and gave the go-ahead; at 2315 hrs that evening the Commandos dressed for battle.

Of all the lessons learned from Dieppe the most important was that there had to be a fall-back position in the event that the landings did not go according to plan. Peter went into action as confident as he could be that every eventuality had been covered. As ever, the plan did not survive first contact with the enemy which, in this case, included the sea.

93

The heavy swell made the business of embarkation on the LCAs more difficult than it needed to be. The night was dark, and there was a headwind which, together with the swell, made life very uncomfortable. The LCAs moved away from the side of the *Dunera* to form up before beginning the run ashore. The Flotilla Officer, Lieutenant Russell RNVR, also commanded Peter's boat.

Whether through incompetence, as Peter suggested, or a reluctance to go into action, Russell contrived to make the landings as fraught as possible. In Peter's view, Russell moved the flotilla off too quickly, before all the LCAs had formed up, and in the process managed to miss one of the six boats he should have had with him. Their orientation was further confused when Russell took them to the port side of the *Duchess of Bedford* when they had been ordered to pass to starboard. It is hard to see how this could have happened; in his post-operation report Peter says baldly:

> He was . . . hailed by a voice crying through the night on a magaphone [sic] that he was to go to starboard of the *Duchess of Bedford*. He promptly went to port of this vessel, thus losing the M.L. [motor launch] which up to that time had been in sight. He did not hail the M.L. although advised to do so by the Military Officers.

In Russell's defence there was considerable confusion in the area where they had massed to lower the boats, and it is vividly captured in John Durnford-Slater's account: 'Ships were going in all directions. The *Sobieski*, a large transport, appeared on our [i.e. *Prinz Albert*'s] port beam, going very fast and heading straight for us. A large ship appearing out of the dark like this is most alarming, but she just missed us.'

Lash's boat broke down within ten minutes of moving off and the men returned to the *Dunera* to be re-embarked on the spare LCA, however they could not locate the *Dunera*. The three remaining LCAs continued their run ashore, but almost immediately Russell declared that the boats had been lowered in the wrong position off *Dunera* and that he had to get a new course from the *Duchess of Bedford*. In effect, he was lost. Peter fumed at the time this wasted, particularly as the eventual response was an exact repetition of the course that had been given out at the briefing: N53W. They proceeded along that course, although the delays had cost them precious time. When Peter urged Russell to pick up speed he refused, saying that the other boats could not keep up with him.

Concern that he was going to miss his landing time turned to alarm as they came up to port of the flotilla carrying the Royal Scots Fusiliers – whose landing time was 45 minutes after their own – when they should have been to starboard. In order to move to the correct position, 'Lieut Russell,' Peter noted dryly, 'with more courtesy than wit, decided to pass astern of this Flotilla despite my protests.' At only half strength Peter's Group continued on its way with Russell still lost and saying so to anybody who would listen. They missed both a sonic buoy which had been deployed to help them locate their position and a folboat – a small canoe deployed by a submarine with a flashing light to act as a marker.

Ahead the men could see fires on the horizon which they surmised – correctly – to be Syracuse. The beacon which was their marker at Scoglio Imbiancato shone to the left, but Russell was unconvinced, and Peter did not recognize the unusual angle at which they were viewing the rocky outcrop at Beach 44, their destination. Instead of disembarking, therefore, they turned north. When Peter asked Russell to keep close inshore so that he could look out for land-marks Russell took them much further out to sea, claiming that he had to 'clear the point'.

Before long they entered Murro Di Porco bay, just outside Syracuse. Both Skrine and Peter realized where they were and asked Russell to turn around. He took some persuading. As they turned back they were fired on by an observation post at Torre Ognina which was enough to convince Russell that they should return to the *Dunera* without delay.

Peter joined Roy Cadman, positioned in the bows of the LCA with the Bangalore torpedo, to get a clearer view of the shoreline. Cadman's job was to be first out of the boat and up the beach so that he could blow a hole in any beach defences. He did not, therefore, wish to surrender his position even to his commanding officer who was clearly in a towering rage. Peter's language was extremely ripe and the state of his temper surprised even his own men.

They should have been ashore long since and they could hear gunfire which indicated that the action had started, so Peter ordered the signallers to break radio silence and establish W/T communica-tions. This Russell attempted to forbid until Peter told him that he could not lawfully issue such an order.

At this point they encountered the remains of a glider which had crashed into the sea and was sinking. There were twenty survivors clinging to the wreckage and despite the delay Peter decided to rescue them, a decision opposed by Russell who clearly just wanted to get away. In no mood to be contradicted, Peter informed him brutally that he must be out of his mind. They agreed to take a third of the men in each boat and succeeded in completing the rescue before the remains of the glider sank.

It was clear that Russell's mental state was cause for concern. Peter tried to adopt a more conciliatory tone, realizing that any other approach would result in Russell suffering complete collapse. He could not keep this up for long, however it was now getting light and Beach 44 was positively identified at last. When a shell landed close to the beach during the final run-in Russell tried to turn the boat around 'until,' according to Christopher, 'PY stuck a revolver into his ribs'.

Peter says in his report on the incident that since Russell 'seemed much depressed from the outset, I told him not to worry and that things might be much worse,' an attitude for which Russell was apparently grateful, but Peter adds in his report that 'as a matter of fact I was much annoyed by his pessimism'. He concluded with some understatement: 'I have previously made four landings, all in the right place, twice from LCA Flotillas. Lieut. Russell's Flotilla is not in the same state of training as that to which I have been accustomed.'

As they finally went ashore all firing ceased and they landed un-opposed. Ironically, they came upon another landing craft carrying Brigadier Tarleton who was somewhat surprised to find the spear-head of the landing arriving after him. Graciously, Tarleton suggested that the two forces should go in together.

After this, the remainder of the action was something of an anti-climax. While still on the LCA, Peter had reorganized his soldiers to take account of the fact that half his force was not with him. Their objective should have been the Casa della Tunara but they had landed in the wrong place, being to the right of the line when they should have been to the left, so they had to improvise.

The group reformed near Fontane Bianche Farm where Tarleton asked Peter to deploy along the railway line between two points where the railway and road intersected. This they did, encountering no opposition. Colonel Cator was concerned that contact had not been made with the troops to their left and ordered a patrol out to accomplish this. Peter meanwhile took a patrol of three men up the railway line to Cassibile station and the road junction at Strada Statali. When he got there he discovered that Cassibile had fallen, enabling 17 Brigade to pass through and advance towards Syracuse. He had not fired a shot.

It must have been galling to hear of the successes of the day from other units, although there was a friendly fire incident which resulted in the death of one trooper. For Durnford-Slater things had gone like clockwork and he was in high spirits. Peter was philosophical: 'At Dieppe he had had a series of misfortunes whilst I had been lucky. This time the boot was on the other foot.'

They spent the night of 10 July in Cassibile where, according to Christopher, 'the local inhabitants were very happy to see us.' The following morning General Dempsey ordered the commando to clear the area between Torre Ognina and Cassibile. Durnford-Slater sportingly allowed Peter to organize the operation for which he used 3 Troop under John de Lash, who had been similarly thwarted by the botched landings.

They advanced with good speed along the railway line until they reached the road and railway junction where an RASC company told them that there had been firing during the night from the direction of a farm called Torre Cuba. There had been no activity since daylight, however, and the RASC troops assumed that the occupants had either surrendered or withdrawn. The party turned off the railway onto a track leading towards the farmhouse. Peter told Lash to deploy his men in extended order on either side of the stone-walled track while they were still a good distance from the objective. This was just as well, because as soon as they got within 100 yards of the farm they came under fire from several Breda machine guns and a number of snipers.

As an observer in the rear, Peter advanced with his runners, Christopher and Craft, 'exercising,' as he put it 'the divine right of commanders'. The burst of fire caused Christopher to vault off his bicycle and over the wall in one fluid movement while Peter and Craft flung themselves onto the ground. In his operation report he wrote that 'the engagement lasted about 15 minutes and during most of that time I was busily engaged crawling backwards on my stomach, to get out of the line of fire of two of the . . . M.G.s.' Ever mindful of the need to report on operational improvements, he added: 'A point of detail as regards equipment to be improvised is some better method of carrying hand grenades than the present one of sticking them on

97

the belt by the lever. I, several times, had to crawl back for mine when I least wished to do so.'

Meanwhile Lash crawled forward under covering fire from Herbert who plastered the walls of the farm with bursts from a Bren gun which he fired from his shoulder – no mean feat. It did the trick and Lash got close enough to the machine-gun post to lob a grenade. It missed its mark, but made the Italians manning it run away. Lash and a party of others now rushed into the farm firing as they went. As they did so, another party succeeded in entering the farm from the north, having detoured through the orchard under heavy fire. The wounded included eight Italians and a British paratrooper who had been captured. He was not seriously injured, however, and ran out to welcome his liberators. Resistance was at an end, and Trooper Pritchard came to tell Peter that it was now safe to move.

While the garrison formally surrendered – and eleven British prisoners of war were rescued – Peter inspected the defences and discovered that they were considerable. The two officers and fifty-one ORs of the 206th (Italian) Coastal Division had been able to beat off several fighting patrols from this strong position; the farm was surrounded by thick, square walls with Bredas positioned at each of the four corners. The walls and the buildings around them were loop-holed and the tower contained another machine-gun position. Across the farmyard a 12-foot trench had been dug which held another Breda. The 60-foot water tower provided an excellent lookout point; looking back towards their direction of advance it was clear that the Italians must have seen them when they were about ¾ mile away.

The commando suffered only one slight injury, to Trooper Smith, wounded in the initial burst of fire.

The Italian prisoners were taken to Cassibile by the freed British prisoners and a few of Lash's men under CSM Fawcett, while the rest of the men moved on towards Torre Ognina. Peter had kept one of the Italian officers with him, Captain Covatto, thinking that he might come in useful even though neither spoke the other's language. The Captain seemed keen to co-operate for he pointed out a mine dump and an evacuated strong point as they moved towards Torre Ognina, although this might also have been because Peter indicated, by much theatrical display and some well-chosen words, that if the garrison resisted surrender they would be put to the sword. In the event, they encountered no resistance and reached the cliff-top garrison at Torre Ognina without meeting a soul or hearing a shot fired. Rounding a large rock, they encountered a huddled group of Italians who surrendered at once after Covatto delivered what Peter hoped was an Italian translation of his summons. The bag was one officer and sixteen ORs who were sent to Cassibile with the remainder of 3 Troop.

Peter, Christopher and Craft took, according to Christopher, the coast road back to Cassibile. En route they came across two crashed gliders, one of which contained the bodies of four badly burned paratroopers, but no survivors. When they arrived back in Cassibile that evening, Durnford-Slater noted that Peter was much more cheerful.

Durnford-Slater moved inland with most of the commando that evening to act as flank guard, while Peter remained in command in Cassibile with 3 and 5 Troops. He established his HQ at the water tower and organized the men to defend the village. The night was quiet and the following morning, under the command of Brigadier Senior of 151 Brigade, they were ordered to a farm called Massa Lo Bello, outside Syracuse. Peter commanded the advance party which had to beg, borrow or steal the transport needed to get their equipment to the new location – all the vehicles they had used while they were based in the Middle East had been left there. Colonel Cator had acquired a battered van which arrived carrying twelve soldiers, and together with a car and a couple of farm carts, this constituted the 'baggage train'. It was hot and dusty, but the farm, when they reached it, turned out to be a haven of shade set in orange groves, where the men were able to rest and see to their equipment.

XIII Corps HQ was located in a nearby orchard. Peter and Skrine could not resist strolling over to watch, as Peter put it, 'the great ones from afar'. Dempsey was in conference with Brigadier John Currie, commander of 4 Armoured Brigade, and they were joined for a short while by Monty himself. Skrine was photographing the makeshift operations room – a couple of tables, a radio, a jeep and one or two trucks –when Monty invited him over to take photographs, an event which, though unimportant, Peter included in his account of the operation; he was not above being flattered by the attentions of the C-in-C. Later that afternoon, Dempsey visited the Commandos in their own orchard which further raised him in Peter's estimation. An informal visit by a general at that juncture displayed, to his mind, one of the best qualities of leadership. During the course of conversation Dempsey told them: 'We've got something good for you this time!' The afternoon's deliberations had clearly borne fruit.

Chapter Nine

Sicily – Agnone

After all the meticulous planning that had gone into the landings at Cassibile it was ironic that their next operation, arguably the most difficult they ever undertook, was conceived, briefed and launched all within the space of twelve hours.

On the night of 12 July, the commando received orders to re-embark on the *Prinz Albert*. Although they had suffered few casualties they had not been unopposed. The Allied landings were continuously under attack from German fighter bombers despite accurate work by artillery aboard ship and ashore. The Luftwaffe found their mark on several occasions; one tanker blew up, providing a spectacular pyrotechnic display which concluded with clouds of black smoke that obscured everybody's vision for some time.

During the afternoon Durnford-Slater was summoned to a conference in Syracuse, also attended by Montgomery, Dempsey and Admiral McGrigor. The 50th (Northumbrian) Division were encountering opposition on the road to Lentini, believed to be held by Italian troops, and it was proposed that while they cleared this away two landings further north towards Catania should take place.

Both objectives were bridges: the Primasole bridge, spanning the Simeto River, and the Punta dei Malati, which crosses the Leonardo River two miles north of Lentini. Primasole was to be attacked by an airborne unit while Punta dei Malati was 3 Commando's objective. Punta dei Malati was to be held to ensure that it was not destroyed by the retreating enemy – 50th Division would need it to continue their advance.

Durnford-Slater, buoyed up by a very positive briefing ashore, returned to the *Prinz Albert* armed with maps and grid references.

Monty's final words to him had been, 'The enemy is nicely on the move. We want to keep him that way. You can help us do it. Good luck, Slater.'

His announcement that they were to go into action that night was received with consternation in the wardroom. Since the previous operation – so well planned and rehearsed – had been for Peter an unmitigated disaster, he was less concerned about the lack of detailed briefing time than some others. There was not even time to give the operation a code name – they were discussing it at supper-time and launching the landing craft three hours later. The men who had returned on board earlier that day in need of time to rest and recuperate once more prepared to disembark.

For several reasons Peter expressed concern about this: firstly many of them had foot problems because of the boots they had been wearing; secondly the men had been on board ship long enough to lose a degree of fitness; thirdly lack of transport meant that they would have to carry a great deal of heavy equipment; and fourthly they had left their bedding on the *Dunera*, and there was none spare on the *Prinz Albert* so they had not been able to rest properly.

However, as he later wrote: 'Don't bellyache if you are overworked . . . It only means that people you respect . . . trust you.'

There remained operational difficulties. There were not enough landing craft to get the men ashore in one wave. If the first landings could hope to achieve an element of surprise, the second could not. This increased the risk of casualties but they believed that the area was not heavily defended; the local Italian commander had surrendered and had ordered the coastal defences to do likewise. Thus there was no expectation of resistance from the coastal defence battery on the headland next to the landing site, nor from the four or five pill boxes on the beach. Nevertheless HMS *Tetcott*, a Hunt class destroyer, was to lead them in and bombard the battery on the headland to cover the landing.

The first wave consisted of HQ and 1, 2, 3 and 4 Troops. 2 Troop, with HQ, was to hold the beach until the second landing was effected. 1 and 3 Troop (under Peter's command) were to move inland and take the bridge, whereupon 4 Troop was to send patrols north to contact the airborne troops attacking Primasole bridge, and south to join up with 69 Brigade. The second wave, 5 and 6 Troops, were to move inland and help hold the bridge. In his view, Peter had acquired the plum job.

In the short time between briefing and disembarkation the troop commanders tried to ensure that their men had a clear idea of what they were about to do. Peter, with Skrine, looked at the available maps and plotted a route for their move inland. Skrine, a graduate of the Staff College (most unusual in the Commandos), had a gunner's eye for terrain. The best option available was a railway line which ran directly inland from close to the landing site although it disappeared into a tunnel further inland. Peter also identified defensible strong points around the bridge at Punta dei Malati.

When *Prinz Albert* set sail at about 1900 hrs the men remained below decks preparing their equipment. For the first time they were going into action without steel helmets; the decision to wear berets was a popular one and it may have been the absence of an Operation Order which enabled the commanders to allow this relaxation. For rations, they carried only chocolate, biscuits and bully beef or sardines. They were also handed a packet of sandwiches as they left the ship.

At 2140 hrs the boats were lowered and the first wave embarked. The eight LCAs made uneventful progress towards the shore, while Catania was being bombarded to the north, lighting the horizon spectacularly and giving the boat commanders additional help in locating their position; to the west and south, towards Syracuse, occasional bursts of Very lights and Bren gun fire were also visible, and in the further distance, evidence of a sea battle taking place to the north-east, towards the Italian coast, was discernable as star shells and flares lit up the sky.

As their landing point came into view two Dakotas passed low overhead and flew inland, bound for Primasole; they crossed the shoreline unopposed, which seemed to augur well. All was silent until they were close inshore when the battery on the cliff opened fire on them, as did the pill boxes and machine-gun nests on the beach. The *Tetcott* and the landing craft immediately returned fire. The sight of a steady stream of tracer directed on the pill boxes lifted many hearts and although enemy fire was not entirely suppressed, it was largely ineffective.

Peter's landing craft was to the right of the flotilla as they hit the beach. He felt that the approach was too slow – as soon as the beach defences opened fire they should have gone in at full speed to make it more difficult for the enemy to get their range. As they landed he was suddenly struck repeatedly on the chest and was convinced that he had been hit, particularly as he felt no pain – a sure sign he was dying. When he did not fall down he found that he was standing in

102

the path of the stream of empties which was pouring out of the Lewis gun in the bows.

A short lull in the enemy's fire gave them enough time to dash the 50 yards up the beach and look for cover while the Bangalore torpedoes blew holes in the beach defences. To their left all was chaos – the left-hand landing craft had landed right in front of an Italian machine-gunner. With typical audacity the Adjutant ran up to the position and kicked the gun over which so astonished the Italians that they surrendered at once. To the sporadic bursts of fire and the occasional detonation of a grenade dropped by the enemy from the top of the cliffs was added the confusion caused by whistles blowing, orders being shouted and the blast of the hunting horn used by 1 Troop. Peter, whose temper was uncertain when the adrenalin was running, became infuriated by the lack of control and roared at the men to form up and take cover along the line of the bank he was occupying with his own group. As Brian Butler put it, 'Major Young, with some well-chosen words, eventually restored some sort of order.'

Sometime during this melee he found time to consider the relative merits of the Enfield Mark IV rifle and the Garand, which he did not have on this operation, having lent it to Trooper Fred Walker. Afterwards he wrote in his diary:

I am more than ever convinced that the Mk IV Enfield Rifle is not the proper weapon for Commando troops. The bolt often flies half open with the safety catch applied, and when this occurs while the soldiers are lying on the beach, as it frequently does, the rifle becomes jammed from the outset of the operation. The peep-sight is certainly an advantage but to my mind, it is offset by the soldiers only being able to put 300 or 600 on their sights. The bayonet is . . . too small and the soldiers don't feel much tempted to close with the enemy in the dark as they should, but prefer to fire, which is generally ineffective.

The incident resolved itself when a gap was discovered in the wire and Peter ordered them through, although he realized that it could have been mined. But they were lucky and formed up into a ragged column to begin the 5-mile march inland. Peter sent Lash with 3 Troop out in front and followed with his usual coterie of 'orderlies' or runners. As Christopher relates: 'I took up my usual position on P.Y.s left flank, Craft on the right and two other runners following

103

on behind.' The uneven pace of the march meant that these men had constantly to move between the various troops at Peter's behest to make sure that they were in contact with each other.

Almost at once an explanation for the warmth of their welcome was offered. Herbert sent to Durnford-Slater, without comment, a prisoner he had captured. He was German. Unknown to them, the whole area had been reinforced with elements of the Hermann Goering Division which had been engaged near Lentini; they were clearly there to stiffen the sinews of their Italian allies.

They advanced agonizingly slowly at first and halted altogether when they encountered a party of Italian prisoners coming in the other direction with their rifles slung over their shoulders and their hands up. Peter consigned them to the care of the walking wounded who were returning to the beach, but a man in one of the follow-up sections opened fire on them. The whole column came to a standstill once more as others started firing too. It took several more of Peter's well-chosen words to get them settled again, however the point section could not then be induced to advance. Peter wrote scathingly in his diary: 'This was not entirely due to the failure of Lieut. Nicholas who was leading, because he was not properly supported by Sgt Smith who was creeping along behind and, when I asked him who he was, answered me in a voice like a woman.'

Skrine offered to accompany the leading sub-section to ensure that they did not get lost. Armed with a compass, which he had liberated from a crashed glider during the operation at Catania, and accompanied by his runner, he soon outstripped the pace of the leading sub-section. On the road which led from the beach towards the railway line they encountered a motorcycle with a machine gun mounted in the sidecar. Cox, his runner, put it out of action with a well-directed grenade which induced enemy troops to open fire from positions close by and forced the leading elements to take cover under a bank which ran along either side of the road. During this exchange of fire both Skrine and Cox were hit, the former, Peter thought, by bullets from both sides. Skrine refused the morphine which Ned Moore, the medical officer, offered him and Peter was forced to leave him to his fate.

Lash, well forward by now, was still engaging the enemy to the front, many of whom were German paratroopers. Peter sent Nicholas around to the right to try to take the enemy position from that flank and when Captain Lincoln Leese, commanding 1 Troop, reported to him for

104

orders Peter sent him with the bulk of his force to support Nicholas.

As soon as he could Peter went forward to see how things were going. Word came from Durnford-Slater who offered to send 4 Troop around the left flank, but since he had already committed most of 1 Troop and a sub-section of 3 Troop on a right-flanking movement, Peter declined the offer, feeling that the command and control issues arising from two flanking movements in the dark over un-reconnoitred terrain was too risky.

The advance had stalled. Peter, with Lash, was lying amongst some trees which lay to the left of the road contemplating the enemy positions on the railway line still further to their left. Impatient to break through, Peter called for a Bren gun to be brought forward and fired the weapon himself while Herbert, who had remarkable eyesight, spotted for him. This did the trick and after he had emptied four or five magazines, the enemy firing stopped. During this enjoyable interlude Durnford-Slater came up. 4 Troop, which had been in the rear, also arrived, and Peter ordered them to deploy in the trees just ahead. In the lull they heard ahead the sound of Leese's hunting horn as he closed on the enemy.

3 Troop, which had borne the brunt of the action so far, needed to regroup. In passing, Peter noted in his diary his irritation that 3 Troop had not carried out his instructions, 'which have always been that when fired on at close quarters at night, they should go in with the bayonet'. Had they done so, there would have been fewer casualties and a faster advance, however his observations about the limitations of the Enfield Mk IV indicate that he understood why they had been reluctant to do so.

Resistance melted away; progress would be faster if they continued their advance along the railway line. Peter accompanied the forward elements on the left side of the track, moving so fast that he began to overtake them. Captain Bill Lloyd, now commanding the lead elements, sent a man forward with instructions not to let the Second-in-Command get in front which Peter considered a very thoughtful gesture. He continued to make good progress and sent a man out with wire-cutters to cut as many telephone wires as he could reach. It was not long before they reached Agnone Station.

Here they met 1 Troop and found Leese with four Italian prisoners. Leese had been wounded by a grenade which he feared had blinded him; he apologized to Peter who reassured him and sent him back towards the beach. Veasey was now in command of 1 Troop; Peter told him to reform his men.

Resistance was now minimal and they were able to progress much faster since 'the troops had given up plunging into the ditch' whenever they were fired upon, and they did not waste time searching every house they came across.

Shortly they reached the mouth of the railway tunnel and paused to confer. The troop commanders were all present and Durnford-Slater wasted few words. They had about 3 miles still to cover before reaching their objective; 4 Troop was to continue in the lead, followed by 3 and then 1. Headquarters was to continue to move with the lead troop. Time was of the essence – they had to reach the bridge under cover of darkness before the retreating enemy to prevent them from demolishing it. They had some difficult country to cover in the meantime and Peter took the lead. With a final word to urge the men not to straggle, they pushed on; Durnford-Slater wanted to approach the bridge from the north, which was not the direction the enemy would be expecting.

The going was nightmarish. The terrain was uneven and full of obstacles which served to make a steady advance in good order difficult. After 2 miles, they reached the Leonardo River about a mile downstream from the bridge. It looked wide and shallow and in order to reach the north side of the bridge it would have to be forded. Lloyd led the way and disappeared underwater. When he resurfaced, spluttering, Peter went to find another crossing place. A little upstream he found some stepping stones and sent Christopher back to the column to tell them to follow. On the far bank they negotiated a reed bed followed by terrain which was even worse than that already covered: 'a thicket followed by a field of peculiarly penetrating thistles'. Eventually they reached the road which led to the bridge as the sky began to lighten in the east.

With Peter as pathfinder, they moved at good speed until they came to a bend in the road beyond which they could see a road block; they had reached the bridgehead. Here they found an orchard behind a cactus hedge to the right of the road. Sending the leading sub-section of 4 Troop forward, Peter took his runners into the orchard and advanced along the line of the hedge. It was not long before they encountered an occupied pill box. The ensuing action was confused as Peter recounts in his diary:

Everybody seemed to stop and many voices were heard giving orders and crying for grenades. I had no grenades and, as there was no wire round the pill-box, I ran up to the middle loop hole

106

and fired two or three rounds . . . through it. I could hear an Italian inside shouting in an alarmed manner, but nevertheless he did not surrender, but ran out into the road where he was killed.

Butler now decided to seize the initiative so he ran forward, shouting, 'With me, Movement Group!' When, embarrassingly, no one followed Peter called on his own group to go with him. Christopher was first off the mark, followed closely by the rest; they ran round the pill box and back onto the road. About 30 yards ahead they encountered another unmanned defensive position, a wall shaped like an arrowhead.

From there they advanced to the bridge where they met the leading sub-section. The road along which they had come up from the east intersected here with the main north–south route from Lentini to Catania. Seeing another larger pill box to the north-east of the crossroads Peter went to flush it out; he threw a hand grenade into the basement, but it, too, was unmanned. The only opposition surrendered without a fight – the modest garrison was an Italian captain with a small platoon which had no stomach for battle.

After a gruelling march, this was something of an anticlimax, but Peter, to whom Durnford-Slater had entrusted the defence of the bridge, ensured that the men were effectively deployed. Whether the bulk of the enemy had yet crossed was not clear, but the arrival of the Commandos north of the river had clearly caught them unawares. Erskine, an intrepid subaltern, reported seeing the enemy south of the bridge when he posted a Bren gun on the bridge itself, but feeling that the position was too exposed Peter withdrew him.

4 Troop was now set up north of the bridge, but Peter wanted to take a more aggressive posture, so he ordered Lash – known among his colleagues as a fearless, even reckless, operator – to establish a position south of the river. On the way, Lash was ordered to cut any demolition wires he encountered. 1 Troop was positioned to watch the road to the north and Peter established HQ near the first pill box they had attacked in the orchard.

There followed a short hiatus during which Peter attempted to interrogate the Italian captain he had taken prisoner. He tried, unsuccessfully if cheekily, to persuade him to visit the Area Commander in Lentini and request that he surrender his garrison.

By now, men from 5 and 6 Troops, which had landed in the

second wave, began to arrive. Like the first wave, they had not landed unopposed despite the presence of 2 Troop. The new arrivals, commanded by John Pooley, made the same difficult journey inland and met up with the first wave at the crossroads just as the action began to unfold once more. A PIAT mounted on the bridge successfully hit an enemy ammunition truck and trailer, setting them on fire, the resulting fireworks enlivening the scene for some time. Nobody was able to disengage from the action long enough to brief the new arrivals and Peter, in particular, was extremely busy with a number of developments.

Both he and Durnford-Slater received reports from Lash's party that they were pinned down under the bridge and that most of them had been wounded. Peter's offer of fire support, particularly from the PIAT, a weapon new to the Commandos, was turned down and the news that the enemy was now trying to work round their left flank meant that the troops would have to be redeployed. Peter suggested that he take a party from HQ Group to occupy a house which lay in the path of the advancing enemy, but Durnford-Slater turned this down in favour of sending elements from 5 Troop instead. They advanced under covering fire from HQ.

Just then a Mark IV Tiger tank appeared on the far side of the bridge and opened fire on the Commandos' position in the orchard. Peter and Durnford-Slater agreed that their position was untenable. Their strength was now about 350 but effective deployment of the men was impossible – there was very little cover, nobody carried entrenching tools, and they were becoming targets as the light improved and the enemy began to get their range. They would have to move back from the road and take up positions where they could harry the enemy.

3 Troop, still under the bridge, had to withdraw as a matter of urgency. Peter wrote in his account:

I sent Tpr Christopher to extricate them. He ran forward across the field to the far end of the Bridge where he found about 10 men of 3 Troop. The rest were under the arches at the nearer end – 'resting'. Christopher got across and back very quickly and most fortunately unharmed. 3 Troop fell back to the east end of the orchard. If Trooper Christopher had not carried this message so promptly and gallantly I have no doubt that 3 Troop would have been under the Bridge to this day.

The word 'resting' in inverted commas carries with it a question mark. Although 3 Troop did succeed in cutting all the demolition wires which had been laid under the bridge, they did not get to the south side as ordered. Peter's subsequent comments on the operation make his own feelings clear:

It is very much to be deplored that my orders to O.C. 3 Troop to cross the RIVER LEONARDO and capture the south end of PUNTA DEI MALATI were not carried out to the full . . . Lieut. Herbert, DCM, MM was sent ahead by Captain Lash to recce the southern bank where he found unsuspecting enemy transport parked. He reported this to his Troop Commander . . .

Lieut. Herbert urged him to . . . have a battle, which to my mind would have been carrying out my order in the spirit in which it was given. The Troop was, however, withdrawn underneath the arches where they effected nothing and indeed could effect nothing . . . Had I known on this night what was going on in their hearts, I would have taken charge of 3 Troop personally, and have little doubt that, with the aid of God and Lieut. Herbert, the south end of the Bridge would have been our's [sic].

Herbert was a popular and effective officer; indeed Peter thought he was outstanding and, respecting his judgement and ability, felt that his account was more to be relied upon than any other.

Events were unfolding rapidly; organizing the orderly withdrawal of the men in such spread-out positions was no easy task under fire and casualties began to mount. Lieutenant Cave was killed, shot through the chest, and Lloyd was badly injured while occupying one of the Italian pill boxes, suffering a broken leg and a broken arm. Peter, encountering him lying on a mattress, did not recognize him at first because his face was covered in grey dust. The Germans were rapidly getting their range and shells were exploding all along the orchard, particularly at the end where the men were starting to move away towards Agnone.

Veasey, with 1 Troop, had not yet got the word to retire. Durnford-Slater asked Peter to ensure they were told, so Peter decided to go himself, taking with him Christopher and Clarke – Craft was missing. On the way they encountered several groups of soldiers, mostly from 2 Troop, moving generally eastwards. Some were helping their wounded comrades; many were going, Peter thought, too far northwards so he 'directed them to incline to their right'. Just before he reached 1 Troop's position he discovered that the Adjutant was wounded. Head had been hit in the leg and was sitting propped up against a tree. He wanted to be left where he was but Peter thought this was inadvisable, so he ordered Clarke and Trooper Grant to make sure that the Adjutant was moved from the area under fire. He recorded in his diary:

> I went up to Lieut. Veasey's position and ordered him to retire as soon as the orchard was clear of troops to its eastern hedge, and told him I expected him to carry out his withdrawal by bounds and make it a classic example of what a withdrawal should be. He did indeed conduct his withdrawal in a very cool and orderly manner.

Returning to his start point, Peter found 3 Troop bunched around their commander at the eastern end of the orchard and told them to spread out since they were under tank fire. Then he began to send off the men, staying behind until the end, hoping that he had created enough time for the men helping Head to reach the main body. As first 3 and then 6 Troop began to move to the rear, Peter could not resist returning to have a look at the bridge which appeared to be deserted although there was firing coming from that direction. He waited a few minutes longer to give 1 Troop enough time to pass through. He thought that his party were the last troops on the ground at that point; afterwards Durnford-Slater – in very high spirits throughout this costly and confusing action – told him that he thought Peter had always wanted to do 'this Bonnie Prince Charlie stuff'.

Peter ensured that his own movements were calm and orderly, making his men keep their dressing on him as they moved through the fields. Keeping the men ten paces apart meant that they were less likely to become casualties when they came under fire, but they could maintain contact with each other and could equally provide co-ordinated fire if necessary. It was a formation that they had practised endlessly and it came into its own on this occasion. As Christopher remembered: 'It was good to see the troops withdrawing across the field in open formation, no panic, no bunching.'

With the number of casualties continuing to rise, Ned Moore and his team could not keep up with the stream of wounded. Corporal Hopkins MM, a veteran of Vaagso and Dieppe, lost a hand but when Peter met him he only asked for a revolver. He returned to the beach and was killed organizing resistance there. Others were not so restrained and Peter had to tell one stretcher case to be quiet when he encountered him 'making,' as he said in his diary, 'a good deal of noise'.

Meeting up with Durnford-Slater again Peter was pleased to note that Head had also been brought safely back. The task now was to regroup and, where possible, evacuate the wounded. Those that could not be moved were left with a water bottle and what food could be spared in the hope that the advancing Allies would find them.

A number of 4 Troop were awaiting the signal to begin their withdrawal. Peter sent them on their way then hung around with his runners to give the wounded time to get a head start. They could hear a tank moving around about a quarter of a mile away, but for some reason it did not open fire for which they were grateful. They fell back through an orange grove to a point on the map identified as Tenta Principe. Here they constructed a road block and retired behind a low wall to await events, however the tank did not venture far enough down the road to be ambushed, and after a while they withdrew into the hills south of the river to rejoin the main body of the commando.

Durnford-Slater, in typically bellicose fashion, was still looking for opportunities to engage the enemy. He had assembled a party of men behind what cover they could find to keep watch on the bridge and await events. Although they were under fire it was difficult to assess the direction it came from, particularly a mortar which was more effective than the rest. Peter claimed that he silenced it with a single shot at a range of 2,000 yards – although he self-deprecatingly acknowledged that it was an unlikely story.

It became clear that any sort of counter-attack on the enemy forces at the bridge was impossible and that their best chance lay in withdrawing towards Augusta, hoping that they had done enough to allow 50th Division to get through. Those troop commanders who were available were called together for a rapid 'O' Group (Orders Group) which was succinct to a degree: compass bearing 164 degrees, lie up during the day and move back towards the Allied lines at night.

Peter travelled for some distance with the Colonel, moving west by south, keeping the German armour in sight but at a respectful distance. He could see their own troops moving away keeping well spread out to minimize casualties. Pantall is succinct: 'Owing to the difficult nature of the country . . . contact was extremely difficult to maintain and the Unit eventually split into small parties. The[ir] adventures . . . are epic stories in themselves and many deeds of

111

gallantry and stories of resourcefulness and endurance were told when the scattered Unit reorganised some days later.'

The unexpected presence of 3 Battalion of the Hermann Goering Parachute Division contributed to the Commandos' problems; Peter acknowledged that if they had known of the presence of such quality troops the plan to withdraw towards Augusta would, as he put it, 'hardly have been adopted'.

It soon became clear that Durnford-Slater's own party was too big to be concealed easily and Peter decided to separate from it. Taking Christopher, the only one of his runners still present, he moved south-east to the Massa Pagliarazzi where he was able to provide flanking cover. Here he found an occupied farmhouse whose inhabitants appeared to be friendly, although he could not understand them. They had a rest and some much needed sustenance, and Christopher took his photograph with a camera he had taken from a German prisoner. They also observed the battle going on towards Lentini, which they subsequently discovered to be 69 Brigade's attack on Monte Pancali.

Refreshed by this respite, Peter returned to the offensive. Reluctant to stay where he was he began to form an idea which would effectively exploit his current position. As he put it in his diary: 'I decided that it is not every day that one finds oneself behind the enemy lines and that the best thing to do would be to collect some troops . . . and approaching the road near our original objective to ambush one or more soft-skinned vehicles.' He reasoned that at some stage 50th Division would be advancing to the bridge and they could join them in their advance on Catania. The more he discussed it with Christopher, the better the idea seemed – the journey to Augusta was an unattractive prospect even if the scenery was spectacular. They wanted only a few more men.

They had just resolved on their course of action when they heard footsteps approaching. They belonged to Lieutenant White who was on a foraging expedition; he led Peter to a party made up of a number of wounded men and ten others. The wounded were too badly injured to be moved, so Peter left them with Moore, the MO, and divided the remaining party into two small units which he put under the command of the two subalterns, White and Collins.

With his two scratch sections he and Christopher moved back towards the Punti dei Malati via the river valley, taking cover in the many orange groves there and picking up fruit from time to time as sustenance. On the way they encountered Head once more, concealed in some bushes by the river and accompanied by two other wounded men and Lance Corporal Abbott MM, who was uninjured. Abbott had acquitted himself well at Dieppe and Peter was glad to have him join the party. Head was in good spirits, probably because the morphia that Moore had given him had not yet worn off. He accepted two of Peter's oranges and, assuring him that he had not been disturbed by the enemy, seemed to be in a fairly safe position.

They pushed on towards the bridge, but paused before they reached it to rest. Peter fell asleep for a short while and awoke feeling much better; they continued their advance reaching the Lentini–Catania road shortly before dark. It was now late on 14 July and they had been on the move almost continuously since dawn the previous day.

Posting most of his men in an unoccupied house near the road he took a small party on to the embankment nearby where they could observe the traffic. He could see that there were troops moving north-wards while armour was manoeuvring along the side of the hills about 1½ miles to the west. It seemed pretty clear that they had broken through the main German attack. This was confirmed when one of the men from the house came to tell Peter that the Northumberland Hussars had made contact with them. Peter went to meet them and found them very friendly, even offering him rations, which were extremely welcome.

During his absence the house they had occupied was approached by a party of about eighteen German paratroopers. One of Peter's men attempted to lure them into the open by calling out to them in German, a trick which might have succeeded if someone else had not called out in English. There ensued a brisk exchange of fire which ended when the Germans withdrew leaving behind a quantity of equipment.

Peter set up his headquarters in an undamaged house called Sanciolo which lay about ¼ mile south of the bridge on the Lentini road. From there he contacted the liaison officer from 151 Brigade who undertook to inform Durnford-Slater of his whereabouts, and to send ambulances to collect the wounded. In relative safety and comfort, therefore, they were able to rest during the night of 14/15 July.

Peter spent the following morning accompanying the ambulance to recover the wounded. He was impressed by the performance of these wounded men, mostly from 3 Troop who had been held up under the bridge the previous day. One of their number, Trooper

113

Winkworth, who was uninjured, had even persuaded a passing German patrol to give them cigarettes by posing as the Unit MO. That kind of audacity always appealed to Peter. They were evacuated to a Field Ambulance in Lentini and Peter returned to his men at Sanciolo.

Here he met another party led by Lieutenants Donald Hopson and Aubrey Moody, who had arrived in the company of three ambulances and five Bren-gun carriers in order to continue with the mopping-up operation. Almost at once they were engaged by a party of German parachutists in an orchard to the east of the road, however even Peter decided to move out of harm's way when he felt a shot whistle over his head during this skirmish. As he moved back to the road General Dempsey drove up in a jeep and they exchanged a few words. The General expressed his pleasure that the bridge had not been blown up and waved away Peter's caution that there was a firefight going on just down the road. He continued northwards towards the Primasole bridge and Peter began to move his men back towards Agnone to regroup, using the Bren-gun carriers as transport.

It proved impossible to reach Agnone because 151 Brigade was still heavily engaged in that area with the Germans. In an extraordinary coincidence the party met a Sicilian man on the road who was carrying a letter from Walter Skrine asking for medical assistance – he was successfully recovered although he was to spend a year in hospital.

Peter decided to move towards Augusta since that was the direction the men had been sent the previous day. He picked up a lot of his men en route, particularly at Villasmundo where many of them had congregated. The following day he located the *Prinz Albert* lying off Syracusa.

Although fighting was still going on, 3 Commando's part in it was over. The people who mattered, Dempsey and Montgomery, both told Brigadier Laycock and Durnford-Slater that they had done as much as could be expected of them and more. Indeed Dempsey told Laycock that the 'men of No 3 are the finest body of soldiers I have seen anywhere'. High praise indeed.

Monty instructed Durnford-Slater to have a piece of stone engraved with the words '3 Commando Bridge' set into the masonry on Punta dei Malati. It is there to this day.

Durnford Slater put Peter up for a bar to his DSO. The citation reads:

1. Barbara Young with Peter and Pamela c.1920. *(MCD)*

2. Peter Young aged about 8. *(MCD)*

3. Peter Young at Knebworth playing cricket aged about 12. *(MCD)*

4. Second Lt Peter Young with Dallas and Barbara c.1939. *(MCD)*

5. A group of men on HMS *Prince Leopold* returning from Vaagso. *Back row:* Smith (12) of 6 Tp and 4 sailors; *3rd row:* Durling, Leishman, Bingham, Smith (81), Hogan; *2nd row:* TSM Emmott, Sub Lt Hall RANVR, Peter Young, Sub Lt Oram, L/Cpl Harper; *Front row:* Tpr Nicholls. (*MCD*)

6. Ain-el-Turear, Oran 1943 *l. to r.* Tpr Torrens Maj Peter Young, Tpr Christopher, Lt Frans d'Esposey, L/Cpl Craft MM, Cpl Charleswo Capt J. N. De W. Lash. (

7. HMS *Prinz Albert* off Sicily. (*OC*)

8. Beachhead at Cassibile, Sicily. (*OC*)

9. Major Peter Young in Sicily, 1943. *(MCD)*

10. On operations in Sicily – Peter Young is on the left of the picture. *(OC)*

11. Italian soldiers surrendering to soldiers of 3 Commando. *(OC)*

12. The orange grove at Lo Bello. Monty departs after a briefing session. Brigadier John Currie stands by the side of the staff car. Taken by Walter Skrine. *(OC)*

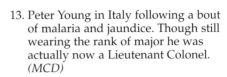

13. Peter Young in Italy following a bout of malaria and jaundice. Though still wearing the rank of major he was actually now a Lieutenant Colonel. (MCD)

15. Studio photo taken in Molfetta after the operation at Termoli. On the back Peter wrote: 'Taken at MOLFETTA, Italy. October 1943. To L/Cpl R.W. Christopher as a *reward* (in lieu of E.D. Pay). PY Lt Col.' (OC)

14. HMS *Ulster Monarch* showing LCAs slung off the ship's side. (OC)

16. The Young family: Pamela in WRNS uniform, Peter, Dallas and Barbara in ARP uniform 1943. (OC)

17. 3 Commando in Limehouse practising street fighting. The area had been heavily bombed and was used prior to D-Day to rehearse tactics for house-to-house fighting.

(Author)

18. King George VI inspected troops at Petworth House shortly before D-Day. As a regimental commander (or equivalent) Peter was presented to the King. *(OC)*

19. Peter with John Durnford-Slater in France, 1944. (OC)

20. The memorial erected by the citizens of Pétiville to commemorate the liberation of their town in August 1944. *(Author)*

21. Street sign in Pétiville. *(Author)*

23. The Brigadier outside The End House
with Sgt Christopher 1945. *(OC)*

22. Studio portrait taken when Peter was
Deputy Commander 1 Commando (1944-5).
(OC)

24. East Grinstead 1945, a photograph demonstrati
the different orders of dress: *l. to r.* Lt Wilkins
CSM Jimmy Leech MM (walking out dress),
Christopher MM (clean fatigues), Lt Pantall
Cpl Why (light raiding order), Brigadier You
DSO MC, Tpr Walker (D-Day order), Cpl Lo
(Drill order), Cpl Litherland MM (Brigade HQ
Police). *(Author)*

25. Peter playing the fool, 1945. (OC)

26. The Young family home at Oxshott, 1947. *(OC)*

28. The officers of 9 Regiment with Glubb Pash[
Zerqa, 1955. (MC

27. Peter Young briefing King Hussein of Jordan
during an exercise. (Author)

29. Peter Young with CGS Field Marshal Sir
Gerald Templer in Jordan 1955. (Auth

30. Peter and Joan Young outside their quarter in Jordan. (MC

31. Peter with some of his collection of wargaming figures c.1965. *(MCD)*

32. Gaming figure, Field Marshal Graf von Grunt, Peter's eighteenth-century alter ego. *(Author)*

Field Marshal Graf von Grunt (1699-1788).

33. Peter acting as father of the bride at the wedding of Gill and David Chandler in Beverley Minster, 8 Feb 1961. *(Author)*

34. Arab Legion cocktail party, 1971: *left to right* Peter Young, John Adair, Joyce Condon, Sir John Glubb, Lady Glubb, Thea Talbot (later Adair). *(MCD)*

35. Peter Young and John Adair at Missenden Manor c.1968. *(MCD)*

36. Peter Young in the uniform of the Trayne of Artillerie c.1973. *(Author)*

37. Patrick Caron Delion,
Peter Young and the
author outside Broughton
Castle, 1974.   (Author)

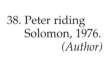

38. Peter riding
Solomon, 1976.
(Author)

39. Peter at the Glosters
Museum in 1982,
taken during the
filming of a TV
documentary.
(Author)

40. Peter with
Dobson, 1987.
(MCD)

41. Sketch by Stephen Beck of Peter and Dobson with the artist at Edgehill. *(Author)*

42. Letterhead designed and drawn by Stephen Beck for Peter as Captain Generall. *(Author)*

The Sealed Knot, Ltd.

from: Easter Monday 1

The Captain Genera

Brigadier Peter Young,
D.S.O., M.C., M.A., F

Bank House, Ripple,
TEWKESBURY, G

On night of 13/14 July, 1943 after landing at Agnone, and during the advance to Punta dei Malati, Major Young maintained pace and direction of the advance. He personally led several assaults on enemy posts encountered. Under heavy fire at Punta dei Malati moved continually in the open, coordinating and encouraging the troops, showing a complete disregard of danger. Later he moved around all day behind the enemy lines, helping and directing the wounded and parties which had been cut off.

He was outstanding throughout the operation and showed a wonderful example of offensive action.

He was awarded a bar to his MC instead.

It came at a price: 28 killed, including 5 officers (Captains Lloyd and Ruxton, Lieutenants Tony Butler, Cave and Pienaar), 66 wounded and 59 missing (including Captains Lash and Long, and Lieutenants Westley, Voyevodsky, Nicholas and Buswell), mostly taken prisoner.

One of those captured, Fred Walker, remembered particularly that the German officers who interrogated him asked about Peter Young – the Mad Major – and John Durnford-Slater by name. As with many of the men taken prisoner by the Germans, he subsequently escaped and rejoined his unit. (The Garand rifle Peter had lent to Walker became a casualty of war.)

This had been their longest battle by some margin. If they had known about the German paratroopers they might have taken different decisions, but it is unlikely that the outcome of the operation would have been affected. They maintained forward momentum and did not allow the unexpected to alter the way they executed their plans. Their rigorous training regime must take much of the credit for this.

Among those killed in this operation was Lance Corporal Freddie Craft. On 26 July, Peter wrote: 'It appears . . . there was a burnt body, with a Garand rifle and ammunition at AGNONE. We fear it was L/Cpl Craft MM.' As Christopher observed: 'a very costly battle'.

A few weeks later, Peter confided to his diary:

Bob [Laycock] has read my report . . . and liked it. He said what he liked about it and John's (D-S) was that our men had obviously been sticky at first and had got better as they went on. He said it made all the difference to have CHARACTERS like you and John!! Also that he was beginning to think Commandos were quite good. I said in the words of John that our people may have been bloody windy on the beach, but that most units wouldn't have got off it at all. There is no doubt that No. 3 are very high in his estimation.

Chapter Ten

Sicily – Life as a Liaison Officer

The men of 3 Commando found themselves back at Lo Bello, just outside Syracusa where they had so recently been. Their strength was down to about 270 men, of whom twenty or so were returned to their units as being unsatisfactory, and with no prospect of reinforcements, they reorganized into Headquarters and four troops, Nos 1 and 3 being temporarily disbanded to make up numbers in the remainder.

After a few days' rest the men began to recover; many had already had foot problems before Agnone, which Peter put down to the fact that they wore SV (Soulier Vibrum) boots with rubber soles. Being young and fit they soon returned to fighting form with a period of respite but they had no idea what operations might be forthcoming, and they were billeted in an area which limited their ability to do much training beyond working on their general fitness.

Peter grew bored. When Laycock visited 3 Commando at Lo Bello on 24 July as he was in the area, Peter took the opportunity to ask if he might do some liaison work between the Special Service Brigade and other units in the area. Laycock 'said certainly, but that I had done enough and was not to stick my neck out. I told him I was very cautious. He said, "That's not what John told me the other day."'

The night before Peter's departure to XIII Corps HQ the men organized an impromptu entertainment. Sergeant Jimmy 'Knocker' White and Lance Corporal Bruno Magnoni did the talent spotting, and Trooper Gates cast the show, a melodrama in which each of the characters had one line to say. Peter was cast as the Villain, and had to say:

'Be mine, be mine, Oh love, be mine,
And I will love you till I'm ninety-nine.'

Durnford-Slater was cast as the Hero, and at the end he had to shoot the Villain. 'Actually,' Peter wrote, 'he just pushed me off the stage.'

'I have little doubt,' Peter opined, 'that it was really a put-up job and cast beforehand by the wicked Magnoni.' (Bruno Magnoni, also from the Beds and Herts, had a theatrical background. After the war when they were all back at Kempston Barracks there was talk that Peter had his eye on Magnoni's wife. He certainly had a reputation among his men of being – in the vernacular – a 'randy bugger'.)

On Sunday, 25 July Peter moved up to XIII Corps' Headquarters near Lentini to take on a fortnight's attachment as the Liaison Officer between XIII Corps and the Special Service Brigade. He took Christopher with him – and, according to his diary, Mussolini's mattress which had been 'liberated' from one of the dictator's residences, a local villa.

He enjoyed renewing acquaintances in the Corps Headquarters, many of whom he had met through his friendship with Skrine. The military situation remained fluid and although there was little trouble from the remaining Italian forces, the Germans were still reinforcing in the east; Peter hoped that the Americans, who had landed in the west, would drive eastwards and keep the Germans on the defensive – the less they were able to regroup and dig in the easier it would be for 50th Division to take them on.

The day after his arrival at Lentini Dempsey addressed the staff to tell them how the battle was going. 'He is very impressive,' Peter wrote in his diary. 'Something in his voice and manner reminds me irresistibly of Geoffrey Anstee.'

In the ten days since Peter had been in action in the area much had changed. Several airfields were operational and the RAF was in impressive form – on 25 July they shot down twenty-one JU52s over the Straits of Messina. The terrain enabled both sides to observe each other with comparative ease. Peter had some new field glasses which helped, but the lie of the land was such that when he was visiting Tac 75, a small tactical headquarters, he had fantastic views of Pianura de Catania and Etna as well as the troop movements in the area. He was, therefore, puzzled to learn that although an airfield had been laid at Agnone it was not yet deemed safe for use as it was under observation by the enemy. 'I don't really understand this,' he wrote, 'for so is LENTINI WEST. PACHINO was made ready in a day, because Monty would not accept the excuses of those who said it would take 5. Good.'

118

He continued to analyse his own role at Agnone, particularly 3 Troop's failed assault, and visited Punta dei Malati, looking at the situation as it presented itself during the battle, concluding that 'my orders to Capt Lash were, without any doubt, eminently feasible.' The visit appeared to remove once and for all any doubt he might have harboured about the orders he had issued to 3 Troop. He also examined the beach where the landings had taken place and determined that the defences were poorly sited which had enabled the landing forces to get ashore and beyond.

His diary entries contain a running commentary on the developing military situation, but it is for his personal movements and meetings that they are chiefly interesting. He continues to consider the future use of the commando, informed by his ability to see at XIII Corps HQ how the battle was progressing. The pages are shot through with his own observations of his fellow officers and of himself.

I heard an illuminating remark by that rather junior Lt-Colonel of whom Walter Skrine did not particularly approve in the DUNERA, to the effect that he didn't like to go right forward to Brigades and Battalions, because he didn't want to worry them. This is how Regimental soldiers get hold of the idea that Staff Officers are too Olympian to understand their difficulties ... I get the impression that our Air Superiority is being supplied to the Support of ground troops in a wasteful manner and not as effectively as it could be. This will improve with practice.

I have an idea that a Commando could be effectively used on deep patrols in the North: Object to help keep the battle fluid there, BUT, particular objectives should be selected. This being the US 7th Army Front, my plan is probably ruled out, as Monty is not over the Americans, and it is a disadvantage I think that Alexander isn't here.

Peter records several hard-hitting conversations which reveal much about his own feelings as well as how some of his colleagues viewed him. On the evening of 26 July, during a visit to the headquarters by Bob Laycock, he had a chance to have a discussion with him during which several topics were aired.

They went over the operation at Agnone, and Peter remarked that he, Durnford-Slater and John Pooley were the only three officers who had survived unscathed since before Dieppe. Peter thought that Pooley was very upset by the loss of so many of his friends at Agnone, but that Durnford-Slater did not care very much, however Laycock disagreed. Peter's response was: '"I suppose I must be a callous sod. I can't say I was particularly upset about any of the Officers we lost." (I forgot Ruxton, who I confess I am sorry about.) I told him, however, how I regret losing Cox and Craft.'

Peter was delighted when Laycock revealed that Monty was keen to send more Commandos out to the theatre; he felt that the way the campaign was developing was 'an ideal wicket' for Commandos. This led to a discussion about replacements for the casualties they had suffered at Agnone. Peter had been keen to make up numbers before he had left Lo Bello:

> I told him that he could say 'Goodbye' to No. 3 if we had any more jobs like the last one, before we were made up to strength . . . He doesn't want to risk Units losing their Identity as 2 nearly did after St. Nazaire . . . I told him that our men were shaken by the last Operation, but were beginning to recover . . . which I hope is true.
>
> I got the impression when talking to Brigadier L that he is either a bit thick and doesn't get one's more subtle remarks or passes them off with a frivolous comment – as when I proposed my version of the reorganisation of the Commandos. I suggest that it is the latter because he has always handled the 'political side' of Commando life with success.

He was only a Major (substantive Lieutenant, war substantive Captain) at this time but the tenor of his diary entries betrays his ambition to take Durnford-Slater's place at the head of No. 3 Commando. He knew that there was talk of a change in the way in which the Special Service forces were organized and he realized that Durnford-Slater was in the frame to become a brigadier.

On 27 July he accompanied two Intelligence Corps officers on a visit to 30 Corps which was in the vicinity of Ramacca. Moving on to Palagonia and Mineo they were intercepted by a military policeman who informed them that they were out of bounds – not something that was likely to cause Peter to change his plans. He goes on:

> We went into a convent and the (?) Mother Superior opened the door of the Church for us. It was about 1300 and a service was toward. She brought Holy Water and put it in our hands,

crossed herself and said she was going to pray for us. A lot of trouble to go to for heretics; but she was a jolly old person who didn't look as if quibbles about doctrine would bother her as much as the physical difficulty of getting down on her knees.

Lunched near the house of some extremely friendly Sicilians. I suspect one man was really a soldier! He wore Italian Army boots like mine. They gave us oranges, apples and mulberries and bread. We gave them 'bully' and biscuits.

No detail, it seemed, was beneath his attention.

That evening control of the Special Service Brigade reverted to the Eighth Army from XIII Corps which meant that his job as a liaison officer ceased to exist. Although he was told he did not need to leave until the following day, he resolved to report to Laycock at once. Arriving at Brucoli at about 2200 hrs, he found Laycock playing bridge – badly, he thought. They had not yet heard the news of the transfer of command which caused Peter to wonder if it were true. After an uncomfortable night on the floor of Laycock's office where 'it was very hot and I was never so plagued by mosquitoes', he returned 'with . . . Christopher and my baggage (I don't mean femme de campagne)' to XIII Corps. There the change in command was confirmed so he reported to Eighth Army. It was 28 July, his twenty-eighth birthday and the anniversary of the investiture of his MC.

Eighth Army had a much bigger staff and Peter soon discovered that there were already fourteen liaison officers. Of more interest to him was the fact that his point of contact there, a South African major called Ingledew, had as his assistant one Captain Young who wore a signet ring with his own family crest on it: a hand clasping a dagger. 'He said his family motto, like ours, is "Press Through" but he did not know his coat of arms. I gather he is from Scotland. I told him we had originated from Perthshire.'

Young gave him a tour of the Headquarters where there were 150 staff officers, 'some of whom,' Peter recorded, 'are never seen at all; I am assured they all do something. Napoleon himself need not have been ashamed of a staff that size or indeed, of the pavilions, which are the quarters of the ascetic Monty.'

He took at once to the G2 Liaison Officer, Major Llewellyn, who briefed him on the current situation and even went so far as to put a motorcycle at his disposal. Major Maitland, G2 Maps, gave him his first look at the next planned attack which he considered straightforward, though likely to prove sticky. When Maitland expressed some criticism of XIII Corps, Peter 'made a point of praising General Dempsey and Brigadier Sugden'.

Understandably, he was interested in discussions about the employment of the Special Service Brigade and he fretted about 3 Commando's future role. They were still badly under strength and his diary is littered with comments about the lack of reinforcements.

He recorded some interesting gossip about Winston Churchill's son, Randolph, whom Peter had first encountered in Scotland in the winter of 1940/41. Llewellyn knew Randolph and had helped him when he had first tried to get elected to Parliament. At this time, Randolph was serving as an Intelligence Officer on the staff of Eighth Army and they agreed that Randolph probably acted as a spy for his father; there is some anecdotal evidence that Peter had met the Churchills at parties in London.

The talk continued to centre on the Commandos and their future. Over breakfast on 29 July:

> [Laycock's staff officers] said I was a shit, to which I replied that I had never pretended to be anything else. The fact is that I am most anxious to get command of No 3 and think I stand well to do so. I don't want to take it over at a strength of about 100 all ranks!! On the other hand there was never a more suitable theatre for raiding than this and we might as well make the most of it while we are here . . . If only someone would produce replacements for No 3!!

He continued to attend briefings to ascertain future roles for the Commandos, but little information was forthcoming, which he found frustrating.

That afternoon the weather broke. Peter had established a sort of camp for himself under a tree since he disliked the claustrophobic atmosphere inside the HQ buildings. Christopher, meanwhile, was the sole occupant of a lean-to shed with a tiled roof not far away. As the storm clouds built, Peter moved himself and his war booty – Mussolini's mattress and an Italian gunner officer's uniform case, liberated during the previous operation – into Christopher's billet. Thus, although plagued by ants and flies, they remained dry during the ensuing storm.

On 31 July he attended the 0830 hrs conference, 'a pictureseque gathering outside the office Trucks of G. Ops'. Toby Low, G2 Ops, told him that it would be safe for him to be absent until 1600 hrs so he decided to visit the Special Service Brigade and XXX Corps.

He arrived back to find that deployments had been announced in his absence: Nos 2 and 41 RM Commando were to take part in Operation Buttress, while Nos 3, 40 RM (commanded by Lieutenant Colonel 'Pops' Manners) and the Special Raiding Squadron (commanded by Paddy Mayne) were to be deployed to Operation Baytown. The former were to move with Laycock to North Africa where they would come under the command of Lieutenant General Horrocks in X Corps. The latter were to be commanded by Durnford-Slater.

Peter returned to Brucoli immediately he heard the news. There he dined well, savouring the knowledge that he was finally in command of No. 3, if at the moment only temporarily. He spent the night there, moving back to No. 3 Commando HQ on 1 August to take up his new appointment. 'I should,' he wrote in *Storm from the Sea*, 'have been sobered by the thought, but in fact it was one of the happiest days of my life. It had long been my ambition to command a unit, and to have the good luck to get the one I had served with so long was unusual good fortune.' He was more than ready to go back to offensive operations and was already talking to Durnford-Slater and his staff about his plan to land forty men on the southern tip of Italy to cut both the lateral roads across the toe.

Chapter Eleven

Italy – Bova Marina

The first weeks of August were spent getting 3 Commando ready to go into action once more. The introduction of commando brigades meant that the Commandos had to give up officers to staff the head-quarters. Peter gave some thought to his own deputy. '[The] 2 i/c,' he wrote cryptically, 'should excel in those matters in which the CO is deficient.'

Peter's plan to interdict the roads which ran across the southern tip of Italy was shelved when Dempsey asked him to undertake a series of reconnaissance raids to establish the state of the coastal defences in the area where Allied landings were planned. The raids had the following objectives: to take prisoners; to ascertain whether the bridge at Bova Marina was prepared for demolition and to blow it up if it was; and to collect information about the nature of the beach so that troops could be prepared for the landings.

Peter reconnoitred an anchorage at Taormina on 24 August with a view to using it as a base for operations; the town was south of the Straits of Messina, about 25 miles from the closest point on the Italian mainland. Although it was 40 miles from their projected landing area at Capo Spartivento, the harbour was sheltered, with a narrow and rocky entrance, and big enough to accommodate the men and materiel which would be required. At 1930 hrs on 25 August, despite poor weather, they set out but the heavy seas forced them back to port and it was agreed that they should attempt the crossing again the following night.

The weather improved the following day and they re-embarked, clearing the harbour entrance by 1900 hrs. They proceeded due east in an LCI until they reached a point South of Capo Spartivento where they transferred to the LCA they were towing. As they began the run-in they realized that they were much further out to sea than they thought and it took an hour and twenty minutes to reach the beach. It was not, Peter noted, a mistake repeated on subsequent landings.

'Owing to the curiously odd rule of our methods of navigation which we had been forced to adopt, we landed at a place which I immediately recognised to be the wrong one.' There seemed to be no opposition ashore and the first party landed at 0240 hrs. An hour later one of the men returned with an Italian prisoner; shortly afterwards two flares were launched and they heard LMG fire from the same direction. Taking a few men with him – including Christopher, now a Lance Corporal – he advanced towards the apparent firefight. Meeting his patrol en route he discovered that there was no opposition and the village was, after all, Bova Marina, their original objective. They laid a couple of mines at strategic points where the road and railway crossed the river and then re-embarked, with their prisoner, for an uneventful journey back to base, arriving back in Taormina at 1000 hrs on 27 August. The prisoner was taken to Special Services Brigade HQ and thence to XIII Corps HQ for interrogation, being subsequently released and sent home.

Dempsey ordered that five groups with wireless sets be put ashore immediately at Bova Marina so that they could pass information back to base. As they were to embark that evening, the plans were necessarily hasty. There were not enough men at Taormina to mount such an operation, so Peter stopped at Cannizzara, where 3 Commando was based, to pick up the necessary forces. The five parties each consisted of four men and were commanded by Captains Waldie and Ellis, Lieutenants Reynolds and Cummings, and Second Lieutenant Pollard. They were joined by signallers from 156 Field Regt RA as the Commandos' wireless sets were not powerful enough to broadcast over the required distance.

The first wave landed at 0300 hrs on 28 August, 3 kilometres west of Bova Marina. Peter took his orderlies – Christopher, Lance Corporal Turner and Trooper Dix – and Captain Nixon with him and moved inland to find the road. They took four prisoners whom Nixon took back to the LCA where Cummings' group secured the area, setting up a beacon consisting of a hurricane lamp set up inside a petrol 'tin' with one side ripped out. This faced out to sea to act as a guide for the second wave.

When the second wave arrived at 0445 hrs, Peter disembarked Reynolds' and Pollard's men and re-embarked Nixon's party and his own men. Leaving Reynolds, Cummings and Pollard ashore, they put back about 200 yards out to sea and moved eastwards searching for the tower they had seen the previous night. Although they did not find it they landed unopposed as dawn approached. While they brought rations and wireless sets ashore, Peter once more took his orderlies and Nixon to find the road which lay about 200 yards inland behind a cactus hedge – a ubiquitous feature of the landscape – and a railway embankment. As they returned to the beach they heard a vehicle approaching and went back to the road, arriving in time for Peter to empty his pistol into a passing truck, which halted too far away for the results to be observed. Leaving Ellis and Nixon ashore he took his own men back to the LCA.

The only incident of note on the journey back to Taormina was that they were fired on as they passed Melito. Seven rounds were sent in their direction, the first four of which were ranging shots; the remainder were in range, but fortunately dropped behind them. Peter assumed the Germans stopped firing because they thought they had sunk their target; when they got back to Taormina they discovered that the LCI had been hit and would need dockyard repairs.

When Peter reported to XIII Corps with his prisoners he discovered that there had been little radio traffic from his shore patrols, though whether from poor reception or lack of information was not clear. At all events, Dempsey told Peter to return the following night with a wireless set in his LCI and to speak to all the patrols ashore from 5 miles out to sea. Following that he was to go ashore and make contact with Nixon's patrol. He was to give specific instructions to light bonfires between 0200 and 0300 hrs on the following two mornings in order to guide the possible landing forces to the right beaches.

Peter picked up a new LCI (107) from Catania, under the command of Lieutenant Prebble RNZNVR, and sailed back to Taormina as soon as the wireless set had been installed. They arrived at dusk and Peter himself piloted the vessel into the anchorage where they picked up enough men to man the Oerlikons and accompany him ashore. The party included: Christopher, Dix, Waldie, Moore, Leyland and Corporal Davison. They sailed at 1930 hrs and, arriving on station without incident, they tried to contact the shore patrols. In this they had no success, so rather than waste time continuing the attempt they decided to go ashore at once.

The run-in seemed very fast but once they had gone ashore to reconnoitre Peter realized that they were in the wrong place. He had already sent Waldie east to find the elusive tower, but when he decided that it would be best for the others to go by sea he discovered that it would be impossible because Prebble, following orders to go ashore at two-thirds power, had grounded the LCI so thoroughly that it could not be budged. No one could now get off the beach. While Prebble and his sailors made strenuous efforts to refloat the LCI, Peter began to put together his own emergency Plan B. 'I told [the men] there might be a landing on either of the next two nights and in any case there would be an invasion in a week. If they could do anything to harass the enemy so much the better, but the main thing was to remain free.' He divided the party into four groups under himself, Moore, Leyland and Davison – Waldie was still searching for the tower – and told them to conceal themselves in the hills and woods, but to remain close by until it was certain that the LCI was hors de combat.

With that he took Christopher and Dix off eastwards towards Bova Marina. It was not long before he encountered Nixon and was annoyed to discover that Nixon had lost three of his men as well as his wireless set and notebook. This last was a particular problem as it contained codes and call signs which could be of help to the enemy. Wishing to pass this information back to Taormina as soon as possible, they returned to the LCI to use the radio but discovered it was dead. Waldie had also returned, having failed to find the tower. Then Pollard reappeared, having lost his party, so Peter detailed him to go to Bova Marina and light the fires Dempsey wanted to guide the Allied landings. They concluded that the LCI was stuck fast. Prebble was apologetic, explaining that he had always been taught to run in at that speed, but that he had been at fault for not deploying his kedge anchor. At this point the days when raids were meticulously planned must have seemed far away indeed.

Peter gave Prebble exactly the same instructions he had given his own men. They moved away from the beach; there had been some desultory fire in their direction from the west, and although it fell short there was every chance that they would be discovered if they remained where they were. For good measure he told Wallis, the signaller, to disable his wireless set and to conceal himself and his men.

With that, they abandoned the LCI and moved inland. Peter had with him Waldie, Christopher, Dix and Lance Corporals Edmunds and Jackson. They moved up the dry river bed of the Amendolea towards the hills where the terrain was mountainous and difficult.

As the men were fit and fresh, this was more an advantage than otherwise for it reduced the chances of discovery. After a while they took to the hills east of the river; dawn was approaching and Peter did not want to be caught in open country in daylight.

It was hard going and navigation was virtually impossible, but eventually they crested a rise and saw below them a group of three houses concealed in a little hollow, well positioned as a lookout point. Since it was now broad daylight and they were all tired, Peter resolved to make this their headquarters. The door of the nearest house was open and they walked in. There were only two rooms and the first one they entered was almost entirely filled by an enormous double bed. Peter, with Christopher, promptly lay down on it, having detailed Dix to mount guard on the mule track which led to Bova Superiore. Waldie, Edmunds and Jackson took over the highest of the three houses which overlooked the village of San Carlo and the dry river valley to the west.

Shortly afterwards the owners arrived. The complex of buildings belonged to the Maffizi family: father and mother, daughter and teenage son, Giuseppe, who had six toes on either foot. They treated the interlopers very well, their first act being to cook them breakfast: eggs which they served with bread, figs, water, cheese and 'figua d'India', the fruit of the cactus bushes. After a shave, they slept for the rest of the day.

Stranded with no combat supplies and no means of communication, Peter set about creating a routine. They knew that invasion was imminent but there was little they could do in the meantime beyond ensuring that the nightly fires were lit according to Dempsey's instructions.

That night they all walked down the mule track to Bova Marina, about 4 miles as the crow flies, but far longer on foot. When they reached the coast they lay up on the east end of the beach searching for suitable tank exits which they failed to find. They lit a fire at 0215 hrs against the tall chimney stack of the Co-operativa, which they had identified as a tower the first time they had landed. Although they kept it burning until 0300 hrs, there was no sign of life out to sea. Nor was there any apparent interest from the locals, none of whom came to find out what was going on.

As they were leaving the beach they encountered Nixon with his three remaining men. Peter decided to take them back with him, having resolved to try and gather together as many men as he could; none of their previous training had prepared them for a prolonged period behind enemy lines. He installed them in the third of the Maffizis' houses and left them to rest.

During the day he drew up his plans for their next foray, which were to set an ambush in addition to lighting the fire. In order to do this, he wanted to set out earlier and reach the coast during daylight so that he could study the lie of the land. Some of Leyland's party met them as they made their way down the dry river bed and took them to their own observation post. It lay on a ridge which overlooked the road near the abandoned LCI and Peter remained there for the early part of the night; they had a clear view of the LCI which attracted the attention of passing German soldiers.

He detailed Waldie to light the fire, reckoning that Pollard should also be doing so, leaving him to set the ambush. He gave Waldie some of Leyland's men and kept two for himself. In the last of the daylight, Peter took Leyland, Christopher and Dix to another OP which had been set up by Davison and his party. This position was in an orchard on top of a flat hill. While they were there, four German soldiers went aboard the LCI and started firing the Oerlikons. Leyland fired a round back at them. Having searched an abandoned slit trench which lay at the south end of the orchard overlooking the coast road, they returned to Leyland's position until darkness fell.

At midnight Waldie left to prepare the fire, having asked Peter not to spring the ambush until after 0400 hrs so that he and his men would have time to get away. Peter and his group took up positions around the bridge they had mined during their first landing four days earlier, Trooper Jimmy Leech armed with a tommy gun, Dix with a .303 and Christopher with a Garand. Peter had only his Webley pistol. By 0300 hrs they were ready and about half an hour later they heard a group of men moving up the river bed; although Waldie had only five men in his group Leech counted eight. Unsure whether this was Waldie's party or an enemy patrol, they remained where they were. Then they heard engines out to sea and, thinking it was a landing, abandoned their positions to go to the beach, but it was a false alarm so they returned to the road.

At 0445 hrs an army truck approached from the west. Peter's first shot was to be the signal to open fire. When the headlights were about 10 yards away, he emptied his pistol into the truck. Leech followed suit with a burst from his tommy gun and Christopher emptied a clip of ten rounds while Dix also managed a couple of rounds. The truck came to a halt about 50 yards up the road and they could hear groans emanating from it. They could not tell what damage they had done but decided that discretion was the better part of valour and withdrew before the enemy could retaliate.

He later wrote in *Storm from the Sea*:

> Somewhere I imagined some [enemy] Intelligence Officer . . .
> plotting our activities on his map, and trying to calculate for his
> commander how many British troops had landed . . . The LCI
> could carry about a hundred, and he would know that others
> had landed the night before she ran aground. The more coloured
> pins he stuck in his map, the more men he would credit us with;
> the more men we were supposed to have the better.

He discovered when he got back to base the explanation for the eight men Leech had heard withdrawing before the ambush could be sprung: one of their number had sprained his ankle and had been left behind, while Waldie had picked up four sailors from the LCI. These were added to the number of men Peter was collecting at his HQ.

The following morning, 31 August, two Italians arrived, accompanied by a number of armed followers, who said they wished to speak to the man in command. Negotiations were hampered by the fact that neither spoke the other's language, but Peter understood that these men had been looking for him to offer what they called 'collaborazione'. The area was apparently a hotbed of dissent for they claimed that they had the support of 600 Social Democrats who were anxious to help the invaders. When, they wanted to know, were the landings to take place? Peter temporized, his limited Italian restricting his replies to 'dopo domani' and 'subito' which were vague enough to be useless. He was suspicious that they were reluctant to answer even the simplest questions about local defences and the strength of troop concentrations.

When they suggested that they should fetch an interpreter Peter acquiesced, but kept a hostage, one of their young relatives, a soldier whose regiment was in Rome, for which reason he had with Italian logic posted himself to Calabria. Shortly after they left the lookout saw two German soldiers on the mule track about 50 yards in front of their house. They had just crested the rise and disappeared as soon as the alarm was raised. Dix and Christopher, with Peter, were the first to reach the point where the Germans had been seen. They peered over the crest of the hill but saw nothing, then Leyland reported seeing a man stalking along the side of the hill bent double to try to conceal himself, so the party moved out at the double, others joining them as they went. As they advanced, they caught sight of several men and a running fight went on down the hill towards San Carlo. Only four men kept up with Peter all the way down; he deployed the rest to guard their flanks. In the orange grove at the bottom, they found a discarded Italian rifle which was, Peter thought, a good sign.

Peter, with Leyland, reached the river and learned from some local peasants that the soldiers had been there. On top of a rocky outcrop to the south stood a small, stone, square building in front of which stood an Italian soldier. Leyland fired at him which sent him inside, and he continued to fire towards the building to keep the occupants away from the windows. Peter approached the door and demanded their surrender. To his surprise not two, but seven men came out of the house, laden with haversacks and suitcases. 'The capture of these Italians,' Peter noted, 'enabled me to equip the sailors in my party with Italian rifles, boots and water bottles.'

The LCI, already shelled from Melito three days earlier, was now bombed by the Germans. Peter also observed a British plane repeatedly overflying the site and decided that the staff would not conclude that it had been beached because of the shellfire. However, as they had received no information since the LCI had landed, he also thought they would be loath to commit a landing to the area.

With the capture of the Italians they had acquired a map showing the locations of Italian coastal divisions and their sub-units in the toe of Italy. Peter was anxious to get this document back to the staff at XIII Corps, but the only way they could think of doing it was to disguise one of their number as a local peasant and try to bribe a local fisherman to take him across the straits to Messina. Lance Corporal Thornton volunteered, but as Peter admitted, 'we disguised him as best we could and when we had done he looked exactly like a British soldier in disguise.' Reluctantly, therefore, they abandoned that scheme and instead decided to sail back, using a boat one of them had noticed on the beach. Ten men volunteered to go, with Nixon in command, but this scheme came to naught as well – they left at nightfall and returned the following morning saying that the sails were rotten.

The Allies bombed Bova Marina that day, 1 September, and at the same time the enemy began to close in. One of the sentries reported that a truck had arrived at a building outside San Carlo which they thought was a platoon HQ, hoping that it was there to take the occupants and their gear out of the area. There was some reason to suppose that might be the case, as they could see soldiers and civilians moving north, away from the bombing.

They received a nasty shock, therefore, when about twenty soldiers appeared from the direction of San Carlo, running in open order towards their own position. Peter realized at once 'from the businesslike way in which they moved, and from their dress', that they were Germans. He knew that the enemy kept a squad of 'lorried infantry' at Melito or Catanzaro which could be rapidly deployed if needed. Their depredations over the previous few days had evidently borne fruit.

Although they were in a strong position Peter knew a few bursts of rapid fire would use up their ammunition. He noted also that if the Germans continued their line of advance they would come up on their rear. Giving the order to stand to, and leaving Waldie to observe, he took Leyland with him to go up Mount Triolo to assess the German advance. This proved impossible as 200 yards to the rear of their post there was a steep ravine, which also precluded the Germans attacking from that direction. They would advance up the hill as the Italians had done the previous day, and as he reached that conclusion he was given the 'close' signal from the OP, so he returned there without delay.

'In the pathway,' he related, 'two Officers strode about exercising the "divine right of commanders". A runner with his rifle slung ambled back towards the river-bed. I thought only Germans would behave like this.' When Leyland advanced he was fired on, and then the house in which they were sitting came under fire. Peter assessed their chances: there were at least twenty-four enemy and he had eighteen, four of whom were sailors and one of whom was sick. They also had a prisoner. The shortage of ammunition clinched it: they would have to withdraw.

He gave the order to move and Leech, suffering from malaria, arose from his sickbed. The Maffizis had spontaneously hidden all their kit during the alarm the previous day and Peter asked them to do the same again as they hurriedly descended towards the river bed. They had, Peter reckoned, about a fifteen minutes' start by the time the Germans reached their position and secured it.

To his surprise they had not been long on the move before they were joined by Signor Maffizi.

He was about sixty-five and had fought . . . in the last war. His shoes were made from sections of motor-car tyres, with just a

132

sole, no heel or instep, and uppers largely composed of string. He kept up apparently without any difficulty at all and was an invaluable guide. I was about to ignore him the first time he tried to stop me going my own way, but in a few yards I came to a steep precipice.

They moved on, always eastwards and always up gullies, making sure they kept the shoulder of hill between themselves and the advancing enemy. Gradually breaking up into smaller parties, orders did not get passed as they should have done and contact was lost. Leech soon dropped out and was left hidden near a house along with an exhausted sailor. Once they were on their way, Maffizi bade them farewell and returned home.

They came across one of the men who had visited Peter to discuss 'collaborazione', the murderer, as Peter described him, who gave them all wine, water, bread and fruit. This fortified them for their final push up a mule track between Bova Marina and Bova Superiore where at last they found a house which gave them good visibility in all directions. Peter's party consisted of Christopher, Dix, Leyland and Griffiths (a signaller). They were joined that evening by Nixon who had with him Smith, Turner and Thornton.

They took stock. Most were suffering minor injuries which stopped them operating effectively: Nixon's hands were covered in sores and bandages, Peter had cuts on his wrists which were going septic and a couple of the men had foot problems; Turner's feet were already septic. From their position they could see their old hideout and as evening fell Peter swept the scene with his binoculars; he could see the sun glint on metal and knew the Germans were still there. As he watched he saw them turn slowly – disconsolately, Peter hoped – and march back towards San Carlo. He counted the better part of 100 men. Their change of location had been well timed.

They rested all night and the following day, watching the gathering activity around them. Bova Superiore was not, as far as Peter could tell, garrisoned but was nonetheless bombed by the Allies. An old woman who had brought them some eggs was wounded in the attacks, however as Peter noted in his diary: 'Nobody tried to do us any evil as a result.' Everybody except the sick stood guard duty for an hour at a time; in order to keep movement to a minimum the guard sat on a chair with his back to the house. Peter included himself in the roster. The men slept in their boots with one eye open and were only allowed to take their footgear off one at a time to wash their feet.

It was now 2 September. Peter knew that the landings were due the following day, but he was concerned about the condition of his men. The locals were still bringing them food but their ammunition remained low. He had not made contact with other members of his party although he was fairly certain that they would be able to fend for themselves. Their clothes were in a dreadful state and the Maffizis' daughter had washed their socks from time to time, a vital service for which they were all grateful, for keeping their feet relatively sound was possibly the most important service she could have rendered them. In addition, they had left everything behind in their hasty departure. Those who had had shaving kit – and Peter was not amongst them having used Dix's throughout – no longer even had that. Peter was now reduced to being shaved with a cut-throat razor by the owner of the house they were occupying – an act of courage in itself for the man's hand shook uncontrollably as a result of the terror he had felt during the bombing of Bova Superiore!

At 0340 hrs on 3 September Peter took Leyland with him up a hill near their billet from where they had the best view of unfolding events. From there they could hear the barrage being put down on Reggio di Calabria no more than 30 miles away to the north-east as the crow flies.

Peter intended to watch for Allied landings in the area around Bova Marina; by now he had a pretty shrewd idea of where pockets of resistance were likely to be and whether they would be Italian or German. During the morning he decided to go back to the Maffizis' compound. Instructing Nixon to meet him there at 1900 hrs he moved off with the rest, encountering no enemy en route, though he did catch a glimpse of Waldie's party. On the way they called at the house where the murderous 'Social Democrat' had fed and watered them. He had nothing new to impart so they moved on. On the way they had their first sight of a British destroyer steaming from west to east along the coast.

Further on they found more of their men being sheltered and cared for by a local man who spoke 'good American'. He had set up a tight watch system using his neighbours and, clearly enjoying himself, was ensuring that his guests came to no harm. Peter ordered the soldiers back to Monte Triolo and they moved on at a leisurely pace, using little-used tracks, arriving at their destination well before the appointed rendezvous with Nixon.

Giuseppe Maffizi came out to meet them and told them that all three of the houses had been comprehensively looted. When the troops were told that there were 'Niente Inglese' they were so infuriated that one of them fired shots at Giuseppe's feet. Even this did not induce the Maffizis to divulge any information and the only evidence they found was a solitary British field dressing. Peter wrote in his diary: 'Curiously enough these people welcomed us more cordially than ever on this occasion.'

When neither Nixon nor Jackson had arrived by 1920 hrs Peter went back to the coast where his party – Christopher, Dix, Leyland and Griffiths – spent the night in the slit trench he had reconnoitred three days earlier. Here he was in a better position to make contact with anyone who landed.

No one landed at Bova Marina that night and the following morning the Italians guarding the Amendolea bridge moved out. Peter watched six of the men breakfasting outside a house near the bridge before departing northwards up the river bank. This, he thought, would be an opportunity for an ambush so he took his party on a rapid flanking move and discovered a suitable place for an attack, a steep rise which overlooked the path on which the Italians should be travelling. When no one came he returned to the bridge to find that the men had decamped, leaving all their equipment behind and the bridge intact. At that instant one of the locals approached and asked where the Major was. When he identified himself to the peasant's satisfaction, not an easy task given the state of his uniform, he was shown a large amount of enemy material and presented with three Italian prisoners. He instructed Dix to bring with him the red and yellow naval signal flag they had found there which the Italians had liberated from the beached LCI.

The main body of the garrison had withdrawn to the railway tunnel at Bova Marina but there remained a detachment of men between the bridge and San Carlo who Peter decided to attack. Guided by the peasant the party advanced in open order across the Amendolea. Peter was surprised that no one fired on them as they crossed the river and paused to mount the two LMGs. He sent the peasant forward to demand the surrender of this detachment and was gratified when a heavily decorated officer emerged from the surrounding trees along with eleven men. It was not clear whether the ease of this capitulation was due to the fact that Lieutenant Guidorossi was unsure about the mettle of his troops or whether he was concerned for the safety of his *femme de campagne*, a pretty Red Cross nurse called Rosaria Cotroneo. Peter's bag was now fifteen, all without a shot being fired.

135

Peter instructed his prisoners to collect what kit they could, put on their helmets and to bring with them their water bottles. He also told them to carry their LMG and 'a sort of carbine (Biretta TMC) which their parachutists use'. Thus equipped they moved back towards the Amendolea bridge, moving in single file with Peter and Guidorossi in the centre.

Peter formed a high opinion of Guidorossi, who had seen service in Spain and Ethiopia, and won the Croce di Guerra twice. He told Peter that he had taken up the mines which Nixon had laid near the bridge himself, instructing his men to remain at a safe distance. He also told Peter the outcome of the ambush of the truck on the night of 30/31 August. There had been five men on it: the commander, Major Braga, was unhurt, however his sergeant, Calvi, was wounded and one of the three Carabinieri with them was killed.

They withdrew to a house which overlooked the bridge, sited on a bluff which afforded good visibility and where they could mount their guns to command the road. The property belonged to Cavalliere Rosetti who entered into the spirit of things by offering to ride over to Melito on his bicycle to see if the British had landed there. As they waited they shaved and washed their feet while Rosaria patched up their injuries as best she could, causing Peter to remark, 'we began to think that it was not a bad idea to take pretty girls to the wars.' He dispatched Leyland to recover an Italian Very pistol and cartridges from the first position they had occupied. Peter thought that the best way of getting to Melito was by sea and there were ships out there which could take them.

Shortly afterwards they saw HMS *Quail* steaming eastwards and fired off their Very lights at once. Griffiths, the signaller, made a flag out of a field dressing, using that and the flags Dix had retrieved to semaphore. To their relief they saw her heave to. It so happened that *Quail* was carrying Paul Lee, an Associated Press war correspondent. His account of the end of the operation was carried under the bellicose headline 'Commandos Captured Four Italian Towns' and appeared in the national press some days later.

'Five of us have cleared this place,' Peter signalled, not beating about the bush. 'Two hundred disarmed Italians in a railway tunnel down the road want to surrender. Can you send a boat?'

Quail's captain, Lieutenant Commander Jenks, did not receive this in quite the way Peter might have imagined. 'I don't want two hundred Italians aboard,' Lee heard him say before he signalled back, 'Why do you want a boat?'

Peter responded 'We have been here over a week and wish to report.'

According to Lee, Jenks looked at his watch and said, 'Probably British Commandos. Anyhow, it's teatime, so let's bring them off for a cup.'

Peter watched as a boat was lowered and began to make its way ashore. As it grounded his Italian prisoners rushed forward, to the alarm of the boat crew, but 'at that instant five weary men in khaki and green commando berets sauntered down from the bushes', as Lee laconically recounted it for the Press. The word 'sauntered' perfectly captures the scene. Unobtrusively, two of the men immediately began to herd the Italians into a line, while two others took up position in the dunes to cover the operation. Peter approached the boat and made himself known to its Commander, Sub Lieutenant Gillott.

He wanted to take all his prisoners with him, but that proved to be impossible. There was room for only seven of them, and these included Guidorossi and mistress, described by Lee for the British public as 'a cute but unwashed little brunette Red Cross nurse in Army shorts'. Gillott was reluctant to include her, but Peter's men 'all said: Bring her along. She knows how to look after herself and is a good sport. She volunteered to give us all a shave this morning.'

For form's sake Peter told the remaining prisoners to return to Cavalliere Rosetti's house and they would be picked up the following day. As they pushed off, Trooper Hewitt, who had been with Davison's party, ran down the beach and they took him on board. Once on the *Quail* Peter duly reported to the Captain on his bridge.

Jenks, a large, calm man, was wearing a white sunhat. They chatted for a few minutes while they sent a signal to report that Peter's party had been brought off and then Jenks asked him if there was anything he would like. Peter said that he'd like nothing so much as a bath, so shortly afterwards he found himself with the run of the Captain's cabin enjoying 'the greatest bath of all time' as he described it in *Storm from the Sea*.

Quail landed him at Teresa where he was met by RQMS Fawcett who took him to XIII Corps. He reported to Brigadier Sugden, Admiral McGrigor and Durnford-Slater. There was an affecting scene when they had to let Rosaria go. The Italian men were made prisoners of war, but there was no facility to deal with a woman and according to Christopher, 'there was a tearful scene before she went off', left to her own devices.

The wash-up for this operation was mixed. As a reconnaissance operation it had been a failure; the only order they had been able to carry out was to light a bonfire at the requisite time and place. A major reason for failure had been the inadequacy of the wireless sets they had been given which did not have the required range.

Cummings was seriously wounded and captured, but submitted his operation report on 11 October 1944 after he was repatriated from Germany:

I told him my name, rank and number, and refused to say any more. He [the German interrogator] then told me I was in No. 3 Commando, commanded by Major Young, 'the Mad Major'. He also showed me Lieut. Nixon's notebook and said that a party on the beach had been wiped out, and I thought he was probably right. He informed me that a Commando raid had taken place the previous night and it had been annihilated.

Afterwards Peter wrote:

The Italians invariably tried to help me, I never pretended to be a German or Italian, but always announced myself to be 'Majore Inglese' . . . They are undoubtedly just as cowardly as we have always been told, without having the least idea of what is dangerous and what is not. The only exceptions to this rule were Cavalliere Rosetti, the Maffizi family, the American speaker who housed L/Cpl Jackson's party, my guide on 4th September and possibly Lieut. Guidorossi . . . This cowardliness was indeed an asset because it made the effect of a loud speech in rude Italian much greater, whether delivered to soldiers or civilians, than I would have believed possible.

He felt extremely fit after a week living off the land and he went back to the Maffizi family once the British forces had established themselves at Reggio, just along the coast. So fit, in fact, that he ran up the mountain. He wanted to thank them once again for all they had done – they were reluctant to take any reward – and also to recover the kit that they had left there during their precipitate departure a few days earlier.

He left them on the best of terms and returned to his base only to fall ill the following day with malaria. He was sent to hospital in Messina where he was, by all accounts, a bad patient. After only a few days in bed he felt well enough to go out into the town. While he was out he came across the Commando vehicles drawn up waiting to get across the Straits to Reggio; this was too much. He returned to the hospital and suggested to the staff that it would be easier if he rejoined his unit now since he was feeling so much better. They agreed and after a long and tedious journey he caught up with his unit a week later at Scalea. Here Ned Moore ordered him back to bed, announcing that he had jaundice. Peter complied but refused to go to hospital, a decision regretted since Moore took the opportunity to operate on his ankle to remove the remains of the bullet he had had in there since he was wounded in 1940. As he said, they had been doing no harm to anyone.

The participants looked back fondly on their time at Bova Marina. Forty years later Peter and Christopher, still exchanging frequent letters, would write to each other on the anniversary of Bova Marina.

While his men rested up during what was left of September, Peter slowly recovered and the Commando Brigade geared up for what was to be their final action in the Mediterranean campaign.

Chapter Twelve

Termoli

Peter took some time to recover from jaundice. When No. 3 Commando left Scalea by sea they did so under the command of Captain Arthur Komrower who had recently returned to active duty; Peter reluctantly remained behind with a small rear party which included Christopher and Clarke, who had replaced Freddie Craft as his driver.

As the only Allied officer in Scalea he dealt with local issues arising from food shortages and the results of extensive bombing. Food was distributed centrally and order was being kept by only four Carabinieri. Peter offered his Provost Sergeant to help and the local Carabinieri chief, Antonio Rege, accepted gratefully. It was chaos and the Amgot (Allied Military Government in Occupied Territory) representative seemed unable to help.

After a few frustrating days he resolved to join the rest of the commando and on 27 September his party left for Taranto. 'On the day I left,' he wrote in his diary, 'I gave the whole population a rousing speech.' By his own admission, Peter spoke little Italian and it is unlikely that his listeners understood much English. It is, however, just the sort of theatrical gesture he excelled in – as much about timing as delivery, and he was a master of both.

He was accompanied by Moore, Leyland, Clarke, Christopher, Lance Corporal Moore, Dix and Jones. They had trouble getting out due to the absence of bridges, but they arrived at Senise at 1800 hrs that evening after a journey of about 120 miles. It was gruelling going across some inhospitable mountains but the chief of the local Carabinieri directed them to the best hotel in the place where for 10/- the whole party was accommodated for the night.

The following morning, after Clarke repaired a puncture, they moved on arriving at Special Service Brigade HQ, 4 kilometres north of Bari, at 1700 hrs that evening (28 September). The only person they found there was Captain Ronnie Lunt, the Brigade Padre. Peter discovered that they had captured Foggia, about 80 miles to the west, and that Bari was too far back from the front line to be any use as a base for launching raids. Durnford-Slater was at XIII Corps HQ and they were still waiting for the LCIs containing the troops who had not yet reached Brindisi, about 60 miles down the coast. They were not now expected to reach Bari until late the following day at the earliest.

With nothing else to do Peter got a room at the best hotel, the Albergo Imperiale, and spent the rest of the day familiarizing himself with the area. The Germans were thought to be responsible for the present lack of running water, however it was expected to be restored the following day. There was electric light, although the blackout was not strictly observed, and trams were running in the town. He was surprised to see armed Italian troops moving about freely, even close to Brigade HQ, and noted that there was an Italian camp along the coast road with Italian sentries.

The following morning, after a shampoo and shave he met Durnford-Slater, returned from XIII Corps HQ where he had been explaining to Dempsey how he planned to capture Termoli. It was a straightforward scheme with 3 Commando landing first to establish the beachhead half a mile west of Termoli. When Dempsey pointed out that No. 3 had taken a battering already, Durnford-Slater explained that going in first would be less risky – the initial landings were often easier because of the element of surprise. Besides, he was landing in the first wave and he wanted to go in with the men he had lately commanded.

Peter and Durnford-Slater then discussed the proposed changes to the organization of the commandos. Peter was not at that stage impressed by the reputation or performance of Nos 40 and 41 RM Commando: 'Our private opinion is that the RM are too stupid and too inexperienced to manage Combined Operations properly and we fear that the voluntary nature of the SS will die out.' He was also unhappy with the lack of representation of army Commando units on the new Divisional staff. The new Special Service Division consisted of four brigades, two Army and two Royal Marine, and Durnford-Slater had been put forward as one of the Army brigade commanders. The Army Commandos were concerned that the Commando Depot at Achnacarry, run from the start by Lieutenant

Colonel Charlie Vaughan, was likely to be taken over by the RM.

At noon the following day, 30 September, the LCIs reached Bari. After taking on rations they left again two hours later for Manfredonia, about 60 miles up the coast towards Termoli. The operation had been due to begin that night, but the LCIs arrived so late that it was postponed twenty-four hours. Peter had retired to bed, still not fully fit.

Late on 1 October, Peter, Christopher and Clarke also moved up to Manfredonia, covering the last part of their journey across ploughed fields because the road bridges had all been blown. On 2 October 3 Commando left for Termoli at 1130 hrs. Peter visited Durnford-Slater in his HQ outside Manfredonia that morning and discovered that Dempsey had been over to visit the previous afternoon. Durnford-Slater opined to Peter that Dempsey's commitment to Special Services was exceptional; any other general would have put them under the command of his division, whereas Dempsey's brigade remained effectively independent. Agreeing, Peter wrote, 'This relationship of our's [sic] with Dempsey makes our position much more pleasant.' Dempsey had also found time to ask after Peter suggesting he should be ordered to hospital.

Peter spent most of 3 October in bed, rising only to conduct an Orderly Room on two miscreant lance sergeants. 'Both of them put together would make one rotten private,' he wrote peevishly.

Twenty-four hours later the frustration of not being in action overcame him; Christopher noted that Peter was 'feeling much better and being bored set off for Termoli'. They left Manfredonia at about 1600 hrs, heading for San Severo, about 60 miles west, but bad weather and the parlous state of the roads forced them to halt before they reached it. They spent the night in a village called Largo Sentierone, by common agreement the worst night of the campaign; according to Christopher the beds were full of fleas, a cat yowled all night and the horse in the stable next door passed wind incessantly.

They were back on the road again at 0800 hrs, despite the foul weather, reaching San Severo after negotiating a 'bloody awful railway line' but found that the unit transport they hoped to use to get them to Termoli had already left. Instead, therefore, they filled up with petrol and pushed on, caught up in the general flow of traffic towards the battle. They were delayed once by another blown bridge and had to wait about an hour while Combat Engineers effected repairs. Peter's party used the time to brew up and were surprised to be attacked by a lone German aircraft. There was no cover, so they

142

'just sat there,' according to Christopher, 'watching the bombs coming down and hoping for the best'. The rest of the journey was uneventful; they reached Termoli without further incident where they installed themselves, as ever, in the best hotel they could find, in this case the Albergo Corona.

The operation seemed to be going well, but Peter did not relish his position on the sidelines. When on the following morning (5 October) Durnford-Slater's second-in-command left the temporary HQ to report to Corps, Peter persuaded Durnford-Slater to let him act as Brigade Major until he returned. As soon as this was agreed, Peter went forward to visit No. 3, commanded in his absence by Komrower, and see how they were getting on. They had reached their initial objective without casualties and were due to be relieved shortly; Peter decided to leave Komrower in command until they moved back.

Peter's return journey was more eventful than he would have wished – they went too far forward and came under fire from German mortars, according to Christopher, 'near, but not quite near enough'. They shot back down the road and into an olive grove where they found Komrower with, among others, Lieutenant Colonel Chavasse (of the Reconnaissance Regiment, under whose command No. 3 were operating). Apart from a little shelling, there did not seem to be much going on, so Peter returned to Brigade HQ to report to Durnford-Slater. He left just as the Germans began their counter-attack and before long they were putting down accurate fire on forward Allied positions. Things were not going well in other parts of the battle either. During the morning a liaison officer who went to visit 36 Brigade reported that the Royal West Kents (RWK) had been forced to retire.

In the confusion the exact position of the two brigades was far from clear and the German counter-attack was gaining ground. It had started to rain heavily and positions occupied by some units could be cut off if the watercourses started to fill up. Some units were falling back so the front was poorly defined; by early afternoon there was a general sense that the operation hung in the balance.

Both the town and its approaches were now being accurately shelled. Peter visited the elements of the brigade, commanded by Pops Manners and Paddy Mayne, holding the San Salvo road. The pervasive air of nervousness was not something Peter was accustomed to experience in action; as he stood with Manners observing a carrier platoon of the Inniskilling Fusiliers, the occupants got out and fled.

143

Moments later some men of 5 Troop appeared, a good distance from where Peter knew their commander to be. They said they had been told to withdraw, which Peter thought was probably true, but that they had got lost and had gone too far. A further sign of jitters came when a Bofors ack-ack gun charged towards them away from the action. Peter was amongst those who stopped it and persuaded the crew that they were not, as they feared, in imminent danger.

He knew that they had only to hold on until 38 Brigade came up by sea, and that they were due at any time, but he also knew that it is the general who cannot keep his men committed in the face of a determined offensive from the other side who will gift the victory to the enemy. Now, if ever, was the time to keep the brigade united and moving forward.

At 1445 hrs Peter returned to Brigade HQ to find that in his absence it had taken a direct hit from an 88mm shell which hit the room next to where Durnford-Slater was conferring with Brian Franks. It killed one man and wounded two others who were lying on Peter's duffel coat and looked, according to Peter, 'a bit bad'. Durnford-Slater moved his HQ downstairs, selecting the room with the strongest walls.

Peter's diary now records events minute by minute. The early afternoon was the worst, as the Germans pushed strongly towards the town but the two brigades held their ground despite the fact that 3 Commando was exposed with both its flanks open to the enemy. As it got dark the Germans moved forward once more, using Very lights to signal to each other as each new position was reached. 3 Commando, exhausted and by now short of ammunition, found itself squeezed into a small pocket, surrounded on three sides by the Germans. They did not lose their nerve. Deducing what the Very lights meant, they formed up to match the German front and waited until they were only 50 yards away before opening fire. They were able to pinpoint German positions because they were using tracer and although they succeeded in holding off the attack, causing many casualties in the process, they remained virtually surrounded, the enemy being at most 100 yards away.

38 Brigade finally entered the harbour at Termoli at 2015 hrs. Brigadier Nelson Russell DSO, MC arrived at Durnford-Slater's Command Post shortly afterwards and undertook to disembark a battalion at once to reinforce the threatened positions. The prospect of fresh troops raised everybody's spirits; from then onwards they felt the battle was won.

During the night Komrower's Adjutant, Hopson, and his batman managed to get back to Termoli and report to Durnford-Slater that unless they withdrew they would be annihilated. Komrower was ordered to withdraw into reserve at Termoli forthwith. Hopson made his way back to the commando position, arriving at about 0100 hrs. Peter took Christopher and followed him. The commando was occupying a ridge from which there was only one safe route out. As the men began to withdraw, Peter and Christopher crawled up on to the ridge to meet the men and lead them to safety.

At 0330 hrs Arthur Komrower reported to the Command Post that they had safely evacuated their position. He had had the privilege of commanding 3 Commando in what Durnford-Slater called 'probably their finest performance of the war', while Peter was, perforce, confined to the sidelines. Komrower's last act in command was to billet the men and order stand-to for 0515 hrs when he would, as previously arranged, hand over to Peter whose final action in the battle was to throw a grenade into a cellar where the locals claimed there were a lot of Germans. There was, he reported, a satisfyingly loud crash when it exploded, but he suspected that the only casualties were wine bottles.

Photographs of Peter at this time bear testimony to the severity of his illness – he was very thin and gaunt. The condition of his command was not much better. The nominal roll gave a total of only 146 officers and men, having suffered 2 killed, 28 wounded and 6 missing during the battle. They had only three operational troops instead of six, and all three had enough men to make only one strong section in each.

The Irish Brigade moved through the town and up to the front, leaving 3 Commando with little to do; as the elements of 38 Brigade landed and joined the fight the Germans realized that they were not going to recapture the town and fell back. By 1700 hrs on 6 October the battle was won. Montgomery's objective, to take the town which the Germans saw as a vital part of their plan to continue holding Rome, had been achieved and he was delighted.

Durnford-Slater withdrew the men to Bari that evening. 3 Commando went by sea while Peter, with Christopher and Clark, went by jeep. They were billetted in the little town of Molfetta where they occupied a school as their temporary barracks. The men relaxed and spent their time organizing football matches against other units based close by – Peter's diary contains the team list for a fixture which was held on 24 October against 40 RM Commando – or swimming contests which took place in the harbour. While he was there he had a photograph taken in the local studio, on the back of which he wrote: 'Taken at MOLFETTA, Italy, October 1943. To L/Cpl R.W. Christopher as a <u>reward</u> (in lieu of E.D. [Extra Duty] Pay). P Young Lt. Col.'

On 19 October, Dempsey visited them. Komrower commanded the parade which was drawn up in the school yard in three ranks, with officers forming two further ranks and WOs in the rear. Peter won 5/- from RSM Briggs who had bet him that the unit would be too big to form up on one side of the courtyard; the parade state shows fourteen officers and 150 men on parade. To Peter's approbation, Dempsey did not speak to any of the officers on parade, but concentrated on the men. 'He gave,' Peter reported in his diary, 'a short sketch of our activities in Sicily and Italy to show what emphasis he himself put on each operation. Bova Marina he called a novelty, and most useful. Agnone . . . most important . . . Termoli too.

'I have never,' he concluded, 'served so reasonable a general. If all my general inspections go so well I will be all right.'

On 23 October he wrote:

The astonishing news was heard from the BBC this morning that Brigadier R E Laycock DSO is Major-General and CCO!

The youngest general in the British Army at 36. This ought to do us a bit of good. Much depends on how the SS Bde is regrouped, (but I need not tell my dear hearers that Major Y is now sweating on pulling full Colonel, never mind CO. ha. ha. [sic] However, one thing at a time.

At the end of October the men embarked from Taranto on a US LCI which took them back to Syracuse where Bob Christopher was promoted to Corporal on 17 November. On the following day the men moved by LCI from Syracuse to Bizerta in Algeria which they reached on 20 November. After a period in transit camp at Phillipeville, near Bone, they travelled by road to Algiers in early December where they awaited transport home.

Reflecting years later on the Italian campaign, Peter wrote with some pride that throughout his active service in Sicily and Italy he never shot an Italian.

On 25 December they embarked on HMT *Mojolo*, arriving in Liverpool on 4 January 1944 where they were met by, amongst others, John Durnford-Slater and Lord Lovat. On 1 November Peter had been gazetted temporary Lieutenant Colonel and confirmed in his appointment as commander of 3 Commando. Durnford-Slater, now a Brigadier, had exciting plans for him and his unit once they had rebuilt their strength. Their immediate objective, however, was some well-earned leave.

Chapter Thirteen

Normandy

Commando Leader

Major Peter Young has proved himself at 28, a very able Commando leader. When I spoke yesterday to his father Mr Dallas Young, in his office at the Law Courts, I learned that Major Young's one hobby is military science and military history.

He joined the Beds and Herts Regiment straight from Trinity College Oxford. His decorations include the DSO and the MC to which a Bar has now been added. Quiet spoken Mr Young is obviously very proud of his son, who is carrying on the tradition of a family with a military record which goes back almost 200 years.

Newspaper article late 1943.

They arrived back in England five months before D-Day. Durnford-Slater entertained most of the officers at the Adelphi Hotel that evening before they went off on leave. He was now on the staff planning the D-Day landings and Lovat had taken over the brigade.

After two weeks' leave, spent with his family, Peter arrived in Worthing on 24 January where he found himself billeted, with Christopher, in the house of a Mr and Mrs Mycock, a couple in their late sixties. According to Christopher, Mr Mycock used an ear trumpet and the family air-raid shelter was underneath the dining room table.

They began training at once, but still awaited reinforcements from Achnacarry so Peter could not yet reorganize the troops. Royal Marines were now being trained at Achnacarry alongside Army Commandos, with Lieutenant Colonel Charlie Vaughan still in charge, an exacting and energetic taskmaster who produced Commandos of a very high order. Every skill that Peter had helped to hone in the first generation of Commandos was assiduously developed until recruits were able to demonstrate to visiting generals the pièce de résistance, an amphibious landing carried out in conditions indistinguishable from the real thing.

Peter was amused to discover that one of the training troops at Achnacarry was named after him. During an interview with one new arrival who had been in Young Troop he decided to probe a little:

'Who was Young?' he asked the hapless soldier.

'Oh, some officer who was up there at one time.'

'And what was he doing there?'

'A refresher course or something.'

'And where is he now?'

'I suppose he's been bumped off, hasn't he?'

Antipathy between the Royal Marines and the Army manifested itself when the Provost Sergeant in Worthing, Lofty King, issued a ruling that no Marine was to enter the town. Naturally it was not long before a Marine was found enjoying a pint in one of the local pubs; Lofty demonstrated with his fists that he meant what he said. Such hostility was unacceptable – like it or not the units had to operate together, but when Durnford-Slater told Peter that such behaviour would not be tolerated the Army Commandos felt he was supporting the Marines over them. It took some time for the bad feeling to subside.

Reinforced with about 160 men, the commando could begin training in earnest. Integrating so many men into a core of battle-hardened troops was a new challenge. Peter's focus was to ensure that his cadre of NCOs was the best it could possibly be; most, having lost their rank on transferring to the Commandos, had earned it back during operations. The result was that he now had a core of home-grown NCOs. 'I am deeply conscious,' he wrote, 'that 3 Commando was well served by its officers and men, but it owed its successes more than any single factor to its peerless NCOs.'

On 21 February Montgomery inspected the brigade, now consisting of Nos 3, 4, 6 and 45 (RM) Commandos. Peter was introduced to him and they had a brief conversation about whether they had met before and when; it was a conversation they had three or four times during the war. He noted the men's reaction to Monty; when the inspection was over he got on to a jeep to talk to the men who crowded round to hear what he had to say. 'There could be no doubt,' he wrote, 'of the enthusiasm and confidence he inspired.'

The following day they moved to the Combined Training Centre at Dorlin in Scotland. Peter travelled up with Christopher, driven by his new driver, Samways, in a Humber Snipe. The main objective of this period of training was to integrate the new recruits and carry out exercises which would be impossible on the crowded south coast. They practised shooting and worked with landing craft before returning to Worthing on 10 March.

Later in the month they were inspected by General Dempsey. The unit was drawn up on Broadwater Green in Worthing. After Dempsey was welcomed with a General Salute he ordered the men to slope arms and came forward to shake Peter's hand. The inspection went very well; he talked to the men who had served with him in the Mediterranean and to those who wore his own cap badge of the Royal Berkshire Regiment; the parade ended when the men marched off in column.

'Very excellent,' was his verdict, to Peter's satisfaction. Before he left, he asked Peter how much he knew about the coming operation. Peter responded that he knew he had to be ready by the end of May to which Dempsey responded: 'That's about right.'

It was not until 14 April that the commanding officers received their first briefing which was delivered by Lovat but excluded, for reasons of operational security, all dates, times, locations and place names. The pace of training increased; two days after this briefing Peter conducted a unit exercise at Pevensey Levels which was chosen for its similarity to the terrain they would encounter at the French landing site: flat marshy country with small patches of scrub and trees intersected by deep ditches. The advance and objectives were designed to conform as closely as possible to the plan as it then stood for D-Day.

On 22 April, a Saturday, Peter 'spoke to the Unit in the Rivoli Cinema . . . about 320 of them anyway. We paraded, very clean, at Broadwater Green as usual. Review Order. Only riflemen armed . . . We then marched to the cinema.

'[He] warned the men particularly to be self-reliant and suspiciously alert . . . told them not to say "we've done enough", in action.'

Endless briefings were given covering everything from lessons learnt at Dieppe (by 4 Commando) to the advisability of making all troops run a mile before breakfast, doubling if their clothes were wet.

On Tuesday, 16 May he attended a conference at Ashling House at which a number of players were present. Lieutenant Commander Duff DSC, Croix de Guerre, RN was outlining naval aid, a subject which clearly did not hold Peter's attention since, interspersed with the information he was given about offshore fire support – *Serapis* to support 3 Commando and *Suarez* to support 6 Commando with what he described as 'useful supporting fire' – he jotted down, amongst others, the following notes and then fell to doodling.

> John Pooley [second-in-command] is marrying Mary Rantley, his 'landlady's daughter', on Sunday next . . .
>
> I have no time this week to go to Aldershot to see my first line reinforcements. Nor has my 2 i/c.
>
> I had lunch with Major Nicol Gray [second-in-command] of 45 Cmdo [sic] at the In and Out on Sat last [13 May]. Major Gen Bob Sturges RM and Brig Jumbo Leicester (4 SS Bde) were there. I said to Sturges, 'I see you got your name in the papers last week.' (It was announced that he was 'Commando's Chief'). He promptly slapped me on the head!
>
> I spent Friday and Saturday nights at home at Oxshott, and visited Limehouse St Fighting area with Nichol [sic] Gray in the morning. Called on Maj. Keith Cameron, L Block Chelsea Bks, at 1130, London District School of Tactics . . .
>
> I came up here in Reis' [sic] S.C. [Colonel Charles Ries, Commanding Officer of 45 RM Commando's Staff Car]. Mine is being waterproofed.

The Limehouse Street Fighting Area had been destroyed in the Blitz and was being used to train troops in street fighting. 3 Commando had been allocated 18 and 19 May and Peter took full advantage of the two days. 'The exercise,' according to Peter's papers, 'was practised both by day and night and in view of the unit's subsequent action in and around Amfreville, the time was well spent. A touch of realism was added when the enthusiastic troops succeeded in burning down a house with a 2-inch mortar bomb, let off in the wrong direction.'
On 20 May he travelled to Chichester to hear Montgomery address brigade commanding officers. Nobody below the rank of Lieutenant Colonel was allowed in. He noted that Monty did not like using a microphone but that his voice scarcely reached the back of the gymnasium where they were gathered. When he asked if everybody could hear him, some indicated that they could not, whereupon he asked if any of them were deaf. It was, he wrote afterwards 'quite

151

an interesting and affable speech'. He talked for about three quarters of an hour and divided his subject into five parts: Past, Present, Future, Immediate Future and Points to which he attached importance.

The brigade now took part in a final exercise, a full dress rehearsal of the coming operation. From HMS *Tormentor*, near Portsmouth, the troops embarked on LCIs, each of which accommodated 90-100 men, 'five,' as Peter records, 'being required to lift the whole unit'. They sailed to Littlehampton where a practice assault landing and advance inland was carried out, apparently chosen for its topographical similarity to the area they were to attack. Peter, with hindsight, observed caustically: 'This [decision] will be evident ... to the reader who, knowing the full story . . . will readily see the connection between Littlehampton and Ouistreham; the River Arun and the River Orne; the Arundel Bridge and the Bénouville bridges.'

As planned, John Pooley's wedding took place on the afternoon of Sunday, 21 May. Ned Moore was best man.

On 22 May the King inspected a detachment of Peter's men in Lord Leconfield's park at Petworth. The occasion was photographed by Captain Mallindine.

On 25 May, at 0530 hrs, the commando entrained at Worthing and moved to a camp designated C18, just outside Southampton, which was closed that night. Thereafter only organized parties accompanied by an officer were allowed out for training and recreation. Their austere surroundings temporarily dampened morale – there was little to do but visit the American-run cinema in a large marquee. It did not take long for the men to recover their spirits although they chafed at the inactivity. Peter wrote: 'By the time we had been there a day or two we were ready to face death in practically any form rather than go on living in boredom where we were.'

The tasks given to 6th Airborne Division were crucial: to seize and hold intact the bridges across the Caen Canal and River Orne at Bénouville; to silence the Merville and Ranville batteries which could otherwise fire on the 3rd Division as they came ashore; to destroy bridges over the River Dives and River Seine, delaying the arrival of German troops from Le Havre and Caen; to seize the towns of Franceville Plage and Sallenelles, east of the Orne; and clear the area north to Cabourg.

This last task was allotted to the Special Service Brigade, and 3 Commando were to operate on the extreme left in the Cabourg sector. Most of the men were to be parachuted in; those that were to attack by sea were to land on Sword Beach, just west of Ouistreham and the River Orne. The only problem from Peter's point of view was that he would be landing at H+90, thus missing the initial assault. He felt, as he put it, 'vaguely insulted'.

Now that they had no access to the outside world the operation was repeatedly briefed to all the men, using photographs and models to familiarize them with the landmarks and way points. Although their destination was still not generally known, everybody knew that the first objective was to get to the bridges and join up with the airborne troops.

Durnford-Slater's headquarters arrived in the concentration area on 2 June. He travelled round all the commandos and received a great welcome from No. 3 where he was pleased to note that the troops were laughing and singing, and the officers were confident and content. He left them with regret; this would be their first operation without him at their head.

On 4 June there was a church parade, and on 5 June, Lovat addressed all ranks, ending his remarks by saying, 'demain on les aura'. At 1400 hrs that day the troops were taken to Warsash. While waiting, Nos 3 and 6 Commandos played soccer on the beach. Christopher received a leg injury during a game of shinty (Irish hockey) the day before they left camp. When he suggested to Peter that he did not think he would be able to go, Peter responded, 'You will make it even if I have to carry you.'

At 1630 hrs they embarked; as each man went aboard they were handed a ticket although it was not clear who was meant to collect it at the other end. An hour later they slipped anchor and made for Southampton Water where the invasion force was massing. When, at 1900 hrs, they reached Stokes Bay to join the assault craft which were collecting there in great flotillas the scale of the invasion became clear. At 2130 hrs they received their sailing orders and Peter finally revealed their destination. As the troop commanders issued maps and final instructions the fleet got under way.

As they cleared the shelter of the Isle of Wight they felt the effects of the storm which had delayed the operation by twenty-four hours; the assault craft bobbed and weaved in the heavy seas. Sleep was impossible for most men and seasickness added to their misery.

The high winds which afflicted the seaborne crossing also affected the airborne landings – although some of the gliders found their targets, many men landed some way from their designated drop zone. Regrouping took precious time. By 0830 hrs the following morning the seaborne elements were 2 miles out to sea, awaiting H+90 and their run inshore to Sword Beach – 45 RM Commando on the right, heading towards Queen White, and 3 Commando on the left making for Queen Red, the more easterly of the beaches. Gun flashes were visible but no sound penetrated out to sea. Close by, the battleship *Ramillies*, amongst others, was bombarding the Bénouville Battery with 15-inch shells. Ahead, the forward units were going in to a hazy beach area shrouded in covering smoke. The firefight, begun before dawn on that sleepless night, was an unforgettable sight. As they finally began the run-in the sounds of battle began to be heard, the time-delayed crump from the enemy coastal batteries and friendly tanks adding themselves to the roar of the ships' guns. As if by magic the LCIs formed themselves into a line abreast and accelerated ashore; the adrenalin took hold and seasickness faded.

Peter began to recognize landmarks from the photographs: Ouistreham was just over half a mile away to his left and ahead of him lay a line of shelled houses silhouetted on the skyline like teeth. Suddenly, a hundred yards from the shore, the advance stopped. When Peter queried this he was told that they were five minutes ahead of schedule. His blood now up, Peter responded:

'I don't think anyone will mind if we're five minutes early on D-Day.'

'Then in we go.'

They had now to run the gauntlet of shellfire which had got their range. A shell burst overhead and a splinter of shrapnel hit Peter's flak jacket. As the ramp went down the LCI received a direct hit; Peter, first out on the starboard ramp, found himself in 5 feet of water. Tank tracks running up the beach told him that, in effect, the area had been swept for mines, courtesy, he thought, of the 13th/18th Hussars who had landed on Queen Red in the first wave. At 0905 hrs he hit the beach and ran inland shouting for the men to follow him in single file.

Peter's account of the D-Day landings in *Storm from the Sea* is written in the present tense, giving his words an urgency that pulls the reader into the action. It is hard to exaggerate his pride that he was there as the Commanding Officer of 3 Commando. Whatever happened ashore – and he must have been inured to the certainty that their carefully formulated plans would be drastically modified – he had utter confidence in the troops under his command. They did not disappoint him.

Their first setback was the accurate shelling directed at the landing

154

craft. Apart from his own craft, struck at the moment of impact with the beach, LCIs 512 and 509 were lost, along with many men. Despite this, most of 3 Commando got off the beach in good order. There was little cover behind the houses which lined the beach. Peter stood on the road directing troops and they were soon moving inland in two files. The sand dunes gave way to marshy ground which they had to cover under fire. Progress was agonizingly slow, but the ground absorbed much of the shellfire. They took a few casualties and Peter felt a thump on his shoulder, but discovered to his relief that it had merely been a clod of earth thrown up by a near miss.

As they reached their forming-up place Peter realized that they were already overtaking units which had landed earlier – he had seen as far back as the beach that the infantry was far more cautious than his own men. Whereas they hung back in case of booby traps or concealed Germans, Peter pushed his men on and they went willingly. Although they were exposed, they moved fast and consequently took no more casualties than the infantry did.

Movement inland was becoming difficult. By 1000 hrs they had made contact with 45 RM Commando but the area around them was heavily mined and there was only a single track which was safe to use. Leaving Pooley, lightly wounded but otherwise in good spirits, and Hopson to bring the troops up, he pushed forward to Bénouville Bridge with only Christopher – his injury forgotten – and Leyland to see what had transpired there. Their rear-link wireless set was not working which gave Peter the excuse he needed to push forward.

They moved quickly and were soon passing through other elements of the brigade. In Colleville (now Colleville Montgomery) they overtook 45 Commando and pressed on, encountering little resistance beyond occasional sniping which did not discompose them. By the time they had passed through St Aubin d'Arquenay, about another 2 kilometres down the road, they had taken over the lead in the advance. At the edge of St Aubin the road ran downhill to Bénouville and they covered the remaining kilometre or so at the double. As they entered the village they encountered British airborne troops who were delighted to make contact with them. For his part Peter, having overtaken the forward units of the seaborne Commando landings, had accomplished his own ambition which was to get himself back into the leading edge of the attack. They moved to the bridge over the canal – now known as Pegasus Bridge – where he found a glider which had landed within 30 yards of the road and a number of German bodies lying around it.

3 Troop had preceded him, pressing forward towards Cabourg on bicycles to reconnoitre. In Bénouville they had been ordered by Lovat to support the 9th Parachute Battalion which was to attack Amfreville, a little further north – this village and its château were vital for they lay on a low ridge which overlooked the Orne estuary and beaches beyond, providing a perfect position for artillery observation posts. However, some of 3 Troop were pinned down when Peter got there and had taken cover under a low bank because the bridge was being sniped. Peter told them to cycle across flat out and they would probably get away with it. They did so, and reached the far side with only one loss.

Following their example Peter, Christopher and Leyland sprinted across and reached the east bank unscathed. They had barely set foot there when Lovat appeared. His first words were, 'What kept you, Peter?' His next were to announce a change in plan. The advance to Cabourg was off and 3 Commando was now to move into Le Bas de Ranville in order to protect 6th Division Headquarters and prevent any enemy advance from the south. Le Bas de Ranville encompassed the area in which they stood so Peter could only wait for the rest of the commando to join him. In the meantime he was able to reconnoitre the area to dispose his men in defensive positions as they arrived.

That evening Peter watched as airborne troops of 6 Airlanding Brigade arrived in hundreds of gliders, protected by impenetrable fighter cover. Efforts by the Germans to prevent the landings were in vain.

During the night the Royal Ulster Rifles relieved 3 Commando, which was ordered to concentrate south of Brigade Headquarters between Ranville and Amfreville. By 0430 hrs the move was complete and they had acquired two anti-tank guns, further increasing their security. Well positioned in a sheltered valley Peter's men passed a quiet morning in reserve during which they rested and reorganized.

At 1300 hrs Peter received a message to send his second-in-command with two troops to support 45 RM Commando at Franceville-Plage. Pooley was despatched with 4 Troop under Brian Butler and 5 Troop under Woyevodsky. Peter attended the operational briefing in a field close to the village of Sallenelles; Pooley, it transpired, was to clear Merville Battery while 45 RM Commando attacked the seaside town of Franceville-Plage.

Feeling that Pooley might need explosives to carry out his job Peter

156

visited the Brigade Engineer Troop to see if he could procure anything but returned empty handed. He was restless, however, and determined to go forward to see Pooley and reconnoitre the terrain. He feared, correctly as it transpired, that his men were out on a limb and might need help. He took Christopher and Leyland with him, along with the Medical Officer, his sergeant and a radio operator.

Leaving the Adjutant in charge the party left for Merville. On the way he received word from Hopson that Ranville was under tank attack, but deciding that he wanted to see Pooley he did not turn back. At Merville they found a narrow path through a minefield which they traversed in some trepidation. As they arrived at the far side unscathed they met Pooley, who told Peter that he had simply led 5 Troop in a frontal attack through the minefield while 4 Troop gave covering fire. This was a bold move even by Peter's standards, but they had got through with few casualties to find that the battery was only weakly held. Pooley was now preparing to direct the mopping-up operation and reorganize his forces. He ran on and Peter, taking up an active role in the battle, summoned 4 Troop forward to join the rest.

He had no sooner done so than one of 5 Troop's subalterns ran up to report that Pooley had been killed. This was distressing news; all resistance had seemed to be at an end but Pooley, who was wearing a distinctive jacket, had stood up on a wall near one of the entrances to the battery to attract the attention of his men and had been shot by a lone German. The enemy sniper did not long survive his action. Peter was among those who climbed up onto the grass-covered casemate and dropped a Mills bomb down the air vent. Pooley's death cast a pall over the battle. He had been married less than a week and every man there had helped to celebrate his wedding.

Peter's instincts had served him well: the attack on Merville Battery had put his men in an isolated and potentially fatal position. Leaving Butler to reform the two troops, Peter went to Brigade Headquarters to report. The Brigadier agreed that the force should withdraw, but this was no easy task. The most expedient means of getting out was to split up and move in small groups. This they did but many men were wounded and captured – of Gordon Pollard's section of twenty-three men from 4 Troop only eight returned.

If the guns in the battery had still been operational, which Peter doubted, they could not have been silenced without the use of explosives which had not been forthcoming when requested, reinforcing his view that this was a futile gesture, poorly planned and sketchily briefed. Although he was, with hindsight, philosophical about the inevitability of such jobs, opining that it was better simply to hope that they did not happen too often, he was also angered by its futility.

At Ranville the attack petered out quite quickly, the entrenched troops putting up a spirited performance which convinced the Germans that they were not going to win. They lost two tanks in the process.

That evening 3 Commando was ordered to Brigade Headquarters. By 2200 hrs Peter had deployed his men in and around Amfreville which was to become their base. They had been rejoined about an hour earlier by 4 and 5 Troops, now at about half strength. Peter occupied the château as his headquarters; it had been a German battalion headquarters until the previous day.

The Special Service Brigade now occupied the ridge which over-looked Sword Beach and the Orne estuary, and it was not expected that the Germans would leave them alone. Before setting out from England Peter had given some thought to how the Germans would react to the D-Day landings and had concluded that after a day or two to see how the Allied dispositions were shaping up they would mount a counter-attack, probing along their forward line to attack where they thought there might be a weakness. He expected them to begin doing so at any time and wanted to ensure that his depleted forces – 4, 5 and 6 Troops having taken a lot of casualties – were deployed to best effect. One of his axiomatic military rules was always to keep a reserve and this he was determined to do, although he knew that he would receive numerous requests for reinforcements from other units as time went on. For the moment 4 and 5 Troops were, for obvious reasons, in reserve. If the situation were desperate, he could send his Headquarters Troop into action.

At 0945 hrs on D+2 he received a message from Brigade Headquarters telling him that an attack was imminent – the Germans were forming up in le Bas de Bréville, opposite his position. The enemy advanced at a leisurely pace until contact was made at 1100 hrs when troops were seen in the orchards and gardens surrounding the Longuemare road north-east of the village. They advanced to within 80 yards of the commando's position and occupied two houses on the edge of Amfreville.

The initial exchanges were with 6 Troop which took the fighting to the enemy with a pugnacity which made Peter proud. Their training in street fighting stood them in good stead, as they engaged in a

158

running fight of the sort they enjoyed and were shortly rewarded by the capture of several Germans. Unconventional as ever, they made good – if unorthodox – use of a 2-inch mortar which they fired point blank at the enemy by resting the base plate against a tree. Despite the danger to themselves, this tactic clearly disconcerted and demoralized the enemy which, Peter thought, made the risk worthwhile.

Meanwhile, 12 Section under George Herbert was not making progress as they were pinned down by Germans firing from a ditch. Herbert did what Peter would have done; calling out to his men, 'Come on, we'll go in!' he led the charge into the orchard. As he paused to change magazines a German stood up, took aim and shot him through the chest, killing him instantly. The bullet cut the ribbon of his Distinguished Conduct Medal.

Despite this, the Germans were now generally retreating and Alderson, OC 6 Troop, called off the pursuit, but not before about forty-five prisoners were turned over to Curly Gimbert, now TSM. Peter was gratified to discover that they had faced worthy opponents, men from the 346th Infantry Division, who were smartly dressed and well accoutred; the Germans were equally dismayed to see that the victors were few in number and scruffily dressed: many of them had not shaved and had smeared greasepaint or mud on their faces by way of camouflage.

Late that afternoon George Herbert's body was brought back and he was buried in the garden of the château. Lovat, on a visit to their position, joined the men at his graveside. Herbert's loss was keenly felt. He had been one of the original recruits to the commando and Peter had helped to develop his talents. Herbert had in turn given Peter his wholehearted support. The result had been the making of an outstanding Commando leader whose unique qualities would be missed.

The following day, 9 June (D+3), was quiet for 3 Commando. There was still a gap between 4 Commando and the sea, and if the Germans had found it they could have penetrated the brigade line and turned their left flank. Instead they spent most of the day trying to probe Allied positions to determine their front line, but 3 Commando had a strong defensive position which seemed to deter the Germans from attacking them. Peter was pleased when Durnford-Slater came to visit him in the morning and was delighted when reinforcements arrived during the afternoon, although the two officers and twenty-five other ranks did not go far towards replacing the 124 casualties they had sustained thus far.

The next morning, D+4, the Germans gave notice that they were not inclined to leave the Commando Brigade in possession of the Amfreville ridge, as they mounted a vigorous three-pronged attack against the whole front. The shelling began at about 0900 hrs and although the fire was not especially accurate there were casualties. Peter's chief tactic was to keep the position well defended and to maintain contact with neighbouring commands, 4 Commando on their left and 6 Commando on their right. There had been some infiltration of the line along 6 Commando's position, but the incursions were dealt with by 45 RM Commando.

Shortly afterwards news of the infiltration they had most feared was brought: 4 Commando had been outflanked on their left and were now seriously pressed. Peter was asked to send a troop to support them but he suggested instead that he should take over part of their front, thus releasing one of their own troops to act as reserve. At about 1215 hrs he sent 1 Troop under Clive Collins to occupy the eastern wall of the gardens of the Château de la Rue which had been under 4 Commando's control. He put 6 Troop under John Nixon into the building itself which at once became known as Château Nixon.

During the afternoon he went to visit 1 Troop which was still digging in and taking casualties from continued shelling by the Germans. Peter strolled over to their position, apparently unconcerned by the fire raining down around him or the fact that he might be giving away their position to the enemy. He reached their half-dug slit trench and stood looking down at the men taking cover there; when Peter asked to speak to Bill Britnell he felt compelled to leave the safety of his shelter despite the danger.

'Have you,' Peter asked him rhetorically, 'seen Part 2 Orders today?'

Britnell had scarcely been in a position to do so. Peter informed him that he was incorrectly dressed – he needed another stripe as he had been promoted to Corporal. Britnell thought that if he stood around much longer outside his foxhole he was unlikely to live long enough to reap the fruits of the extra stripe but the incident illustrates Peter's capacity for detail.

Elsewhere the shelling was more pernicious; even Christopher took cover at one point. They found one mortally wounded man in another slit trench and one suffering from shell-shock, the only case Peter said he had ever seen. By now 1 Troop was down to a strength of just thirty-three and when Collins requested reinforcements from

6 Troop, still in the relative safety of the château, Peter had no difficulty in raising the necessary volunteers.

As the afternoon wore on it became clear that the Germans were not going to break through and by early evening they were back at their start line. Peter had been given command of two self-propelled guns. With the pressure on the ridge now eased he decided to patrol with the guns towards Sallenelles and Longuemare. They successfully occupied an empty house and then, to their surprise, they saw a German medical orderly walking towards them from the direction of Sallenelles holding a white flag. When questioned, he said that there were some German wounded on the edge of the village. Not wishing to take this information at face value, Peter advanced cautiously with 5 Troop and a self-propelled gun but faced no resistance when they reached and overran the German position at the edge of Sallenelles, where eighteen men surrendered, mostly wounded. The town had been abandoned by the enemy at about 1600 hrs. Peter took Christopher with him and went down onto the beach where the Germans had tried to turn the Allied flank. A thought occurred to him.

'I suppose,' he said to Christopher, 'I must be the left-hand man of the British Army at the moment.'

'Let's hope Monty doesn't shout "Right form!"' Christopher responded.

At the far end of the village they came across a pill box and half a dozen German troops watching them. Peter brought up the self-propelled gun and sent a couple of rounds in their direction; there was no returning fire. When they arrived back at Headquarters later that evening they found a dispatch rider newly arrived with the news that the shells of their self-propelled guns were incorrectly fuzed and liable to burst prematurely. In the action around Amfreville they had lost six killed (including two officers) and 23 wounded.

According to Christopher's account Peter took him every day to visit each troop in turn, and every day a patrol from one of these troops would be out in front probing the enemy's front line. Sometimes they tagged along behind them and acted as umpires. Over the following two days the Germans continued to try and push the occupying forces from their position on the ridge, but without success.

On D+6 (12 June) Peter decided to move his headquarters from a slit trench into the Château d'Amfreville itself which, concealed by some tall trees, had so far escaped damage from the constant shelling.

This was a more comfortable arrangement and, since it enabled Peter to establish an operations room where he could keep maps on permanent display, a more efficient one. He slept on a camp bed in one corner of the room.

Word reached them at about 1330 hrs that day that there was to be a battalion attack on Bréville, a German stronghold which was being used as a jumping-off point for enemy forays towards Allied positions. To support this, Peter provided 3 Troop as flanking cover for the advancing force. Meanwhile, he was summoned to Brigade Headquarters where Lovat outlined the part he was to play in the main attack which was to take place that night. Peter took three officers and sixty men towards Gonneville – approximately 2 miles north-east of Amfreville – on a fighting patrol. Their orders were to provide a diversion and to take prisoners.

He took with him John Nixon and Keith Ponsford, whose entire troop volunteered to go on the operation despite having been out on patrol all afternoon. They left Commando Headquarters at 2120 hrs and advanced as far as La Grande Ferme du Buisson which they secured but did not occupy. They continued their advance wading through cornfields which could provide cover if necessary. They were unopposed, however, and reached a hedgerow about a hundred yards from the road into Gonneville, now only about a quarter of a mile away to their north. Here Peter divided the party into three, sending Nixon northwards to create a diversion and Ponsford directly up the road to take prisoners. He himself remained with a small reserve to provide covering fire if necessary. All parties were to make their own way back. The only accompaniment to all this was the sound of a distant artillery bombardment to their right as the assault on Bréville got under way and the faint 'wump' of naval guns which were firing on enemy aircraft.

There were Germans in the vicinity, but some of them were so tired that they slept through the ensuing action; one of them only awoke when one of the German-speaking NCOs captured him. Nixon meanwhile encountered resistance from some enemy who were rather more alert, and after a brisk firefight he began to fall back as arranged. Peter stayed in position until he was certain the other two parties had successfully disengaged, then he too withdrew after giving a volley of fire in the direction of the enemy to keep their heads down. When they reached La Grande Ferme they found that it had been reoccupied by some French peasants who presented them with half a dozen eggs as they passed through. Peter reached

162

Amfreville at 0320 hrs to find both other parties had returned safely and without loss.

Peter thought that this action was rather pointless since it was unlikely that the Germans who were in Gonneville would move precipitately in the middle of the night to support their compatriots under attack at Bréville. Still, they had fulfilled their orders and suffered no losses.

The attack on Bréville was also successful, but rather more costly. Early in the action Brigadiers Lovat and Kindersley (6 Airlanding Brigade) had both been wounded. Lovat was succeeded by Derek Mills-Roberts who had himself been wounded, but not seriously, while Kindersley was succeeded by Flavell.

This action saw the end of German offensive operations in the area. Peter could not determine whether this was due to exhaustion, confusion or plain old caution. At all events, 3 Commando established itself firmly at Amfreville and the action resolved itself into a sniping war, which pleased Peter as he had taken some trouble to identify and train snipers prior to the D-Day landings. They had taken the best marksmen for the job but soon found that many of them were not temperamentally suited for the work which required long periods of isolation waiting for the appearance of suitable targets. The best snipers, it transpired, were not the marksmen, but the stalkers who would identify a target and then take great pleasure in creeping up to the victim, getting so close that they could not miss their mark.

On 13 June, Peter took the precaution of occupying La Grande Ferme du Buisson, a prescient move since in the evening a party of about forty Germans arrived, intent upon removing the small garrison. As he had only twelve men, Sergeant Synnott decided that withdrawal was the best option and was on the point of doing so when he discovered that four of his men were missing. As he returned to look for them he was unexpectedly supported by the arrival of a number of British Marauders which – probably by mistake – bombed the crossroads where the Germans were concentrated. As the enemy dived for cover the four missing men made their escape and Synnott revised his plan, sending a runner to request support. 3 Troop arrived just as a French girl ran up and told them where the Germans were laying their ambush. Armed with this information, Hopson opened up with everything he had before rushing the position which he found deserted. The booty consisted of a considerable amount of equipment.

3 Commando continued to harass the enemy on the basis that if they were allowed to regroup and resupply they would rapidly return to the offensive, whereas Peter wanted them on the back foot, unable to do much more than hold their ground. In this he was successful, though there was the inevitable occasional loss.

The headquarters in the château was a hub of activity, subjected to occasional shelling by an increasingly subdued enemy. The Padre was the only person who seemed concerned by this and would cower in the safest place he could find, to general derision. Stanley Scott stood frequent guard duty at the entrance to the château; every time Peter passed him he would tell him to put his beret straight and laugh when Scott instinctively put his hands up to do so. Eventually, guile got the better of instinct and he remained at attention when invited to straighten his headgear, whereupon Peter knocked his beret off his head.

Christopher took advantage of the lull in activity to teach himself to drive Peter's jeep. Henceforward he was now his driver as well as his orderly which was, he thought, more convenient all round. Peter 'liberated' a very smart car which had been abandoned at the château by the Germans. When the commando returned to England he watched anxiously as it was loaded by crane onto one of the transports at the Mulberry Harbour at Arromanches. He subsequently sold it in London for a fraction of its true worth.

In July a number of armoured vehicles belonging to VIII Corps arrived prior to the launch of Operation Goodwood which began on D+42, 18 July. The forward units rolled southwards that day as the advance towards Falaise and Argentan began. It was fine and sunny, and Peter took his jeep to inspect the German prisoners who were caged at Ranville. Their general air of defeat and dispiritedness made a deep impression on him; the Allied bombardment had, he thought, 'shaken them to the core'. Then he watched as their captors began to form them up to continue their march into captivity; a British redcap ordered them to their feet and they got themselves into a rather shambolic line when suddenly a German NCO took command of the situation and began to rap out orders. Instantly the prisoners were transformed once more into a cohesive unit: 'Prussian discipline,' Peter wrote, 'can survive even two thousand bombers . . . How long does discipline take to reassert itself after a shaking like this? This is a question that any soldier may ask in these days of nuclear warfare, days when any battalion commander may be invited to command a unit which has had an atom bomb for its breakfast.'

3 Commando remained on the left flank of the invading force. Enemy resistance was minimal and, although they only had three killed and twelve wounded during July, the losses from the initial battle had still not been made up. Word now came that the Beach Groups were being disbanded and front-line units were to be allowed to take volunteers from them to provide reinforcements. One of the units was 2nd Battalion of the Hertfordshire Regiment (2/Herts), Territorials associated with Peter's own regiment. He arranged to visit them in their quarters near Ver-sur-Mer, about 5 miles east of Arromanches, where their commanding officer allowed him to take as many men as he wanted. Christopher drove him there and was himself delighted to see several old friends amongst the men.

There was no shortage of volunteers, although many of them wanted to stay in the same platoons in which they had already been fighting. This was not possible and Peter tried to ensure that those men he picked understood the conditions under which they would be serving, while Christopher was able to give him background information on a number of them so he was as confident as he could be that he had the pick of the bunch. Christopher also noted in his account that these men, unlike the early recruits to the Commandos, did not lose their rank when they transferred. To Christopher's chagrin one of the new arrivals, Sergeant Kerrison, kept his stripes. Christopher had known Kerrison before the war when they had both played minor league football against each other – Christopher for St Albans, Kerrison for Wheathampstead.

They had now been at Amfreville for some time and had established a good relationship with the locals, however towards the end of July they were told that they were to move. The invading force was gradually starting to expand outwards from its initial positions and 3 Commando was to move south-west into the Bois de Bavent towards the River Dives, behind which the Germans were mounting their next line of defence. Peter held the inhabitants of the village in some affection, indeed he and many of his men remained in contact with them long after the war – from M Bernichon, who traced the ancient maps of the commune so that Peter could make detailed notes of his section posts' positions, as well as marking the precise locations of tank tracks so that he could claim compensation, to M Picard, who became mayor after the war, a position he held for many years.

One night Peter awoke to find a German soldier standing to attention beside his bed. Realizing that from a tactical point of view his position seemed hopeless, he nonetheless groped for his pistol. 'I heard my imbecile followers roaring with laughter. This character was a German deserter who had come in to give himself up.'

Chapter Fourteen

From Normandy to the Arakan

Their new position, which they took up on 1 August, ran from the crossroads at Le Mesnil to the Bois de Bavent. The Germans began to mortar them at once, the two sides so close that they could hear the metallic slither as the mortar bombs ran down the tubes. With most of the enemy concealed behind thick hedgerows, Peter set about responding to this welcome, concentrating his fire on the only occupied building. After scoring several hits a few German deserters came forward to give themselves up.

Peter's policy was to ensure that they gave back to the Germans at least two shells or mortars for every one which landed in his own lines. On the other hand 4 Commando, immediately to his right, believed that shelling the enemy only drew their fire and were therefore happy to let Peter use their mortars. Peter thought that the more weapons he could fire at once the better, believing that only the first salvo of an attack was likely to result in casualties since by the second one everyone would have taken cover.

They spent three days arranging everything to their own satisfaction – the 13th Parachute Battalion had dug small slit trenches which they enlarged to enable two men to sleep side by side and also stand in comfort. Covered in corrugated metal and logs, then with earth, they were safe from everything except a direct hit, though they were damp and uncomfortable after the relative luxury of Amfreville. They faced a more active enemy than before; their task was to locate and destroy enemy positions and it was dangerous work. At the end of two and a half weeks' fighting they had one killed and thirty-five wounded, including two officers.

Peter was summoned from Bavent to Brigade Headquarters by General Sturges, GOC Commando Group, during this sojourn.

Sturges wanted him to leave 3 Commando at once to go out to Burma and take over as Deputy Commander of the 3rd Special Service Brigade. 'No one,' Peter remarked, 'has less objection to promotion than I have.' But, reluctant to abandon his men in the middle of a campaign, he asked for two weeks to think it over. Before his time was up he received a one-word message which gave notice of another advance: Paddle.

He was not particularly surprised – for the previous three days the German rate of fire had considerably increased and he suspected that they were firing off as much of their ammunition stocks as they could prior to withdrawing. During the evening of 16 August he briefed his troop commanders in his dugout and told them that their next objective was Varaville.

The following day they moved east by north towards Bavent, reaching the village without seeing any sign of the enemy. Peter decided to move on ahead. Leaving the main body with his second-in-command, Major Bartholomew, he went forward with 4 and 5 Troops to locate the enemy. Their route took them through the village of Pétiville where the inhabitants hailed them as liberators – the memorial which the residents subsequently erected in their honour was unveiled on 7 June 1994 as part of the 50th anniversary celebrations of D-Day. It lies near the church, round the corner from rue Peter Young.

Peter set up his headquarters at the edge of Varaville in a racing stables with a complex of buildings that the Germans had used before him. A water tower served as an observation post. After the discomfort of their previous position this was a vast improvement, despite a plague of mosquitoes, and Christopher noted that they enjoyed an excellent night's rest.

Their objective was to take the high ground east of the Dives. This required crossing the river over which there were two bridges, one of which the Germans had already tried to destroy, but first they had to determine the state of these crossings and whether they were defended. Two men were sent to reconnoitre Peter's primary objective, the Pont de Vacaville, after dark. They reported that Germans were still occupying the area, but lack of visibility prevented them discovering with certainty the state of the bridge itself. Another patrol, this time in daylight, flushed out the remaining Germans and ascertained beyond doubt that the Vacaville bridge was indeed gone. The next night the Germans shelled the area with their coastal guns, positioned on the heights between Houlgate and Angoville. Keith

Ponsford, who had been on both patrols, was asleep when his bunker received a direct hit. His batman dug him out the following morning unscathed.

On 19 August they were notified that they were to move by motor transport to Briqueville, thence to proceed to the Heights of Angoville, about 7 miles east of Varaville, which lay in German-held territory. The operation would form a salient into the German line which would, the commanders hoped, turn the German right flank and make it easier to force their retreat.

Leaving Bartholomew to get the troops to their start point, Peter went to Brigade Headquarters and discovered that they were to attack at once as Mills-Roberts wanted the heights in British hands by dawn. It was a daunting prospect. They kept the plan as simple as possible because they could only brief the troop commanders once before they set off, and they would be operating in country which they had not reconnoitred but which seemed to be featureless, flat and exposed. The absence of the moon and stars was a hindrance as much as a help.

They moved off at 0100 hrs, led by their Intelligence Officer, Colin Rae, entering no-man's land once they crossed the Dives. They advanced along the railway line which they thought would be watched less than the road which ran parallel to it, though Peter feared that the noise they were making on the cinder bed of the railway track would alert the enemy. Luck, however, favoured them and although there was some sporadic German shelling it was concentrated on the road and flew harmlessly over them.

Peter, as usual, moved with a roving detachment of his own which kept in wireless contact with the Headquarters. He and Christopher kept towards the front; he was anxious not to miss the turn off the railway track, although when they found it there was some confusion for it went in the opposite direction to the one they were expecting, and led not to the church they had been told to use as a landmark, but to a farm. Crossing a tributary of the Dives they were surprised to find the bridge was still intact although there did not seem to be any German patrols or sentries.

They had covered about 5 miles. The Heights of Angoville were on their left but they were still very exposed and the sky was beginning to lighten. Suddenly there came a shot ahead followed by a scream and another shot. For a moment Peter feared that the shot had come from the enemy and hit one of his men. Some of the leading troop thought likewise for they turned and stampeded back, nearly knocking their commanding officer over in the process; a few well-chosen words brought them to their senses. They moved uphill towards the Heights and came upon La Ferme du Manoir d'Angoville. The lead sections, one of whom had shot a sleeping German sentry and sown panic in the ranks, began systematically to clear the farm buildings and discovered a number of Germans whom they took prisoner.

Peter made the farm his headquarters and deployed his troops as it got lighter and he could better appreciate the terrain. At the top of the slope was a feature identified as Point 72 – because of its shape it was christened the Pimple. Peter sent 6 Troop to occupy it.

Shortly after dawn Mills-Roberts visited. Peter was still securing the position and at Mills-Roberts' behest he sent 1 Troop to hold the western end of the hill. Basing himself in a deep ditch which he shared with the Brigadier and the various German prisoners, he realized that he was getting tired when he told Pollard to occupy some houses that did not exist, although he swore he could see them at the time.

The Germans had begun to fire on them so Peter took Christopher up to visit the Pimple where they were being attacked on two sides and had taken a couple of casualties. It was vital that this position be held and Peter made sure that they were in no doubt of its importance before returning to the farm, taking one of the wounded with him.

The day ended on a quieter note – attempts by the Germans to regain their ground were repulsed without difficulty and at length Peter retired to one of the outbuildings for the night. The distinctive sound of jeep engines revving up the hill heralded the arrival of vital supplies and towards midnight they were delighted to hear the sound of the RSM directing vehicles as they arrived in the farmyard. Ned Moore and Slinger Martin emerged from the chaos and explained that 4 Commando had laid down smoke and fire through which the jeeps had made a run for it, arriving miraculously unscathed. Christopher recounts that 'in no time I had a tin of stew and a cup of tea to put before PY. He said it was his best meal ever.'

Using the jeeps to evacuate the wounded the convoy left again at 0200 hrs. Peter slept much better than he would have done had he known that there were two armed Germans in the loft across the yard, waiting for the chance to make a break for it. The following day, 21 August, they continued to consolidate their position and in the evening Peter moved his headquarters to Le Quesnay, which had been lately liberated from the Germans. This position had been cleaned up by German prisoners, one of whom, when told to dig the

170

latrines, was convinced that he was digging his own grave.

They moved eastwards again on 22 August but spent most of their time hanging about in an orchard. Towards evening Peter arranged for his men to move into some nearby barns. Other units waiting with them did not move under cover, an oversight they regretted when the heavens opened during the night. They were, Peter reported the following morning, 'blue with cold and green with envy'.

Later that day they were moved by transport to Drubes and the troops, quartered in a farm at Vasse, were able to enjoy a good night's rest. Peter carried out an inspection of three of his troops the following morning. The mere fact that they had time to undertake such a task showed that at last the pressure was easing.

Passing through Pont l'Evêque that afternoon they concentrated in Le Bas de Surville just east of the town which was, as Peter put it, 'pretty much shattered'. While they were there 1 Troop produced a German prisoner who claimed to be a deserter and a non-Nazi. Peter disliked the look of him, but carried out his interrogation through one of his German speakers, discovering soon enough that the captive spoke excellent English. Resistance, it appeared, was melting before them. Having extracted as much information out of him as possible, Peter sent him off to Brigade Headquarters and tried not to give way to the feeling that nothing could now go wrong. There are times when soldiers get a sixth sense that an operation will pass off without a hitch because the enemy has not got the stomach for battle. Peter had that feeling on D+4 when they marched into Sallenelles and he felt it again now, as they prepared to advance on Quetteville.

3 Commando were to spearhead a flanking movement to the north of the main body, followed by Brigade Headquarters and 4 Commando. This required them to move across terrain that was as difficult as any they had dealt with in France so far. Leaving at 2030 hrs they found themselves going 'across fields, up steep banks, through woods, up hill and down dale'. The lead troops carried Sten guns with orders to open fire and charge any opposition; others carried the wherewithal to destroy any obstacles which might delay their advance. Officers and NCOs harried the men to keep them moving; at one halt Peter actually fell asleep on his feet and was awoken by Christopher after the men had moved on.

They moved into a more conventional formation as they neared Quetteville, fanning out and advancing as stealthily as possible. At this crucial point Peter was horrified to see a rifle being pushed through a gap in the hedge and bellowed: 'Care of arms!' at the offender. Through the gap stepped Mills-Roberts who had retrieved the German rifle earlier. Quetteville, as he had suspected, had been abandoned by the enemy when they arrived there shortly afterwards.

The following day it was decided that the Commando Brigade would move another 5 miles or so north-east to occupy Boulleville, cutting the roads and trapping a substantial number of Wehrmacht troops. Each formation contributed a unit to the operation – in 3 Commando's case it was 3 Troop. The force set off after dark on 25 August and achieved its objective at 0600 hrs the following morning, only to discover that the Germans had left two hours earlier. They had now been pushed back behind the Seine and Operation Paddle was at an end.

3 Commando moved into quarters at Boulleville. The weather was glorious and the countryside superb; after eighty-five days in the line the men could at last relax. On 27 August Peter invited Mills-Roberts, Durnford-Slater and Philip Dunne to supper, Bartholomew having carried out some ingenious foraging to provide excellent fare. Twelve days later, on 7 September, the commando was shipped back to England.

Having had considerably longer than two weeks to think about his decision to go to Burma, Peter decided that he did not want to leave 3 Commando. Nevertheless, in a remarkably short time he found himself on a plane bound for the Far East. Before he left he asked Christopher if he would be interested in continuing to serve with him and Christopher risked the wrath of his wife by agreeing to do so. While Peter completed the first leg of his journey Christopher prepared all the paperwork for his own move, working in the interim for Lieutenant Colonel Bartholomew, now commanding 3 Commando.

Peter's journey was reasonably short – it took five days to fly to Ceylon via Malta, Cairo, Shaiba and Karachi; on 5 October, he deplaned in Colombo and the following day was formally posted to 3 Special Service Brigade as Deputy Commander in the rank of Colonel.

The brigade was at Trincomalee, a location which must have touched the historian in him. When he got there he found two regiments, Nos 5 and 44 (RM) Commando. Nos 1 and 42 (RM) had moved to the Arakan, which Peter found unusual since no one in London had seemed to be aware of the fact. Ten days later, therefore, he left Trincomalee and travelled to Burma via India, arriving at Teknaf in the Arakan on 24 October. A week after he arrived Brigadier Nonweiler was evacuated back to the UK leaving him in temporary command.

Peter knew that he needed to understand the operating conditions, and the tactical opportunities and limitations which the enemy and the terrain imposed upon an amphibious force. Although the Allies in the Far East had inflicted a crushing defeat on the Japanese Fifteenth Army, forcing them to retreat with heavy losses, they were likely to regroup and begin the offensive again as soon as possible. 3 Special Service Brigade was part of XV Indian Corps which, based in the Arakan and together with the Fourteenth Army under General Bill Slim, was poised to pursue the defeated enemy back across the Chindwin Valley.

Things worked differently from Europe, but he enjoyed the business of discovering how to get things done. One of the bonuses of his new job was the chance to work again with Lieutenant Colonel Ken Trevor of 1 Commando, whom he had last seen during his brief time on the Combined Services Staff in 1942. He discovered that the units which made up his brigade had had varied careers, 1 Commando having served in North Africa and 5 Commando in Madagascar. 42 and 44 Commandos had seen no active service and the brigade as a whole had scarcely been employed since its formation. Faced with these circumstances, Peter took steps to organize an operation which would get the men working together; by the beginning of November Nos 5 and 44 had arrived at Teknaf from Trincomalee.

They had no landing craft at their disposal so their first operation was conducted using the Eureka which Lieutenant General Sir Philip Christison, commander of XV Corps, retained for his own use. Peter organized a small raiding party which he accompanied in order to discover for himself what operational conditions they were likely to encounter. The objective was to gather intelligence, and if they could take any prisoners, so much the better. The Japanese rarely allowed themselves to be captured, preferring to die rather than submit to their enemies.

They travelled down the Arakan coast to Hunter's Bay without incident, indeed Peter described the journey as a pleasure cruise, and landed near the village of Ondaw. The Marines went on to attack a Japanese outpost 2½ miles away, returning unscathed. The withdrawal was not without incident – the surf got up and the Eureka broke down, leaving Peter on the beach with his Brigade Major feeling increasingly idiotic. Eventually they got the landing craft going again, but they had to swim for it. Despite the circumstances not one Marine lost his weapon during the rather chaotic withdrawal. They returned to Teknaf with two civilians who had volunteered to be taken prisoner.

This was very different to warfare in Europe and it was clear that the men would not be on active operations in the short term. Peter could not predict how green troops would perform unless he could get them some battle experience. He recalled his feelings, four years earlier when his own battalion had been sent into the Saarland to discover the realities of war. There was, he thought, much to be gained from doing something similar; accordingly he requested XV Corps to give him a sector of the front line so that he could put his own men there. Late in November, therefore, Nos 1 and 42 Commando moved up to Maungdaw, in the foothills of the Mayu Range, and took over positions lately occupied by 6 Ox and Bucks Light Infantry.

Given the Japanese reluctance to be captured it was not surprising that not one prisoner had been taken, and it fell to the Commando Brigade to break the divisional duck. Peter offered £5 to the first man who took a Japanese prisoner and shortly afterwards 1 Commando produced a captive. Peter found that interrogation was easier than he expected since the Japanese, not expecting to be captured, had not instructed their men what to do in the event that they were. The man refused food on the grounds that if he ate rice his captors would pour water down his throat and jump on his stomach.

In mid-December the new Brigade Commander arrived. Brigadier Campbell Hardy DSO, a Royal Marine, stood high in Peter's estimation; he rated him 'one of the best'. Hardy's arrival invigorated them all, for his style of command was such as to inspire confidence and make the men feel that anything they undertook was certain to succeed.

Early in 1945, XV Corps was part of the final push towards Rangoon which they had to capture before the start of the monsoon in May. Their first objective, the island of Akyab, had been abandoned before they got there. Peter got his feet wet during the landing and sat on the beach to remove his footwear and dry off which was, he thought, a gentlemanly way to conduct war.

Their next objective, the Myebon peninsula, was not so easy. Lack of intelligence made planning impossible beyond allocating troops to landing craft, of which there was a motley assortment. They landed at Agnu at high tide after the beach defences had been largely obliterated by heavy air and sea bombardment. The tide turned while the landings were under way and the water receded at an alarming rate leaving the troops to wade ashore in deep mud, an exhausting process during which they were dangerously exposed. Harry Winch, serving in 1 Commando, reached the shore waist deep in the peculiarly slimy mud of the mangrove swamp and looked up to see a pair of perfectly blancoed gaiters belonging to Peter who had gone ashore on a little causeway at one end of the beach without even getting his feet wet.

The brigade established a beachhead virtually unopposed but as they pushed inland towards Kantha they began to encounter resistance. Three Sherman tanks of the 19th Lancers (Indian Army) were brought ashore on an adjacent beach which gave them an advantage over the Japanese who had no long-range anti-tank weapons. By the end of the day, 13 January, they had occupied Kantha, abandoned by the enemy along with documents and supplies, and were able to celebrate 3 Commando Brigade's first victory, achieved with the loss of four killed and thirty-eight wounded.

The following day Christopher joined Peter, having travelled via Deolali and Teknaf. The two men were delighted to see each other again. Shortly after Christopher arrived he accompanied Peter on an unusual mission. There was continuing difficulty acquiring equipment for the brigade; motorized transport was hard to come by and Peter needed a vehicle of his own, so he struck a deal with Headquarters: he would bring back a Japanese prisoner in return for a jeep. He went about this task with his usual disregard for the rules, disappearing into the jungle with Christopher one evening and reappearing the following morning with a naked and bound Japanese prisoner. He got his jeep.

On 20 January the brigade was briefed on its next operation, the battle for Kangaw, a crucial position for the Japanese as it was a junction in their lines of communication as well as being a small naval base and supply point. 3 Commando Brigade's part in this reflected the increased confidence XV Corps had in Commando operations. The operation was an ambitious one. The 54th Japanese Divison was falling back along the road which ran through Kangaw, pursued by the African Division. The Commando Brigade's task was to cut off the Japanese retreat and kill or capture as many of the trapped Japanese as possible.

While it was encouraging to know that the Corps Commander reposed enough confidence in the Commandos to entrust this task to them, the odds were daunting to a man of more sanguine temperament than Peter. He had considered his chances of survival on less fraught operations in Europe and come to the conclusion that he could only play the hand he was dealt and hope that his luck held; this was to be his severest test yet.

On 21 January, Hardy, accompanied by Peter, embarked on HMS *Narbada* with 1 Commando. It was a crowded ship, but after less than twenty-four hours they transferred into the LCIs and began the run-in. The lead unit was 1 Commando, the most experienced. They advanced unopposed up the Daingbon Chaung, a wide river flanked by dense undergrowth which fortunately did not conceal any Japanese positions. Their objective was a long, narrow ridge known as Hill 170 which lay about a mile and a half inland and would have to be occupied if the force were to have any chance of securing the area. Nor could they entrench in the mangrove swamp which surrounded it. 42 Commando was to secure both sides of the chaung to protect the landing site, 5 Commando was to reinforce 1 Commando and 44 Commando was to advance from the beachhead to Kangaw the following day.

Peter landed with the Headquarters party on the heels of 1 Commando which immediately pushed inland. By nightfall they were in possession of most of Hill 170, at a cost of three killed and nine wounded. To their south lay 5 Commando and Brigade Headquarters. The Royal Marine commandos were still on the swampy ground near the landing site, but during the night 44 Commando captured the hill immediately to the east of Hill 170, towards Kangaw, adding depth and strength to their position. The Japanese did not leave the British in undisputed control of Hill 170, counterattacking during the night, but were beaten off leaving the defenders with one man killed and ten wounded.

The following morning Peter reconnoitred a landing site for brigade reinforcements but came under fire from 75mm guns as he approached it with the recce party. When their own gun jammed they were forced to retreat. During the afternoon he visited 44 Commando and found the men barely dug in. Their position was liberally provided with Japanese trenches which provided good cover but they had been rejected on the grounds that the enemy would know where they were. Peter pointed out that it was better to be protected in a position which the enemy theoretically knew than remain vulnerable due to lack of cover, but 44 Commando, which had limited operational experience, ignored his advice.

Returning to Brigade Headquarters, Peter reported his concerns to Hardy so neither of them were surprised when, later that night, the Japanese opened up a severe bombardment on the position inflicting eighty casualties, a figure Peter thought must be exaggerated until Hardy visited them and found they had sixteen dead and forty-five wounded, thanks to the 75 mm gun which the Japanese had used from only a few hundred yards away. The defenders had held their ground and performed well; there were twenty Japanese dead.

Peter and Christopher spent the morning creating their own shelter on the reverse slope of the hill, which was not, they acknowledged, up to the standard achieved in the Bois de Bavent. Three days later Hardy requisitioned their 'abri', and they were obliged to move further down the hill where Peter built a bigger and better one using a bomb crater, although Christopher recorded that he hurt his back in the process.

Meanwhile, there was a continuous build-up of troops at the landing site. To Peter's surprise the Japanese made no serious challenge and this provided the brigade, and particularly 1 Commando, a welcome respite. 51 Brigade was ashore by now and engaged heavily with the Japanese, and on 24 January they succeeded in cutting the road at Kangaw as planned; the enemy was trapped. For a day or so nothing happened, but on 27 January the Japanese opened up a heavy artillery barrage (or 'stonk'). It caused few casualties, although a direct hit on a trench occupied by three gunners upset even Peter, inured though he was by now to the bloody results of battle.

The following day he was provided with a change of battledress, a great luxury for he had not got out of his clothes since landing a week earlier. He was annoyed when almost at once a piece of shrapnel hit him in the thigh, though it drew only a trickle of blood.

Three days later the Japanese counter-attack began. Assaulted on all sides, the brigade was subjected to wave after wave of ferocious enemy attacks against Hill 170. They began just before dawn and by 0830 hrs the first onslaught had worn itself out. From Hardy's position Peter went up to visit Ken Trevor, commanding 1 Commando. Trevor's position commanded a view of the paddy fields below where Japanese soldiers could clearly be seen. In the lull Peter decided to go out and get a Japanese prisoner, but none would allow themselves to be taken alive.

Abandoning that idea he took Christopher with him to visit the three Sherman tanks which had been in action at the western end of

177

the hill. Only one was still operational. While he was there he found a wounded Japanese whom he succeeded in getting evacuated to the medical station before the battle flared up once more. Four troops of Commandos led the counter-attack, two from 1 Commando and two from 42 Commando. Although strongly opposed they succeeded in securing the flank of 4 Troop's position, ably supported by the remaining tank. In the thick of the fighting, Peter took cover in a slit trench from where he was able to watch and admire Ken Trevor's direction of the battle. Casualties were heavy and the landscape altered visibly as vegetation was shot away due to the intensity of the gunfire.

Much of the action was borne by the twenty-four men of 4 Troop, commanded by Lieutenant George Knowland who had arrived from England with Christopher, newly commissioned. They fought like demons; Knowland was last seen firing a 2-inch mortar at the advancing enemy, resting its base plate against a tree. His first round killed six men. At the end of the action their position was partially overrun and Knowland was dead but their stand ensured that Hill 170 remained in 1 Commando's possession. Knowland was awarded the Victoria Cross for his action.

The heat was so fierce by midday that Peter retreated back to Brigade Headquarters. Christopher produced a tin of pears for lunch and thus fortified they went to find Hardy who was visiting Ken Trevor. At the top of the hill Peter found some men waiting to reinforce 1 Commando. They were in extended order to reduce the risk of casualties and as Peter stood there, under fire but with no Japanese in sight, the man a yard away from him suddenly gave a choking noise and slid to the ground, dead. It was as close a call as he ever experienced.

By late afternoon the ferocity of the attack was beginning to slacken. 5 Commando was anxious to relieve 1 Commando which had been in continuous action. The changeover went smoothly and reports began to come in that the Japanese were retreating northwards. Peter's last act of the day was to visit all six peaks on the ridge to ensure that they were secure. By the time he returned to Brigade Headquarters it was dark and the Brigadier had given orders that there were to be no more counter-attacks.

Unable to sleep Peter went to see Major Robin Stuart, in temporary command of 5 Commando, in the early hours. Stuart believed that the Japanese had no more stomach for the fight but they still retained a foothold at the north end of the hill and he wanted to see them off despite the Brigadier's orders to the contrary. Peter sympathized; they were due to hand Hill 170 over to Indian troops of the 25th Division later that day and neither of them wanted to leave the job unfinished. Peter undertook to square it with Hardy but when Stuart went forward he found the position had been abandoned, leaving so many dead that it was difficult not to tread on the bodies.

Both sides fought the battle for Hill 170 with an intensity Peter had not seen in Europe and 'the murderous onslaught of the Japanese and the almost incredible staunchness of the forty men who had held a battalion at bay' made a deep impression on him. In the aftermath of the battle he examined some of the Japanese bodies, most of which had two or three wounds, any of which would have been fatal. 'They had,' he remarked, 'to be very thoroughly slain.' Casualties for the brigade amounted to 135 dead, while the Japanese lost in the region of 450.

On the evening of 2 February they returned to Myebon. From there Peter and Christopher went by jeep to Akyab, the first leg of their long journey back to India whither the brigade was now bound. From Aykab they hitched a lift as far as Calcutta on a Dakota, Christopher's first trip on an aeroplane.

In Calcutta Peter found a room in a hotel while Christopher was billeted in a nearby boarding house, but they spent most of their time exploring Calcutta in a borrowed jeep. They had some time before the brigade caught up with them, so they drove on to Bangalore, a hill-top town much favoured for its climate. Peter stayed in the Officers' Club while Christopher lived in a tent in the club grounds and ate in the club kitchen. Christopher would happily have stayed on, but by now the brigade was approaching Madras and they rejoined it there.

Life was very relaxed; one day at the races Peter picked five winners out of six which provided a welcome windfall. They moved on to Poona by the eastern coast road, the rest of the brigade travelling by train. At Poona they spent a couple more leisurely days until 20 April, the same date he relinquished his appointment. While Peter boarded a plane to return to England, Christopher returned by sea with all their kit.

179

Chapter Fifteen

The End of the War
and its Aftermath

Peter arrived at Oxshott on Friday, 4 May: 'Suddenly Peter walked in 11-ish – thinner, sunburnt – fine. Heaven. All v. happy,' wrote Pamela. The following day he went up to London. He had received a letter appointing him to command 1 Commando Brigade which would mean his return to the Far East, for these troops were earmarked to fight the Japanese in Malaya. His war was not over yet, as Pamela implied in her entry for 8 May: 'Peace in Europe. "V" Day. Tears of gratitude that AT LAST one war is over and us spared so far.'

The strain of the past months was catching up on him for on 7 May he was suffering from a sore throat and looking, according to Pamela, 'yellowish'. He was well enough to accompany the family to church, St Andrews Oxshott, the following Sunday for a Service of Thanksgiving, and on 18 May the whole family went up to Buckingham Palace to join in the general celebrations.

On 25 May Peter had lunch with Durnford-Slater who had returned from Germany. He was delighted with the way 3 Commando had performed during the last stages of the advance into Germany; the two men had much news to impart.

The following day Peter travelled down to Petworth to attend a party being hosted by General Sturges before leaving the following day for Germany. He toured the country for the best part of two weeks and the letter he sent home made it clear how much he was enjoying himself. It was an instructive trip during which he was able to see for himself the aftermath of the final days of the struggle, a battle that he had wanted to be part of until Sturges had moved him on. His family were concerned to hear reports that there were still

180

pockets of Nazi soldiers who refused to accept that the war was over, however by 11 June Peter was back in England and he spent the night at home with his driver, Samways.

On 15 June he went up to the Beds and Herts depot at Kempston Barracks for the weekend but by 18 June he was in bed with malaria and a temperature of 104°. The family doctor prescribed Metapan, he was soon on his feet again and on 23 June lunched with General Lushington, a cousin of his mother's.

One other piece of good news had greeted him on his return from Burma: on 4 June, while he was away in Germany, Walter Skrine had passed his Medical Board A1 and was therefore able to take up the offer Peter had made him to be his Brigade Major. On 24 June the two men were reunited and departed together from the Young family home in Oxshott in a staff car to take up their new appointments. Brigadier Peter Young was not quite thirty years old.

The Brigade Headquarters was at East Grinstead where Peter's predecessor, Derek Mills-Roberts, had been quartered since his return from Germany. The units making up the brigade were Nos 3, 6, 45 and 46 Commandos, variously stationed in Brighton, Eastbourne, Worthing and Tunbridge Wells. Peter's job was to prepare them for jungle warfare in the Far East.

Christopher had spent his disembarkation leave with his wife and now rejoined Peter to take over the duties of driver and batman. In addition to being promoted to Sergeant, he was awarded a periodic Military Medal, given for service over time rather than for a particular action; approval of the recommendation, submitted by Peter, is dated 17 July 1945.

While they were at East Grinstead, Peter lived at Oxshott and commuted daily, driven by Christopher in either a jeep or a Humber Snipe. On occasion he allowed Christopher to take the car to St Albans for the weekend. They had barely settled into a routine when, at the beginning of August, the atom bombs were dropped in Japan and the war in the Far East came to an end.

As the reality of peace began to sink in, those in uniform joined in the general jubilation. Peter organized the unit's participation in the Victory Parade. His main task was to handle the demobilization of the brigade, but as a career soldier he also wondered what was going to happen to him. An experienced and much-decorated officer with one-star rank on his shoulders he was, in the peacetime hierarchy, a substantive captain. Having survived the war he would have to revert in both rank and regiment, in a peacetime establishment where promotion would be slow. During the final months of 1945 he marked his wartime achievements by having his portrait painted by John Worsley. Wearing battledress and regarding the world with a gimlet eye and a slight smile it encapsulates his presence very well.

On 5 January 1946 he relinquished command of his brigade and for most of the next four months he was posted to 3 Infantry Holding Battalion and attached to the Headquarters of Aldershot and Hampshire District with the rank of Lieutenant Colonel. In late April he went to Dover where he was appointed to command the 2nd Battalion of the Beds and Herts. Three days later he was posted to the Staff College at Camberley. He knew that if he was to resume his career he would have to undertake all the courses necessary for promotion in the peacetime army. He was billeted at Minley Manor and allocated a servant called Searle.

The Staff Course held no fears for him. He spent much of his spare time with his parents and was a regular presence in the West End attending almost all of the shows. The programmes he kept were briefly annotated with his opinion of the production, when he saw it and whom he had escorted. More often than not it was his mother. She had attended the Blenheim and Minden Day parade at Sandhurst on 21 August where she met Major General Cyril Lomax CB CBE DSO MC, who sent Peter a divisional sign because his mother, it transpired, collected them.

Barbara was not well; by the end of the year the diagnosis was confirmed as cancer. On 11 February, Peter's father Dallas wrote to Margaret Gladstone, the wife of his late brother, Horace:

It would be no use going to see Barbara. In fact the Doctor has strongly urged me not to do so. She passed into unconscious sleep last Saturday from which she is unlikely to waken. It may be a matter of days, it may be a matter of hours and I am waiting for the telephone call . . . it is nearly five months since the Doctors told me what was actually the matter with Barbara and we agreed that I alone would know. They said everything had been taken in time and the prospects were good but of course they could not hold out any . . . certainty. Since then I've been through that long period of anxiety, hope and despair as the malady waxed and waned.

182

Barbara died that day. She was fifty-six.

She had been a driving force in the family, intelligent and practical, volunteering as an ARP Warden as part of the war effort. Like many of her generation she understood the internal combustion engine; towards the end of the war, when Peter was at East Grinstead and Christopher was driving him, Olive Christopher visited the End House. As she walked up the driveway she saw a pair of legs sticking out from under the family car; they belonged to Barbara Young.

Peter adored his mother and fragments of surviving correspondence indicate their closeness: he addressed her as 'My Darling Mother'. Two days before Barbara died, Peter left for Singapore on duty, having graduated from the Staff College on 12 November. This meant that he was able to spend time with his mother before her illness became too severe.

If her death knocked Peter back, it can fairly be said to have devastated his father.

Dallas was twelve years older than his wife and he had doted on her. She had been gregarious and outgoing, creating the happy social milieu in which the family had thrived. Peter, still in the Army and with a career to carve out for himself, took solace in continuing to work. Dallas, at sixty-eight, retired and by nature not an outgoing man, was left high and dry. He found it hard to express his emotions, in common with many of his generation, and had relied, however unconsciously, on Barbara to build a warm and loving environment. It died with her and he could not bear even to continue to live in the family home. He went almost immediately to stay with friends before finally, during May that year, returning to live in London.

He began a journal, an exercise which he found cathartic, although it reads somewhat stiffly:

> I came up to . . . try out my philosophy i.e. that memories and associations are only sad if they are suppressed. If they are kept constantly in the front of the mind as time goes on they become a delight. I was a little afraid . . . as to how this philosophy would work but it has worked and is working every day and all day.

Written on 5 May 1947 this first, self-conscious journal entry movingly shows how he tried to convince himself that he would get over his grief and move on. The fact that Peter kept it amongst his own papers demonstrates that he understood the depth of his father's feelings and was able by this act to acknowledge them as he probably never did during Dallas' own lifetime.

183

The change in domestic arrangements meant that Peter was living alone in The End House. From the Holding Battalion he was posted as Officer Commanding the All Arms Methods of Instruction Team. He travelled a fair amount, evaluating course requirements for a post-war army that was still in flux. Given Peter's strength in training it was a good choice, but Methods of Instruction lacked the elements of innovation and extemporization at which he had excelled, and it was classroom based.

When the committee of the Commando Association, on which Peter sat, decided to erect a memorial to fallen comrades, Peter suggested the correct location should be Westminster Abbey. He was assigned the task of opening negotiations with the Dean and Chapter. The memorial was eventually located in the cloisters; Peter was involved in deciding the site and commissioning the sculptor, Gilbert Leeward RA. The statue, for which Leeward had used Commando soldiers as models, was unveiled by Winston Churchill on 21 May 1948 and still stands in the West Cloister.

Peter remained in touch with many of his wartime comrades. Christopher had returned to his original trade of printer and was back living with his parents in St Albans. This was not ideal since his wife was pregnant, and Peter conceived the notion that the two of them could come and live with him – as Christopher put it, to 'look after him'. Christopher was transferred to a London branch of his firm and they moved down to Oxshott late in 1947. It was a happy household; Peter entertained a good deal and the parties were noisy and full of theatricals. If Olive – who Peter always called Popeye – occasionally feared that she was becoming an unpaid housekeeper, Peter took pains to include her in all the junkets that went on, and he was punctilious about helping her with the catering arrangements. He exercised his considerable charm to good effect, drawing Popeye into the close wartime relationship he had necessarily had with her husband, so that although she might occasionally chafe at the memories and experiences that bound the two men so closely she was able to feel included.

After nearly two years with the Methods of Instruction Team, Peter was posted as a Major back to his old regiment, now part of the East Anglian Brigade. The regiment was then in the Middle East, so on 9 July 1948 Peter left to join his unit and spent eleven months based in

Egypt. He was also attending the round of career courses that he would have done had the war not intervened. For eight months, beginning in October 1948, he was at the 1st Infantry Division Battle School, returning to England in June 1949 to become Second-in-Command of 5 Beds and Herts, a TA regiment based at the Depot at Kempston.

Peter's relationship with his father was never close but was superficially cordial. Several letters from Peter to Dallas during the first part of 1950 survive. In one, dated 13 March, he describes how he has been clearing out the loft at The End House and then says: 'It was most thoughtful of you to buy a typewriter . . . I congratulate you on the progress you have made in that difficult art. I notice that your machine occasionally leaves words out.' He adds: 'I hope to spend Easter in Paris, where I have a little business!' He asks his father not to advertise for research work as he had plenty for him; his cast of mind was ideal for such a task and Peter felt that it would take his mind off other, darker, thoughts.

Father and son carried on a lively correspondence, mostly concerning matters of research; both men had an interest in their own family history and genealogy was a frequent subject. Dallas also spent his time in the London libraries researching the history of his son's regiment, research that remains unpublished in Peter's papers at the National Army Museum.

Occasionally Dallas travelled to Kempston, just outside Bedford, to visit Peter in his barracks, but at the end of January he wrote wistfully: '[Pam] is off to Hong Kong . . . on Friday week. The three of us [Peter, Pam and Dallas] dine together. The first meeting of the kind for four or five years . . . Peter leaves for Bedford, saw Pam into the tube.' In February he wrote in his journal of Pam's departure abroad with her husband: 'Sad break in a way . . . Such a tiny crowd left. Peter, Pam and I. Peter seems drifting further.' And then, on 12 April, a bombshell: 'A letter from Peter that he contemplates matrimony. No name given but an introduction promised.'

Dallas had no inkling that this was coming, which in the circumstances was understandable. Earlier that year Peter had been included in an invitation to a cocktail party at Melton Court by a friend of his, an American colonel known always as 'Harp'. Among the guests was the hostess's niece, Joan Rathbone, to whom Peter was duly introduced. It was a lively party with games being played, including sardines. At some point during the evening Peter found

185

himself standing behind the sofa on which Joan was seated. 'Never,' he told her, 'take anything I say after six o'clock seriously. But will you marry me?' Her answer is not recorded, but it is clear from subsequent events that they fell violently in love with each other.

Joan was a very pretty woman, with dark eyes and hair, and a most mellifluous contralto speaking voice – indeed, one of the striking things about both Peter and Joan was the quality of their voices for Peter's baritone, too, was very musical. Born Joan Duckworth, she had been raised by her aunt, Winifred Duckworth, in Colwyn Bay, her mother having more or less abandoned her when she was very young and subsequently married Sir George Lacon. Joan trained as a radiologist in Liverpool where she lodged with cousins called Melly – George Melly's mother was her landlady – and in 1939 she married Bertram Rathbone. The following year her daughter, Marilyn, was born, however the marriage failed shortly afterwards. They divorced amicably as soon as they could and Rathbone remarried. The household Peter was introduced to consisted of Joan and Marilyn – always known in the family as Matilda – and Aunt Winifred at whose fateful party they met.

Dallas did not take the news well as his waspish diary entry on 28 April reveals:

> I had a letter from Peter explaining who the lady he intends to marry is: she is Joan Rathbone née Duckworth. She seems to have divorced her husband some two years since and has a little girl aged 9. She herself is about a year younger than Peter. Her mother . . . divorced her husband and married a Colonel Sir George Lacon Bart who has died quite recently . . . Divorce seems to be rather the rule these days than the exception. I notice . . . in the wedding announcements that the mother of one or the other of the bridle (sic) couple has a different name from the father. I take it divorce no longer carries with it the stigma it did in the old days.

He continued to feel antagonistic throughout the couple's swift courtship, the engagement being announced in *The Times* in May 1950. Dallas continued to visit Kempston Barracks but his pride was tempered with a possessive attitude towards Peter. On 17 June 1950 he wrote: 'Left St Pancras for Bedford . . . Peter somewhat remote and occupied but the egregious Colonel Harpur (sic) je n'aime pas.'

His entry for 23 June, Peter's wedding, could be described as curmudgeonly. Curiously it is the only record available since there are no photographs. 'Pouring wet morning . . . After the Registry ceremony they asked her [Juliet Durley] to join the party for lunch at the Hyde Park Hotel. She and Walter [Skrine] saved the somewhat strained atmosphere . . . We met [Juliet at the Albert Hall] at 6:15 and walked across Kensington Gardens to the cocktail party at Westbourne Terrace [Lady Lacon's home].'

Thus, in typically unconventional style, Peter renounced his bachelorhood shortly before his thirty-fifth birthday. The lack of any previous serious relationships, a situation at least partly explained by the war and his prolonged absences, has also been attributed to his close relationship with his mother. Her death in some way released him emotionally to get on with his life. She would have been unlikely to countenance his marriage to a divorcee – indeed, any woman trying to compete with that neat, practical and accomplished matriarch would have had her work cut out for her.

The newlyweds moved into a quarter in Ampthill, a flat in Dynevor House, a Queen Anne building which was their first home together. Peter decided finally to sell The End House since Dallas showed no inclination to move back there, and put the contents of the house, which Dallas had made over to him, into storage; they were all lost a year or so later when the repository caught fire.

Marilyn, who lived with them during the school holidays, remembered a man whose girth was increasing, but who nonetheless possessed a surprising turn of speed. Early on, during one school leave out, Peter and Joan took her out to lunch. Afterwards they all went for a walk round the cricket pitch on the village green and Peter challenged Marilyn to a race which she thought she would easily win. Despite his bulk, she discovered he was still a very fast runner, and competitive with it.

As a legacy of the supreme fitness he had enjoyed during the war he was, in fact, very light on his feet, and one of his party tricks was to do an impression, with extraordinary grace, of the dying swan. It always brought the house down.

Dallas, meanwhile, continued to struggle with the idea of Peter's marriage. He clearly felt, from letters he wrote and his diary entries of the time, that he was being excluded. In November he attended the Armistice Day parade at Kempston Barracks and wrote:

187

Arrived . . . and found Peter grinning from ear to ear in front of the Barracks very busy and apparently on top of the world in anticipation of the arrival of Queen Elizabeth [the Queen Mother] to lunch, as Colonel of the 16th Foot . . . After that he seemed to disappear . . . After the ceremony she spent fully an hour inspecting the troops on the Barrack Square. Peter appeared once again during the final inspection and then disappeared . . . without a word.

This did not accord with his ideas of filial duty.

In December 1950 he received a letter from a cousin, clearly in response to one he had written complaining about Peter's attitude. This clear-sighted exposition throws light not only on Peter's relationship with his father, but on the pressures they faced in the early days of their marriage. The unknown writer, a serving Major, was at the time on the War Office Selection Board, choosing candidates for National Service Commissions:

I wrote to Peter the other day, the first since before his wedding, almost. He has been much taken up with settling his life and re-orienting himself . . .

But the point of all this, is my attempt to draw an analogy between Peter's present attitude towards Father and friends. Would you not agree that his interests are temporarily divided and that it is inevitable? Also that Joan must be expected to display some possessiveness, when you consider the great reputation which Peter has made and her own matrimonial and family troubles. She wants him for herself for a while at least. I do feel that the past has been a nightmare to her which will take years to overcome and her only refuge is Peter, who is above all that.

Joan had a good deal of reserve in her manner borne of a natural shyness, but due also to the difficulties she had had to overcome. She was thirty-four when she married Peter and neither her affection nor her devotion ever wavered towards him. His sudden appearance in her life must have seemed like unimaginable good fortune, and in return for the support and stability he gave her she gave unstinting loyalty through thick and thin (knight in shining armour or not, there were times when he would try the patience of a saint).

In between times, father and son met in London, either at the

British Museum or at the In and Out Club, occasions during which Dallas was able to have Peter all to himself. Peter, aware of his father's attitude, tried to ensure that sensitive topics of conversation were avoided. The two had plenty of other things to discuss, including research which Peter was now beginning seriously to undertake.

While they both did their share of genealogical digging, Dallas concentrated on the 16th Foot and the Beds and Herts, while Peter began to devote himself more and more to the Civil War, an interest he had begun while up at Oxford but which had lapsed during the war. His card index of Civil War soldiers shows that he went systematically through the Calendar of State Papers Domestic (CSPD), extracting every reference to men who had fought on the Royalist side. This was a huge undertaking and accounted for his frequent meetings with his father at the British Museum where the CSPD were kept in the great rotunda. His capacity for acquiring information was immense; he had a vast library of publications, made endless notes, wrote copious letters eliciting the answers to questions, and by the end of his life he did not have room to house it all. Although much of this research remains unpublished, the raw material is there.

None of this stopped Dallas writing, on 21 February 1951: 'Peter and Joan are I gather so rapt [sic] up in one another that they have no time for anybody else.'

Peter's next posting was GSO2 Inf[antry]Training, a Major's staff job which entailed his return to Egypt and MELF. The Army was doing its best to extract from him the fruits of his successful wartime career and Peter was beginning to chafe at the restrictions which peacetime soldiering entailed.

On 9 November that year he landed in Fayid, in the Canal Zone. He did not, he made it immediately clear, relish the idea of being in a desk-bound staff job, even if they were in the Middle East, and he spent as much time as he could organizing exercises which would require his presence in the field. One of these, Exercise Dry Fly, was a re-enactment of one of the North African campaign battles for which former German officers were flown in to give their view of the battle as it had unfolded – a brilliant learning exercise for which such opportunities rarely exist.

His staff soon became accustomed to the sight of Peter's impressive figure, other more senior officers seeming to pale beside the ebullient figure who exuded confidence and energy. They also rapidly came to know that when Peter was bored sitting at a desk he would gather them together and organize a spontaneous exercise around the Nissen huts where they worked, lobbing make-believe grenades whenever the 'going' got tough. This delight in carrying out manoeuvres never left him – he was still teaching fire and movement in his back garden to anyone who professed an interest twenty-five years later.

As he was unaccompanied much of his spare time was taken up writing and studying. He had brought a huge number of reference books and was continuing to build on the studies he had begun in London with his father, and particularly to work on what he hoped would eventually be the Royalist Army List. He was also pursuing an interest in miniatures, possibly of his own family, and contributed at least one article to a periodical dealing with fine art.

For light relief he took part in the lively amateur dramatics and operatics which were a feature of life in Fayid. As well as exercising his vocal chords in *HMS Pinafore*, in August 1952 he took the part of Lord Augustus Lorton in a production of *Lady Windermere's Fan* for which he had to shave off his moustache, causing much mirth in the office.

It was not enough. He felt isolated and disenchanted. Then, on one of the signals exercises, code-named Hatta, which took place in Jordan in co-operation with the Arab Legion, he encountered two colleagues from the Beds and Herts, Pincher Martin and Morris Brightman, both seconded to the Legion and enjoying themselves enormously. Martin invited Peter to stay and by the end of his visit he was determined, if possible, to get a secondment himself. But this was easier said than done – the Arab Legion was a sovereign organization and opportunities to command were rare and coveted. Of the sixty British officers then serving in the Legion, most offered technical expertise from the service arms, and very few were infantrymen. Peter wanted to command a regiment – the equivalent to a British battalion – for which the competition was still fiercer. Nothing daunted, he wrote to General Cooke, commander of 1st Division, asking to be seconded; one of the four infantry commanders was due to leave in six months' time.

In the meantime Peter was so dispirited by the way his peacetime career was progressing that he decided to leave the Army and on a visit to England began the process of resigning his commission. His papers were intercepted before they reached the War Office and returned to him at Fayid where he was, he thought, awaiting the arrival of his relief. He was informed that he would not be released. Fortunately, hard on the heels of this news was the arrival of the approval of his secondment.

He was going to command once more.

Chapter Sixteen

Jordan 1953–6 – Jerusalem

Despite the vagaries of his peacetime service Peter's military ambitions remained unchanged. Service in the Arab Legion, then commanded by Glubb Pasha (Sir John Bagot Glubb), seemed to be a perfect route upwards.

The creation of Israel by UN mandate in 1948 had created more problems in an area not known as peaceful. The Arab nations, remembering when the British had administered the Palestine Mandate in the 1920s, were generally hostile to the British and felt that their support for the creation of Israel exacerbated the situation. However, as Glubb pointed out: 'Most of the British officers of the Arab Legion were extremely devoted to their troops, completely loyal to their duty to Jordan and intensely proud of the high military standards attained. A few of us had devoted our lives to the service of the Arabs and had been bitterly opposed to British policy in Palestine.'

As soon as Peter's appointment was confirmed he wrote to the present incumbent asking a host of questions. James Watson, clearly a man after Peter's own heart, wrote back: 'Naturally I have to tell you that you are taking over the best Regiment in the Legion – the 9th. I founded it three years ago.'

The Commanding Officer of the regiment was the only Briton on its strength so Peter set about learning Arabic; although his English accent made him hard to decipher he understood enough to glean much from listening to his Arab soldiers. Mastering the psychology of people from a culture at such variance with his own was a

192

challenge, but he knew soldiers and getting the best out of these men was for him simply a case of working out what would motivate them.

On 19 March he arrived at Mafraq to take up his appointment. He wrote to his father on 19 April 1953:

We have a good house, built in the days of the Transjordan Frontier Force, and have taken over most of Watson's staff, including his deeply religious Bedouin batman [Haji Ibrahim], ... Hassan, the good plain cook, is a Soudanese. Salim Matar [a Syrian] ... drives the landrover. There is also a Saloon Car, driven by Awad Ahmed (a Jordanian?). He has been away on a journey to Aqaba with Watson so I haven't seen much of him yet.

He did not mention the Alsatian, Tigla, which Peter took on the basis that he would be there long enough to give her a settled home. She was the first of several Alsatians which the Youngs were to own.

He and Joan moved into the 'good house', an adobe quarter in Zerqa, less than 20 miles north of Amman, which he described as the Aldershot of the Arab Legion, and Peter set about familiarizing himself with the region and the situation. He was enchanted by the fact that he was now in the midst of biblical lands in the most literal sense and constantly identified the places he visited by their ancient names. He was serving a Muslim country, facing the new Jewish state on lands which were also deeply associated with the origins of Christianity. If he was not identifying biblical locations, he was visiting crusader castles built by Knights Templar. It was heady stuff and the historian in him was enthusiastically engaged.

The four-day tour of the country which every arriving British officer underwent began on the West Bank at Jeeb and encompassed Kufr Itsion, north of Jerusalem, Ramallah (the Brigade Head-quarters), the Templar fortress of Le Toron des Chevaliers, built in the twelfth century and now garrisoned by the Bedouin of the 1st Regiment, and Qalqilya.

From there Peter went to Amman to meet the Chief of the General Staff, Glubb Pasha himself. Glubb's reputation was legendary. He was much more than just a soldier and Peter was impressed by what he saw, acknowledging that he was a leader from whom he could learn a great deal. Glubb's style was, he thought, understated and more powerful for it. Like Dempsey he never raised his voice, having a benevolent air so that he asked questions without seeming to be inquisitorial. Peter wrote of him: 'He was really many different people . . . for he was engineer officer, arabist, policeman, tribal judge, author, minister, and general, not one after the other, but simultaneously.'

The 9th Regiment was encamped at Khaw, close to Zerqa. Peter took command on 10 April and at once began to assess the existing personnel and to make such alterations as suited his style of command. He concluded quickly that the majority of his soldiers were an excellent bunch and concentrated his efforts on improving the officer cadre. He wrote to his father:

> I have now been here one month and I am enjoying myself very much, but there is plenty of work to do, not that I mind that.
>
> The battalion, we call them regiments here, was formed in 1950 by my predecessor, A J A Watson of the Queens . . . The men are Bedouin except for some specialists, the signallers, the interpreter, the gardener etc. The men are mostly completely illiterate when they join the army. They come from all over the place – Syria, Iraq, the Hejaz, Saudi Arabia and so on. They disregard the political frontiers completely!
>
> . . . It is very interesting to go into the desert and talk to the Bedouin. They are very hospitable people and talking to them improves one's Arabic. I really know quite a lot now!

He was fascinated by the Bedouin, comparing them favourably to the men he had commanded during the war. 'The best of the Bedouin would make very good Commandos for they are individualists, but at the same time smart and well behaved.'

He took his colloquial Arabic test faster than his teacher, Ahmed Qasim, thought wise. He feared that Peter would fail and that as a result they would both lose face. Peter, however, was determined to acquire the extra two shillings a day language pay which he would get once he passed. He therefore rehearsed a speech to answer the obvious question he thought he would be asked: how is it that you are able to take this exam so soon after your arrival? When, inevitably, the question was asked he merely performed his speech.

The young King, Hussein, arrived by air at Merka on 6 April and was welcomed by a guard of honour provided by 9th Regiment. After the ceremonials were over there was a reception in one of the hangars where Peter was presented to the King by Glubb Pasha. At the parade held on 3 May to celebrate the King's formal accession a contingent of 348 officers and men from 9th Regiment represented Peter's new command. They performed the march past in excellent style, but Peter was almost more impressed by the trot past of two troops of the Desert Patrol: 'the Bedouin with their red sashes and their flowing white sleeves adding a touch of barbaric splendour. No words of mine can describe the disdainful expression on the senior camel's face!'

After Ramadan, he travelled to Aqaba in mid-June to collect his car, which was due to arrive by ship from England. After a journey of twenty-four hours he arrived to find that the ship had not yet docked so he took the opportunity of visiting the ruins at Petra on horseback. 'Nothing in Petra,' he wrote, 'is as impressive as its entrance through a gorge, at no point wider than six yards. We rode through the shadowy ravine, a high cleft where a score of resolute men could hold an army at bay, until suddenly the most perfect of all the tombs, the Khazneh, stood before us, rose-coloured in the morning sunshine.' After a day spent exploring the area they returned to Aqaba to collect the car.

Once Ramadan and the Festival of Eid were over, the regiment got down to some serious training. Peter concentrated on night attacks, observing that the biblical Midianites, trounced in darkness by Gideon, were none other than the Bedouin. 'The Midianites,' he wrote, 'were worse than useless at night without discipline and training, and I now found myself in command of a Midianite regiment!'

He shortly found himself organizing a demonstration night attack for the edification and entertainment of two monarchs, King Hussein and his visiting cousin, King Feisal of Iraq. It took place in a valley just east of Zerqa and closely resembled a manoeuvre described in detail in a booklet entitled *The Infantry Battalion in Battle*. In the opinion of John Harrison, a former officer from his own regiment, 'so long as you've got this little book, you can play the battalion like a piano.' It was a great success.

Every so often an event occurred well outside Peter's previous experience. When the regimental Education Corporal, Khalil Moussa, murdered his sister as an honour killing, Peter discovered to his astonishment that there were already several murderers in the ranks. 'Arabs,' he noted, 'do not look upon murders of this sort as a crime, and I daresay that Ahmed Qasim tactfully failed to tell Khalil that I expected him to be hanged.'

195

In late August 9th Regiment took over guard duties from 3rd Regiment and were deployed all over the country. Few men remained at Khaw which meant that Peter spent most of his time on the road inspecting detached units. Once they had settled down into a routine he went on leave to Cyprus with Joan, leaving on 15 September and returning on 6 October. The family visited Cyprus several times while they were in Jordan and Peter took many photographs, mostly slides, of their travels; in the early 1950s the unspoilt scenery was stunning and the ruins largely unadorned by tourists.

He had now been with the regiment for six months and felt that it was time to 'reshuffle the pack'. The most significant change was to make Saoud Rashdan his Adjutant. Immediately afterwards the uneasy international situation began to boil over. On the night of 14/15 October the Israelis crossed the border with a battalion-sized force to attack the Palestinian village of Qibya, killing fifty-two people and retiring unopposed. Peter was umpiring an exercise in the desert when the attack took place, his own regiment being still on guard duties. The incursion was considered so serious that most of the Legion was sent over to the West Bank, leaving 9th Regiment to guard everywhere else. With no Divisional Headquarters to intervene, Peter reported directly to the Chief of Staff at Qiada [Headquarters], Colonel Jim Hutton.

At the same time trouble was brewing in Amman itself. On 20 October Peter was summoned to a conference at Qiada and he was given command of such troops as remained in Amman, as well as his own regiment. The former, including the staff and students at the ALTC, he deployed to guard vulnerable buildings so as to leave his own men as a quick reaction force. The King was due to arrive in the country at any time and ensuring his safety during the journey from Ramthe on the Syrian border to Amman was vital.

Early on 21 October the King returned safely to his capital and Peter based himself at the Police Headquarters building to await events. During the day there were two anti-British demonstrations – the population felt that the British officers had restrained the soldiers from being firm enough with the insurgent Israelis. Peter's men confronted the most persistent demonstrators with bayonets fixed and shemaghs over their faces. Although a few stones were thrown, no shots were fired and in the end the crowd became bored by the stand-off and dispersed. By late afternoon the trouble was over. There had been thirty-three arrests. The incident became known as the Qibya Riots and served to emphasize to Peter the precarious position the British were in – during the demonstrations he had heard isolated cries of 'Death to Glubb Pasha!'

In the lull following the riots 9th Regiment remained virtually alone, while the rest of the Legion stabilized the situation on the West Bank. Peter took the opportunity to call in all the favours he had in the Quartermaster's department to make up unit deficiencies in weapons and vehicles.

A small-arms expert ran courses on firing pistols and Sten guns, and Peter ensured that men from each company became qualified instructors. In the process he also learned his own firing technique was not all he had imagined. By the end, the straight-armed duellist had acquired the battle crouch, a very different style: 'We were taught to shoot from the hip, and were amazed to find that by pointing the barrel as if it was one's right forefinger you really could put a couple of bullets in the target's stomach.'

Christmas was enlivened by the presence of Walter Skrine. Peter took him to visit the fortress in the Druze village of Azrak which had been Lawrence's headquarters in 1917–18. On the way home they encountered a fox which his driver Juma'a, fired by an earlier conversation about foxhunting in England, decided to pursue across country. The only occupant of the Land Rover who enjoyed this diversion was Tigla who watched the fox's progress with great interest, standing on the back seat with her nose on Peter's right shoulder. Eventually, it became too much for her and she bounded out of the vehicle to take up the pursuit for herself.

The regiment moved to Jerusalem in February 1954. They relieved 4th Regiment who made them very welcome, providing a royal feast at the end of the handover period. Peter also found himself in temporary command of the brigade when Arthur Green, the Brigadier, was recalled to England on compassionate leave the afternoon Peter arrived in Jerusalem. He viewed the change positively: life in Zerqa had been that of a typical garrison regiment 'not,' he noted, 'to be compared with the active life that a regiment leads in the border zone, with the chance of an incident ever present'.

He was operating in a region full of religious significance, posting his men on the towers built by King Herod and the massive walls thrown up by Suleiman the Magnificent. Indeed, he was living on the reverse of the slopes where Saladin had drawn up his army to attack Jerusalem in 1187.

He began to ensure that the defensive positions he had inherited

197

were sound and practicable, and where required, his men also constructed their own field works. Peter's war experience was helpful – he had frequently built his own and had seen how the Germans had built theirs, particularly in Normandy. The area of operations he controlled was slightly different from his predecessors and he had to requisition sites to create a strong defensive line. Glubb Pasha visited regularly, supporting Peter and helping where necessary to acquire such sites. Many of the buildings they occupied had two storeys, the top one of which he converted into a barrack room where the men could live, leaving the lower storey as the defensive position which could easily be reached in case of an alarm. Peter enjoyed overseeing the construction work and visited the sites as often as possible during the months they spent working on the defences.

The regiment settled into a routine of guard duty enlivened by regular visits from officers who were passing through, but who did not want to leave without a visit to the Holy City. Peter's tour began with a visit to the village of Et Tur on the Mount of Olives where a panoramic view of the city of Jerusalem unfolded from the top of the mosque. He lyrically described the magnificent panorama:

> Far away to the West we could see Nebi Samwil, the place from which Coeur de Lion had his only glimpse of the Holy City and the key to Jerusalem in the 1917 fighting. Then the Sheikh Jerrah suburb to the North of the Wadi Joz; St George's Cathedral, with its tower like an English country church, standing just inside Jordan, and the Italian Hospital whose narrow tower now forms an Israeli observation post; the Nôtre Dame with the great breach battered in its East wall by the guns of the Arab Legion, and nearer the earthquake-proof Museum, founded by one of the Rockefellers. The Old City with the Dome of the Rock standing alone and beautiful in the great enclosure of the Haram es Sharif, its delicate mosaics still scarred by Israeli mortar bombs; then the Mosque el Aqsa, the Far Mosque. It was in the doorway of this building that King Abdulla was murdered in 1951. In the midst of the City the white pointed tower of the Lutheran church stands up, with the two domes, one white and one black, of the Church of the Holy Sepulchre a little to its right. The great square yellowish towers of the Citadel, easily seen in the morning light, and beyond the tall plain rather ugly tower of the YMCA over in the Western suburbs where the

Israelis have made their capital. The South wall of the Old City zigzags down from Mount Zion towards the Far Mosque and over against it is the Church of the Dormition with its Israeli garrison. To the South on the tree-crowded summit of Deir Abu Tor is another Israeli post; while far away behind on the far horizon stands Government House, now neutral and the head-quarters of the United Nations Observers, and a little nearer, beside the Brook Kedron, Silwan village, the ancient Siloam, stands on the steep hillside, a natural fortress.

Turning around and looking Eastwards into the sun, far below we could see the Dead Sea, blue and hazy in the heat. In the foreground are Bethany and Abu Dis. The mosque, which affords such a perfect view, stands at the place of the Ascension.

The military visitors were then taken down into the city to examine the situation on the ground. Occasionally Peter's zealous Intelligence Officer, Naib Majid Ibrahim, would arrest a bewildered pilgrim, often on grounds that only he could understand. Peter's task was to soothe ruffled feathers and send the poor penitents on their way.

The Israelis constantly mounted small incursions. The Legion's rules of engagement were not to fire unless fired upon, so the Israelis tried to tempt their opponents into breaking this rule by, for instance, throwing stones at them. Whenever there was a disturbance Peter would get to the scene of the action as quickly as possible. It was diffi-cult work for soldiers who are by temperament excitable and it says much for Peter's control over them that they kept their trigger fingers still.

While Green was away there was a serious incursion at Wadi Foukine, when the Israelis crossed the frontier and were fired upon as they advanced towards the village; three were killed. Although Peter suspected that the Israelis were trying to tempt their opponents into action, he agreed to allow them to visit the Legion side of the line to carry out their own investigations. When they withdrew the request five minutes later he wondered whether the Israelis had made the demand in the hope that it would be refused. They could then have complained to the Mixed Armistice Commission (MAC), made up of UN observers and headed by Commander Hutchison USN.

Wadi Foukine was the precursor to a concerted attack which took place at the end of June. On 30 June Peter spent the day in a landing craft on the Dead Sea and arrived home in the evening looking forward to a bath. Hearing the telephone ring he answered it to find that the caller was the first in a series from posts along his front line. They were all simultaneously finding themselves under heavy fire. Peter gave them all the same orders: 'Do not return fire unless I say so.'

While he prepared to visit Brigade Headquarters he contacted 9th Regiment Headquarters and told Saoud Rashdan, his Second-in-Command, to get down to the Citadel and determine what was going on. Remembering that Colonel Jim Hutton was spending the night close by at Nablus he rang him and asked for clarification on the rules of engagement. He pointed out that the firing that had broken out simultaneously all along the front could only have happened by prior agreement on the Israeli side. Under those circumstances, he was told, they could fire 'bren for bren, round for round, and mortar bomb for mortar bomb, but on no account . . . more than the enemy did'.

Juma'a drove him into Jerusalem. It was mid-evening and some shops were still open in spite of the firing. Peter got out of the car and walked through the streets to show his presence and reassure people. He was well known by now and was greeted with relief: 'The Qaid of Kateba Tis'a [The Colonel of 9 Regiment].'

At the Damascus Gate the firing from the Israeli side was intense – even to Peter – but he instructed his men not to return fire and they stood firm, although at each post the firing grew louder. At about 2000 hrs he visited one of his platoon headquarters to phone Glubb Pasha who related the ensuing exchange thus:

'Can you hear me sir?' said a distant small voice. 'I'm speaking from the walls of the Old City, over the Damascus Gate. There's rather a lot of shooting. I have pretty well succeeded in stopping our chaps shooting, but the Jews are giving us all they've got. Can you hear me?'

I could not only hear him, but I could hear high explosive bursts too. 'Can we shoot back, sir?' went on the thin, small voice. 'Troops are getting annoyed. Can you hear me?'

'You know orders,' I said. 'Shoot back on a less scale than the enemy, but enough to keep up morale. Use the same calibre and weapons they are using. Is there any sign of movement? Any chance they are going to attack?'

'I don't think so,' replied he. 'Haven't seen any signs of an attack. They seem to want to get rid of their surplus ammo.'

Peter Young had been in the commandos in the war . . . and had commanded a brigade. He liked battles and sounded jovial – if not facetious.

200

A ceasefire was negotiated. It should have begun at 2100 hrs but the Israelis did not finally fall silent until 0030. The Legion had stopped well before the initial time fixed because Peter had concluded that it was a waste of ammunition. When he got home some time in the early hours Joan told him that the firing had been so loud that she thought the Israelis had attacked Et Tur, just over the hill from their quarter.

The night passed quietly, but with an alacrity that seemed suspicious to everybody on the Jordanian side the Israelis made known their view of events, claiming that the Arab Legion had opened fire on the Israelis in Jerusalem, 'a deliberate attack, without the slightest provocation, obviously planned and centrally directed,' as *The Times* reported. This was, however, the only version of events which was reported in the international media.

Glubb Pasha was not fooled. He noted:

Peter Young, commanding the battalion in the line, was in his bath when the shooting commenced . . . As the firing was said to have begun simultaneously in many places, the only assumption, if the Arab Legion did begin it, was that the 9th Regiment was mutinous, and had arranged a battle unknown to its commander. Anyone who knew the Arab Legion in those days – and especially the 9th Regiment – realised that such an idea was ridiculous.

Peter was summoned to report to the Minister of Defence, Anwar Nuseibeh. The minister, Cambridge educated and with a thorough grasp of the military realities, was a sympathetic listener. Peter's decisive actions and the troops' behaviour were wholly endorsed. 'An eye for an eye, and a tooth for a tooth,' he told Peter, with which sentiment he heartily concurred.

As he left the meeting there was a long burst of machine-gun fire, followed by a volley of small-arms fire. It was late morning and the markets were all open. The firing came from an Israeli position overlooking the Damascus Gate and Peter gave orders that the Vickers gun positioned in one of the towers of the Damascus Gate should return fire. Another ceasefire was negotiated. Peter's cook, Ali Muhamad Ali, was caught in the incident and arrived home grey with fear having witnessed all from his vantage point beneath a bus.

By 1730 hrs it appeared that the firing had stopped and Peter decided to visit his outpost on Deir Abu Tor. Juma'a drove him and

201

Peter recalled the journey seemed to take a long time: 'The Humber seemed the size of a haycart and about as fast. Nobody fired, and with a mixture of disappointment and relief we reached the cover of the houses.'

He found his troops in good heart, despite one casualty. He explained that there was now a ceasefire in force and then walked up towards the headquarters. As soon as they were seen on the street they heard shots, fired from above them and to their left. The only casualty was a young girl whom Juma'a recovered from the road by the Humber. Peter continued his approach to the headquarters, ensuring that he kept a house between himself and the enemy sniper. He immediately contacted Divisional HQ to report the breach of the ceasefire. As he was speaking he heard more shots being fired, this time at an old man who was hit in the foot. This incident Peter also reported.

A little later they heard firing coming from the direction of the Musrara quarter in Jerusalem, and then mortar bombs started falling on the Mount of Olives; the ceasefire was in serious jeopardy. Conscious of what had happened the previous evening, Peter rang Joan to find out if all was well. When he told her that mortars were landing on the Mount of Olives she retorted, 'Like hell they are, they are coming right over!' He could hear the servants panicking in the background.

As soon as darkness fell they returned to Jerusalem where the Old City was being mortared. Tempted though he was to respond in kind he resisted because he feared that all the casualties would be civilian.

The following morning, 2 July, the Jerusalem Post reported that the Israelis had suffered several casualties following the start of the ceasefire the previous evening, four of them at Deir Abu Tor at the time when Peter had been present. Determined to ensure that his men could not be accused of initiating any firefights, Peter gave orders that no weapon was to be loaded and he inspected troops on the walls to ensure that his orders were obeyed. When, therefore, firing broke out from the direction of the Nôtre Dame he knew that his men were not involved in the altercation.

By 3 July the activity was largely political, but Peter received information which led him to suspect that the Israelis were reinforcing their positions more than necessary for the operation that was taking place. He wondered whether the firefight which had broken out on 30 June was merely the prelude to something much bigger, and if so what he could do about it.

Later that day, he confided what he knew to the British Consul General who suggested they ask the Civil Governor on the Israeli side whether there was any truth to the story. The suggestion that the Israelis were planning any kind of incursion was vigorously denied. Peter thought that asking the enemy outright what their intentions were was an interesting concept.

The Jerusalem Incident was now over. The regiment had behaved well and leaving Saoud Rashdan in charge had enabled him to deal with the other tasks for which, as acting Brigadier, he was responsible. He relished the role he played during those fraught days, though he felt that time spent attending high-level meetings, liaising with other services, briefing politicians or talking to the press was time which would be better spent with his men at the sharp end. Unusually, as commander of both the regiment and the brigade, much of the conduct of the operation had been under his control.

Reflecting on the aftermath in *Bedouin Command* he wrote wryly:

The United Nations Organisation . . . produced a long report, containing no account by either commander. If you were going to write up the battle of Waterloo I presume your first step would be to see what Wellington and Napoleon had to say on the subject! Most of the statements were from casualties on either side; the one person who never knows what has happened in a battle is someone who was hit!

Once when someone was asking me questions about the Jerusalem incident he said: 'Who stopped it?' and I replied half in jest and without pausing to think: 'I did,' which, up to a point, I suppose, is true.

Chapter Seventeen

Arabian Nightmare

During 1954 an Ensign from the Scots Guards, John Adair, was doing his National Service in the Canal Zone. Visiting the Legion – as Peter had done before him – he expressed a wish to be seconded to the 9th Regiment. Peter made the necessary arrangements and in August the young man arrived to join the regiment in Jerusalem.

Adair was an immediate success with his Arab colleagues, who being unable to pronounce his name, dubbed him 'Sweillim', 'friend' in Arabic. The name stuck – Peter and Joan called him Sweillim for the rest of their lives. From a regimental point of view Peter found him invaluable for he ran NCO refresher courses, undertook the athletics training and took weapon training in hand. Under his guidance the regiment won the coveted Lash Cup in 1954.

On a personal level the two men struck up a friendship which was to have momentous consequences for them both. Their mutual passion was the English Civil War, although they took opposite sides – Adair as convinced a Parliamentarian as Peter was a Royalist. Peter lent Adair books from his own library and they discussed in detail the prevailing theories of seventeenth-century military operations.

Adair arrived with the regiment in August and stayed until December, spending much of his off-duty time with the Youngs. When Peter and Joan went to Cyprus on leave, Adair held the fort and kept Peter informed about any developments, but he left before the regiment returned to Zerqa for Christmas.

Returning to their old routine, Peter drilled the men every day. They were visited and inspected by various senior officers; when General Sir Gerald Templer had completed his inspection he asked Peter to convey to the men that in time of war he would rather have them on his side than against him.

At weekends he and Joan would visit some of the magnificent places which lay close by: the castle at Ajlun, Qala't-er-Rabad – built by one of Saladin's amirs in 1184 – the ruined Byzantine city of Um el Jemal or, their favourite, the ruined Roman city of Jerash (Gerasa), one of the cities of the Decapolis. They also bought rugs, a pastime which they both loved, for it combined the rituals of Arab hospitality with the convoluted and ancient skill of bargaining.

For six months the regiment was based at Zerqa, then in June 1955 its turn came round once more for Palace guard duty. As usual, Brigadier Green went home on leave in June and July, leaving Peter in command. He organized a series of demonstrations for the King to show how the Arab Legion could defend the frontier along the West Bank between Jordan and Israel. The initial display showed how a battalion could be deployed defensively and what sort of frontage it might reasonably be expected to defend. Peter gave the commentary for this demonstration, following which the whole party adjourned to the Mess of the Divisional Signals for lunch.

In the afternoon they toured the West Bank to show the King the 400-mile front they had to defend with the troops at their disposal. Peter explained to the King how the Northern Sector was laid out. He found Hussein polite and pleasant, but noted with some misgiving that he seldom asked questions. After they had retired to a makeshift mess it became clear that the only military subject which really animated the King was discussion about the Air Force. He returned home convinced – correctly as it transpired – that they had failed to convince the King of the merits of the defensive plan they had devised.

During the summer he took Joan on a trip south which he had long promised himself: a visit to the castle at Kerak which lies on the road to Aqaba. This spectacular fortress was built by Baldwin II in the twelfth century and variously occupied and besieged by crusader armies during its heyday. To photograph its southern aspect they had to negotiate a narrow track which was no more than a donkey path running along the edge of a precipice. They could not turn back once they had set out and having reached the South Moat – where they took pictures with shaking hands – they had to turn around and retrace their steps.

At the end of October the President of Turkey, General Bayar, paid a state visit to Jordan. Bad feeling lingered against the Turks who had ruled the area prior to 1918, and when Peter organized anti-riot training he was amused to hear the 'Turkish' rioters (members of 1 and 2 Companies) shout 'Khurrb el hukumat Young Bey!' (Down with the government of Young Bey!) as they charged the Vickers Platoon. He was gratified that they had added the honorific 'Bey'.

After Bayar's visit the regiment moved once more back to Palestine. In their new sector, north of Jerusalem, they had to defend a porous border through which both sides frequently penetrated. He set up his headquarters in a fort but spent most of his time travelling to visit the outlying positions as the border was ill defined and he wanted to acquaint himself with the terrain. There were a few cross-border incidents during his tenure of the line, but few demanded any military reaction. As he got to know the demarcation line better he became aware that it was – at best – an arbitrary device. It divided, he noted, a house from its garden, the girls' school in a village from the boys' school. A man could even pick the dates from one side of his tree but not the other. 'The line was laid down far away in Rhodes, apparently with the aid of small-scale maps and strong drink.' He dealt with the villagers with a light hand, conscious of their justifiable anger. Much of the ill-feeling was directed against the British.

Bayar's visit had political repercussions. In 1955 Iraq and Turkey had entered into a defensive alliance known as the Baghdad Pact and Jordan was now invited to become a member. When the Jordanian Government suggested that the Turks might like to strengthen the armed forces in the Hashemite Kingdom, the Turks suggested instead that the British might increase their own commitment. A letter was sent to London detailing the formations which Jordan hoped that Whitehall would wish to fund. Peter suspected that the British re-action came as a surprise in Amman: the Jordanians received a favourable response and the offer of a visit by the Chief of the Imperial General Staff to finalize details. Before this could take place General Hakim Amer of the Egyptian Army visited, the outcome of which, Peter believed, changed the Jordanian position. When Templer arrived the talks, instead of being straightforward, became unaccountably difficult to complete. At the same time a wave of anti-British feeling began to sweep across the country. There was clearly huge resistance to accepting any alliance with the Turks and Iraqis, or increasing dependence upon the British. The general feeling in the country was in favour of Nasser's Egypt; the battle lines for the ensuing struggle were clearly drawn.

In 9th Regiment's area this took the form of incidents, small in themselves and often involving schoolchildren, in which the soldiers

206

would unexpectedly encounter roadblocks manned by chanting boys. Peter treated them with kid gloves, offering them nothing more threatening than a lift back to their villages. He realized that the motivating force was the teachers and he therefore assembled them to deliver a lecture on the follies of trying to stop his men from carrying out their duties. The only people they were helping, he told them, were the Israelis and he was not prepared to allow them to do that.

On 19 December he heard from Joan that the trouble had spread to Nablus and that the house of the British Vice-Consul in Rafidia, next door to his own quarter, was under attack. No sooner had he visited the area and deployed enough troops to disperse the mob than more disturbances sprang up, this time in Jenin. He drove there in time to help the police disperse the crowd who left him alone because, he discovered, they thought he was a Circassian. On their way back to RHQ they encountered more schoolchildren with their teachers on their way to Jenin. Although he had no authority to do so, he persuaded them not to continue their journey; he carried a long piece of bamboo such as the Bedouin used for their camels and it made a satisfyingly threatening noise when whipped in the air.

A little further on they encountered a road block, fortunately incomplete, since Juma'a was travelling so fast that they stopped 40 yards beyond it. Only one of the boys who were responsible got away, but Peter stopped him by firing his Luger into the air, so frightening the youth that he gave himself up. Apart from another small demonstration his sector seemed peaceful. Elsewhere the unrest was much worse.

Peter and Joan spent Christmas quietly, visiting Jerusalem on Christmas Day to hear their friend, Pat Leonard, preach the sermon at St George's. Early in the New Year 9th Regiment moved to Jiftlik as the central reserve for the Legion. Less than a week into the New Year the unrest broke out again and Peter received orders to concentrate the regiment near Salt. No other information accompanied this signal, which reached him at 0400 hrs on 8 January.

Peter went into Amman to see if he could glean any further information. Reporting to Hutton, he was told that he was under the command of Brigadier Parry, based near the Citadel in the capital. His first job was to do a sweep through the city and arrest those not observing the curfew. This was easier said than done since most of the people were treating the curfew as a holiday, sitting around outside enjoying the weather for it was a perfect day. As soon as the soldiers appeared they disappeared, popping up again like rabbits as soon as they had passed by. It was a frustrating business, but they took about two dozen prisoners who were sent to a camp at Abdalli.

Henceforth the regiment was fire fighting. Every time they quelled one disturbance another one broke out elsewhere. It was dispiriting, particularly because Peter knew that some of his men had divided loyalties. His own Second-in-Command, Salameh Etayek, epitomized this ambivalence and knowing that his own officer cadre was not fully engaged in the difficult tasks it was undertaking was a source of real concern.

At Zerqa an English officer, Lieutenant Colonel Pat Lloyd, commander of 4th Light Anti-aircraft Regiment, had been killed. Arriving there, Peter was briefed by Brigadier Lupton, commander of the Arab Legion Artillery. The most persistent offenders, he discovered, were refugees whose grievances he knew and understood:

> The problem dates from 1948, when four-fifths of the Arab inhabitants of what is now Israel were driven from their homes. Half a million of these people now live in Jordan, some on the East Bank and some on the West, mostly in squalid camps administered by the UNRWA.
>
> An Arab boy of fourteen, whose world crashed about him in 1948, is now twenty-one, and so a bitter and revengeful generation has grown up in exile, and what we have seen so far is nothing to what may lie ahead if the Palestine problem is not settled.

The British officers were increasingly operating in isolation. When Peter was summoned to Amman to a conference at Qiada he returned to find the curfew had lapsed and everybody was out on the streets. Peter's personal contribution to its restoration consisted of an encounter with a man who sat in his doorway with a defiant mien. As Juma'a drove Peter by, he drew his Luger and put a bullet through the fanlight above the door which terrified the miscreant as much as it amused Juma'a.

Shortly afterwards Saoud Rashdan took over as Second-in-Command. Peter's misgivings about the loyalty of the regiment were well founded; visiting the men he found the prevailing view was that it was impossible to serve two masters. If they were forced to choose, Peter and his British compatriots would be isolated.

The tension eased as the curfew was ruthlessly enforced. Peter found that the refugees regarded infantry as beneath their notice; what got their attention was cavalry. Fortunately, the cavalry school was located at Zerqa and Peter enlisted the services of a dozen horsemen who were able to persuade the inhabitants to obey his orders.

If things were quiet in Zerqa – so quiet that Joan rejoined him – the same could not be said of the rest of the country. The regiment took part in a raid on a refugee camp at Ain-es-Sultan on 22 January, during which Peter's men searched for weapons and questioned the ringleaders. They achieved nothing worthwhile – the agitators had found hiding places for their weapons, and the ringleaders, if such they were, had concocted such plausible stories that it was impossible to arrive at the truth.

They imposed a curfew and moved on 26 January to Karameh where the refugee camp contained about 6,000 able-bodied men who had been unable to work for the best part of a decade. Peter was to perform the same operation as he had at Ain-es-Sultan, but here the task was more challenging. Although they announced that they were returning to Zerqa to try and disguise their true destination, word had reached the camp before they did so and by the time the search started the inhabitants had concealed their weapons. The curfew was successfully imposed, although the atmosphere was hostile and sullen.

On 28 January the operation ended and the regiment moved back to Jiftlik. In his absence a rumour had been put about in Salt that he was seeking revenge for the killing of Pat Lloyd, and many people believed he had killed refugees during the operations at Ain-es-Sultan and Karameh. One corporal reported the rumours to Peter's head-quarters, adding that the men from 42 Regiment said, 'Had we been there we would have shot this Qaid.' It was, Peter thought, an idle threat, but when he visited General Cooke a few days later he was astonished to learn that his name featured on a list of people – including Glubb Pasha – which had been drawn up by the Mufti Haj Ameen as targets for assassination. Cooke told Saoud Rashdan that he was not to allow the Qaid to go anywhere without two body-guards for escort. Peter later told his father that Nasser had offered a bigger reward for his death than for anybody else in the Legion.

His bodyguard was duly detailed, men whom Peter knew well and who performed their duties with zeal and enthusiasm. As the days went by and nothing happened he returned to what he believed was the primary threat: Israel. He thought that an offensive strategy was likely to be effective, concluding that he could regard the problem objectively because he was, essentially, a hired gun and his task was to provide military solutions to a situation in which he had no emotional involvement.

Signs of disaffection persisted, but the regiment continued to prepare a contingent to take part in the Arab Day Parade. Peter dealt with matters of discipline severely, particularly amongst the officers, which did not endear him in all quarters, but he believed that strong action was necessary to contain the mutinous element.

He was due to return to England in July having completed his tour. However, before that he would take over the brigade during Green's home leave so he was beginning the handover of 9th Regiment to his designated successor, Major Irshaid Mershoud. The beautiful spring mornings, vividly green after the winter rains, with almond blossom transforming the valleys, brought home to him how attached he had become to the country.

On 1 March he and Joan went with some friends to the cinema to see *Desirée*. It was the first time they had been out in months and Peter had even evaded his bodyguards. Before they had watched the first reel of the film someone appeared at his elbow to say that Qaid Young was wanted below and he realized that someone had had to do some slick detective work to find out where he was. Green's driver awaited him and drove him at once to the Brigadier's house.

Green gave Peter a whisky and soda and told him bluntly that Glubb Pasha had been relieved of his command. Peter swore. Others were also out, but so far, the two of them remained. Although direct communication with 1 Brigade was impossible because the line was dead, Green had heard the news via Brigadier Galletly. There followed a bizarre scene during which their conversation was punctuated by phone calls from various people who reported the latest changes of command. The third phone call was from Ali Hiyari. 'There was,' Peter recalled, 'a bit of talk, then he [Green] beamed at me: "You're out," he said. It was like being given lbw in a cricket match.' By the end of the evening one of the few British officers still in post was Green himself.

When Peter returned home he summoned his Second-in-Command and his Adjutant who were stunned. To make sure that he had understood correctly, Peter rang General Cooke and was surprised to get through. He spoke to Hutton who assured him that the orders had come directly from His Majesty and were to be obeyed. After as good a handover as possible he was to report to Qiada with Joan.

That same night he received a phone call from Salameh Etayek who was to take over the regiment, asking if he had any orders for him. Peter had for some time doubted Salameh's loyalty and had not been pleased to learn that he was to succeed him. He told him to go to bed and that the handover would begin in the morning.

It took a superhuman effort of will not to lose his temper the next day. Salameh was affability itself, saying he had only known about the changes when he had been summoned to Qiada the previous evening. While Peter was clearing his office, the phone rang. It was Qiada. Peter asked for an aeroplane which prompted Salameh to ask when he put the phone down if he did not want to stay on.

'I explained as clearly as possible, but without heat I trust, that if I was behaving myself nicely, that was not to say that I was prepared to stay on, after being relieved of my command without any reason being given.'

He did not visit the regiment because he did not want to stir up trouble. Although many of his officers came to see him, there were many more who were delighted by his departure. He was more concerned about the soldiers than the officers and noted that the Bedouin were extremely upset by what had happened to Glubb Pasha, even going so far as to threaten a revolt against the new regime. It was ironically their British officers who tried to dissuade them from doing so. Nevertheless, over a thousand of them deserted the Legion over the coming few months, mistrusting their new masters despite assurances that they would be well treated.

Peter's preparations for departure included the sale of everything which could not be shipped back to England. Everything, including the car, was sold at a fraction of its true value. They travelled to Zerqa on 6 March where politics openly collided with the military, and those Bedouin who had accompanied Peter were made to feel threatened; Peter sent most of them back to the regiment as soon as he could, keeping only Juma'a and Abdulla Heikal with him.

In the days following this last alarum they made final preparations; on 12 March Peter visited Qiada for the last time. Ali Hiyari, now Chief of Staff, bade him farewell with the words, 'We will never forget what you did in the Jerusalem incident.' The award of the order of El Istiqlal (3rd Class) acknowledged his vital role in that operation.

They flew out of Amman the following day, accompanied to the airport by a number of friends who kept them company until the time came to leave. It was, Peter remembered, a cheerful gathering. The last people he said farewell to were Juma'a and Abdulla Heikal.

Years later, Glubb Pasha recalled Peter's time in the Legion with warmth: 'He was an unforgettable person, an officer of resource and subtlety who constantly amazed and delighted me. I don't know,' he added, 'what effect it had on our opponents but I would always hazard a guess. He was very much a practical soldier with the common touch which always sat well with the bedu.' This, from Glubb Pasha, was high praise. Of his professional skills he said, 'He was brimming with ideas and strong opinions which he always expounded with charm and erudition. He was a great friend and companion and I was flattered by his book [*Bedouin Command*] in which he catches the feel of those days – he is a splendid writer.'

Lady Glubb had the last word. 'He was a man of enormous charm and wit with a fund of stories. Although he was self deprecating he always had a sly smile which one could seldom resist.'

Chapter Eighteen

An Academic's Life

Peter had loved commanding 9th Regiment; he admired the rugged independence of the Bedu and their unique code of honour which had required no little leap of faith on his part when they borrowed money from the Canteen Fund or expected nepotistic advancement through a cousin or an uncle. He had given his all to the venture, and he had gained much in the understanding of human nature.

For all these reasons he settled down to write an account of his time in Jordan once he was back in England. When he sent the manuscript to be vetted by the War Office they banned its publication on the grounds that it was too sensitive a topic given the continuing problems in the Middle East – the coup staged by the Young Officers' Movement presaged the Suez Crisis by months. When the ban was lifted *Bedouin Command* was published on 24 September of that year, just after Nasser had nationalized the Suez Canal, and a month before the ill-fated military intervention by Britain and France. The book, for which Glubb wrote the Foreword, was well reviewed.

After two months at the Beds and Herts Depot he was posted in July as an instructor to the Joint Amphibious Warfare Centre (JAWC) in Poole. Here Peter and Joan bought their first house together, Church Cottage at East Morden, near Wareham, which they renamed Edgehill. Renovation work on it took six months to complete.

In October he visited the US and Canada; surviving letters from Joan show that he had visited the Harp – she hoped that he had not consumed too much alcohol – and had sought the wisdom of a palmist. This practitioner gave an optimistic reading, even if the life-line was clearly not what she expected, for Joan responded: 'Dear noble, constant, faithful, determined and loving Bear. I'm sure the palmist was right in that part of the hand reading, though I must admit I hadn't realised that you were dead! Obviously the poor thing didn't penetrate your disguise!' She signs off: 'All my love darling, and I wish you were here, Mousie.'

On 29 October she wrote sending on letters, one of which was from John Adair who had decided, she revealed, to be ordained. Whether seriously or not, Joan wrote that she hoped he would not persuade Peter to join him.

By now Peter felt that his military career, at least in the Regular Army, was at a dead end; he was a Lieutenant Colonel once again, but unlikely to advance any further in the peacetime army. As his posting wore on he began to look for other opportunities and by the time he was due to move on, in the summer of 1958, two possibilities had presented themselves.

The first was to return to the Middle East to a command there, possibly Bedouin levies in Aden. He had originally accepted second-ment to the Arab Legion in the hope that it would lead to advancement, for he wanted to become a general and saw that as a possible route – he was ambitious enough to believe he could succeed Glubb Pasha himself had the political situation not overturned his plans. The offer of command, and possibly a brigade, in Aden was not something to be turned down lightly, however Joan did not relish the thought of going abroad again.

He had a second string to his bow. Already a published author and something of an authority on war-gaming miniatures, he had further literary ambitions. He was continuing his research into the Royalist Army of the Civil War and had begun to work with several authorities on the military history of the period, including Lieutenant Colonel Alfred Burne, whose book *The Battlefields of England*, published in 1950, he regarded as seminal. Together they wrote *The Great Civil War*. In addition he published his war memoirs in 1958 under the title *Storm from the Sea*. It had been in preparation for some years for he had been working on it in Jordan. He referred to it to Dallas as a potboiler, but it was a success and remains a lucid account of his wartime experiences, written in the laconic style which he was making his own.

This advance into the groves of academe was to prove decisive. Sometime before leaving the JAWC he received a letter asking if he was interested in becoming the Reader in Military History and English at the Royal Military Academy, Sandhurst. So interested was

214

he that he did not pause to write his response, but rang up and responded in the affirmative. The current incumbent of the post, Professor Ken ('Bos') Boswell OBE TD was due to retire the following year; Peter was to be his successor.

There were formalities to complete. Peter had to apply for Premature Voluntary Retirement (PVR) in order to retire from active service. While his application was considered he left the JAWC on 28 August and took up his final posting as the Deputy President of the Regular Commissions Board at Warminster, a job he held for seven months. He retired from the army on 17 June 1959, a month before his forty-fourth birthday, and was granted the honorary rank of Brigadier.

On 19 June he joined the staff at RMA Sandhurst as a civil servant, having exchanged one branch of government service for another. His job title was Reader in Military History but he was also Head of the new War Studies Department. The position came with a quarter, and as soon as Bos had moved out, he and Joan moved in. It was convenient although somewhat smaller than they were used to, and it was not long before they bought a house in Yateley which they called Hindford after Dallas's childhood home on Brompton Road. Here they had plenty of space and as Peter's renewed interest in war gaming increased, he had an extension built over the garage which housed his gaming table and his expanding collection of miniatures.

A war-gaming table should not be wider than 6 feet across because the players have to be able to reach far enough to move their soldiers. Peter thought this was too small, so his table was rather larger (8x12 feet according to Charles S. Grant). Don Featherstone, a war gamer who played frequently with Peter at this time, wondered how it was possible to get to the pieces in the middle. Delighted to demonstrate Peter ducked under the table and after a short pause there was a minor earthquake, then a panel in the middle of the table suddenly moved aside and Peter's head appeared. 'There you are, dear boy,' he said to Featherstone, 'perfectly simple.' The act of opening the panel usually knocked his soldiers down and in being set straight they edged rather further than the rules strictly allowed. Peter was an incorrigible cheat, but he was also a crafty player, making unusual moves which revealed a shrewd tactical grasp of the battle as well as on occasion applying to the sand table lessons he had learnt during the war. 'You used to find,' Featherstone recalled, 'that you were outnumbered or outflanked . . . because he thought ahead of you.'

One of the attractions of the job at Sandhurst was the opportunity to create a War Studies department which would be unique. With the end of National Service the structure of the commissioning course at RMA was being redrawn to include a greater element of academic work; Peter's job, which he relished, was to provide the cadets with their military history, to build their historical appreciation of their chosen career as well as to give depth and insight into their military and tactical studies.

When he arrived the department consisted of himself, his secretary, Mary Russell, and Rollo, Mary's Alsatian, both of whom he inherited from his predecessor. Rollo was joined by Peter's two Alsatians, Honey and Jasmine, which accompanied him to work – the reaction of visitors who had to negotiate a heap of dogs in the outer office always amused him.

In short order he began to hire lecturers, most of the men he picked being young, bright and academic. As he had proved during the war, his instincts were sound. Within two years of his arrival his department included on its staff several of the most eminent military historians this country produced during the twentieth century, including John Adair – who had not, in the event, been ordained – Antony Brett-James, David Chandler, Christopher Duffy and John Keegan.

He encouraged them to continue their studies and publish their research, as they would have done in a university, and the results of this policy continue to reverberate today: Adair on Leadership; Chandler on Napoleon and Marlborough; Duffy principally on eighteenth-century European conflicts; and Keegan, author of the seminal *The Face of Battle*, commentator on modern warfare. This body of work – with Peter's output principally, though not exclusively, concerning the English Civil War – would rival a department of history at any of the finest universities, but it was all delivered from a uniquely military perspective. It may be taken for granted now, but in the early 1960s such an approach outside the learned journals was completely new.

Peter would help anybody who asked, giving generously both of his time and his resources – loaning books from his own extensive library, passing on the fruits of his own research. He even lent his name to a book if that would secure its publication where an unknown author might struggle. Despite personal revalries, the members of his own department came to look upon him with the same kind of affection he had inspired in his troops, and his desire to see them bring their scholarship to the wider world meant that he supported them in their endeavours and was the first to applaud their successes.

When David Chandler became Head of the War Studies Department he asked Peter how he had done things. Peter responded:

> This is a useful tip. Avoid Departmental Meetings! . . . When I was CO of 3 Cdo I used to wander round from Troop to Troop and give my orders to the captains with nobody else there. My precedessor [Durnford-Slater] used to have long, boring, bolshie conferences. A Lt Colonel can sink a captain with one salvo. But can he sink SIX? This great Truth followed me to Sandhurst, and . . . I did always endeavour to deal with you all singly! . . . Moreover, always give them GOOD news YOURSELF. Convey BAD news to them through your 2 i/c. Ce sont les lois de la Guerre.

He signed himself, as he often did, 'Your loving fiend'.

On 7 January1960 he was elected a Fellow of the Society of Antiquaries (FSA), at the same time as the distinguished biographer, Carola Oman; his credentials as a serious historian were beginning to grow. He was a frequent contributor to publications such as the *Journal for the Society for Army Historical Research* and the *Army Quarterly and Defence Journal*. The first of the twenty-two articles he wrote for the Society for Army Historical Research, the vast majority of them on subjects connected with the English Civil War, had appeared in 1938.

He began to take on other appointments: military adviser to Chambers Encyclopaedia, Chief Examiner in Military History for the Staff College exam – prior to which he had been Lecturer for Southampton University to Staff College candidates – principal lecturer at a course on warfare in England run by Buckinghamshire County Council.

Most importantly, he was President of the Old Comrades' Association of Army Commandos, which kept him in constant touch with many of his wartime associates. Their annual reunion was a popular event even as their ranks began to thin with the passage of time. Regular trips were organized, particularly to Normandy for the commemoration of D-Day. His wartime exploits were now memories kept vivid by the lifelong friendships that he continued to nurture.

217

On one occasion he took a group of cadets to Dieppe. Peter, now in his fifties and somewhat portly, risked both his life and his reputation by scaling once more the cliffs he had climbed in 1942. To his relief, and the admiration of onlookers, he reached the top unscathed.

The concept of leadership continued to occupy him. A passage from *The Mask of Dimitrios* by Eric Ambler accurately articulated his own views on the complicated relationship between the leader and the man:

> A man's features, the bone structure and the tissue which covers it, are the product of a biological process; but his face, he creates for himself . . . He wears it like a devil mask; a device to evoke in others the emotions complementary to his own. If he is afraid, then he must be feared; if he desires, then he must be desired. It is a screen to hide his mind's nakedness.

Leadership or conduct in war was a concept to which he constantly returned. One of the themes he refined upon was not why such leadership skills are achieved, but how they worked. He admired those who were cool under fire – Mad Jack Churchill wading ashore playing the bagpipes, men who made witty remarks which almost managed to turn a battle into a social occasion. Peter emulated the seventeenth-century soldier Count Raimondo Montecuccoli who wrote in 1703 that a good leader was a man who appeared to take war light-heartedly and laughed in the face of danger. Peter understood that the crucial word is 'appeared'. The hard work has been done beforehand: the reconnaissance, the planning, the logistics, the positioning of forces and above all, the training; both halves of the equation had to be in place for the concept to work.

Peter's physical presence at this time was powerful and though his smile could charm, it could equally well betoken a foul temper so that those who recognized the glint in his eyes would earnestly wish to be elsewhere. He was genial and erudite, excellent company and generous to a fault. It was, perhaps, not surprising that the abiding desire of all those around him – colleague and cadet alike – was to earn his approbation; his good opinion mattered.

He was not infallible. He was obdurately impractical which required everybody around him to deal with the minutiae of everyday life on his behalf. It was Joan who bore the brunt of this trait, and she did so uncomplainingly, whether it concerned domestic finances or his reluctance to drive. His tendency to self-indulgence manifested itself partly in a fondness for the bottle which, while it did not quite lead him to overindulge to a dangerous degree, nonetheless led to problems which culminated, in 1969, in his being prosecuted for drunken driving in London. Even after the statutory time ban had passed he never drove again.

His puckish sense of humour, slightly juvenile as it often was in men of his generation – he was a great fan of the Goons – found an outlet in the composition of doggerel verse. He wrote poems about everything. An early example was addressed in 1959 to Alfred Burne who had complained that the publishers of their book, *The Great Civil War*, were putting up the price to a hefty £1 16s.

> Why spend your life,
> In useless strife,
> In battle unavailing,
> By sticking to
> Burnes' point of view
> When Jerrold's is prevailing?
> It is no good
> v. Spottiswoode
> – with Eyre to give him backing.
> Note royaltee
> (see para three)
> And send your sorrows packing!

(Jerrold was their editor at Eyre and Spottiswoode.)

The drive to make money was a constant refrain, driven by an epicurean lifestyle, and the desire to acquire books for research and figures for war gaming. He was for ever hatching plans to embark on a project which would make his fortune. In this he was abetted by David Chandler who possessed ideas and energy in abundance. If none of the schemes came to fruition it was not from lack of trying and he was to continue to try, one way or another, for the rest of his life. The uneven balance sheet caused periodic embarrassment as cheques bounced and horns had to be drawn in, but he never stopped ordering a steady stream of books, old and new, principally from Thorntons of Broad Street in Oxford.

In 1967 Dallas died at the age of eighty-nine; in old age he had withered and become, in the younger generation's parlance, a dry old stick. He had been lonely during Peter's periods abroad; Marilyn remembered that he used to come visiting Winifred Duckworth. She and Aunt Winifred would watch as the letter box opened and Dallas peered in to see whether anybody was there. He was very old-fashioned and could be difficult company. Winifred herself moved eventually into a home just outside Camberley where Peter and Joan visited her regularly until her death.

The year 1964 was the twentieth anniversary of the D-Day landings. Monty, now seventy-six, gave a lecture to the senior officer cadets at Sandhurst, and he began – with an entirely straight face – 'There are three great commanders: Alexander, Napoleon and Myself.' (David Chandler, who was present, noted that nobody dared to laugh.) When the library at Sandhurst mounted an exhibition to commemorate D-Day Antony Brett-James suggested to Peter that it might be a good idea to ask Montgomery if he had any relics of the occasion that he would be prepared to lend for display. Peter thought this was an excellent notion and a letter was despatched to Monty's home, Isington Mill, asking if he would be prepared to look something out. Peter did not envisage anything more than an exchange of letters – the items to be selected, collected and returned as necessary. He was agreeably surprised to receive an invitation to visit Monty's home. A date was arranged and Brett-James, whose idea it had been, drove them over. For the first few minutes, recalling the circular conversations he had had with the Field Marshal, mostly on parade grounds while they had been on active service, Peter tried to establish common ground with people they had known. Something he said must have struck a chord because suddenly Monty relaxed and invited the two men to sit down.

The visit was a great success and they were shown the famous caravan which had acted as his Operations Room throughout the last year of the war. It still had on its walls the maps showing the situation in Germany just after the surrender in May 1945. Peter also noticed framed quotation from a poem by James Graham, Marquis of Montrose, a Royalist Scot whose military prowess he much admired. Monty's verse was:

He either fears his fate too much,
Or his deserts are small,
That puts it not unto the touch
To win or lose it all.

Peter was unable to resist asking if Monty knew the preceding verse, and when he admitted that he did not, Peter was able to supply it:

Like Alexander I will reign
And I will reign alone;
My thoughts shall evermore disdain
A rival on my throne.

It is a love poem, but the military imagery is strong; what Monty thought of Peter's fluency is unrecorded. David Chandler thought, probably correctly, that it smacked of one-upmanship. It did not disturb the harmony of the day, however, and at the end of it Peter persuaded Monty to give him a signed map which they had unearthed showing all his headquarters from Alamein to Lüneberg; the staff at Sandhurst had recently given Monty a new, much neater and cleaner one so he did not mind parting with the original.

Brett-James reports that on the way home Peter was 'almost shaking with excitement' which surprised him, given Peter's war record and the fact that this was not his first meeting with the Field Marshal. Peter's opinion of Monty was not uncritical, but he never forgot the soldiers' reaction to him; it appeared that even now he was not immune to Monty's charisma. Over tea at Hindford the two men regaled Joan with the success of the visit and showed her the articles they had been able to borrow for the exhibition.

In 1969 he wrote a review for the *Army Quarterly Defence Journal* of Monty's *A History of Warfare*. This book was written with Antony Brett-James's help, ironically a direct result of their meeting in 1964. Peter wrote:

To many the volume under review will be of interest not so much as a history but simply as 'Monty on War'; the work not so much of a military historian but of a singularly well-equipped military commentator. The Field-Marshal's views on the art or, if you prefer it, the science of war are of more interest than his relatively brief and selective version of its history.

He then proceeds to damn the entire enterprise with, at best, faint praise. 'For at least 306 out of his 567 pages he appears to be writing of wars which do not seem to have attracted his attention before his 75th year,' he wrote, ' . . . the result is not entirely satisfactory.' But he could not end on a sour note: 'When all is said and done Field-Marshal Montgomery had the great and rare gift of instilling into his soldiers the sure knowledge that his operations were going to come off: that they could not be beaten. That was a pearl of great price. We all owe him very much, and though it be for his fighting rather than his writing, 'tis no matter.' Those are words that he hoped applied equally to his own military career, if not to his academic and literary ambitions.

In his first five years at Sandhurst Peter was establishing his reputation as a historian while working in an environment he found thoroughly congenial. Then in 1966 there was a change of Commandant when Major General Peter Hunt took over from Major General John Mogg. Hunt had different ideas about the Commissioning Course and Peter feared that his department would be the one to suffer. The courses were regularly revamped, he had been brought on to the staff when the army was getting smaller and there was a move to place more emphasis on classroom work in the Commissioning Course. Six years on the financial situation was tight and the first place to cut looked like being the academic content of the course. As they talked of restructuring Peter began to look around for another job.

Coincidentally, he was approached by the Royal Military College of Canada in Kingston, Ontario, who offered him a twelve-month appointment. On 9 November he wrote to them declining their offer, offering as his reason that the RMA was in a state of flux and that he was looking for something at a university in England. Whatever that was did not materialize and for the moment, disillusioned, he stayed on, but he was only waiting for the right moment to make a move.

His career as a writer was now well under way; at the beginning of the decade he had published two books, *Cromwell* in 1962, and *From Hastings to Culloden* (with John Adair) in 1964. The trickle became a torrent as the years passed. In 1966 *World War 1939–1945* came out, and in 1967 no fewer than six books saw the light of day: *The British Army 1642–1970*, *The Israeli Campaign 1967*, *Charge!* (with Lieutenant Colonel James Lawford), *The Civil War diaries of Richard Atkyns and John Gwyn* (with Norman Tucker), *Edgehill 1642: The Campaign and the Battle*, and finally he edited a volume called *Decisive Battles of the Second World War*.

In July 1966, just after *World War 1939–1945* was published, he

222

travelled up to York and read the lesson at a memorial service held to commemorate the Battle of Marston Moor. Afterwards he walked the battlefield and took photographs with his Zeiss Centaflex before departing for home. One of the other participants in the day's events was Peter Wenham, a local archaeologist, who was writing a book on the siege of York. Wenham had given Peter the manuscript to read which he now returned together with his comments and ideas. *The Great and Close Siege of York 1644* was eventually published in 1970 by Gordon Norwood of the Roundwood Press.

Gordon Norwood lived with his wife Ruth in the village of Ratley, on the top of the escarpment in Warwickshire known locally as Edgehill. An idle question one day prompted Peter to look into his voluminous card index to see if any Norwoods had been present at the battle. Gradually the project grew as both men became absorbed in discovering all they could about this first major clash of arms in the English Civil War.

Peter's fascination with the minutiae of military life in seventeenth-century England was now to come into its own. The book which he and Norwood conceived would take existing research and carry it forward to include other aspects of the battle: the logistics; the muster rolls; the casualty lists; everything, in short, to do with the organization and conduct of the battle. Its emphasis on the military means that it does in places read like a post-operation report which is probably what Peter intended. Its narrative, on the other hand, lays out lucidly the course of the campaign as a whole and the battle in particular. If his heart lay with the Royalists, he was even handed when describing events on the field.

The battlefield at Edgehill lies partly on MOD property, the Central Ammunition Depot at Kineton. In some ways this was an advantage since although the site was under cultivation it was not frequented by many people. Peter enlisted the help of a local Territorial Army unit and a dowser in his search for relics. He was able to establish the starting position of both sides for many musket balls – some still embedded in trees – remained from which he could deduce the arc of fire. In the same way he traced the path of cannon balls and estimated the position of the gun emplacements.

From a combination of battlefield research, the considerable, but disparate, source material and his own military judgement, he created an account which was unique and exciting. Dame Veronica Wedgwood wrote in her Introduction:

Brigadier Young enjoys an unrivalled position as the leading authority on the military history of the Civil War. He knows seventeenth century warfare and armies through and through, but he brings to all he writes something more than can be gained from even the most careful study of contemporary sources: a practical understanding and experience such as few historians of this epoch have been able to apply to the subject.

For his part, Norwood was adamant that the book itself should be of the best quality, using Antique Laid Paper and copious coloured illustrations as well as line drawings to enliven the text. Published on 23 October 1967, the 325th anniversary of the battle, the finished product was a thing of beauty and both men felt that it deserved a good send-off. To that end, they conceived a publicity stunt to be held at Edgehill which would involve the participants dressing up and looking warlike in something that could pass for a seventeenth-century idiom.

The event was held in a marquee in the grounds of The Castle pub in the village of Radway. The standards of dress were variable and ranged from authentic headgear – Peter lent Richard Snailham, a lecturer in another department at the RMA, a morion which, typically, he never asked to be returned – to wellington boots and paper doilies for collars and cuffs. The participants spent a jolly day walking about the battlefield admiring each other's headgear, rather self-consciously going through a few rudimentary drill manoeuvres and more enthusiastically quaffing ale. A small diorama of the battle had been set up in the marquee and Peter had prudently posted two 'pikemen' to guard the entrance, for which office they had borrowed a couple of washing-line props. Prophetically, they recalled afterwards that throughout the day small boys had run up to them to ask where they could join. In the end everybody enjoyed themselves so much that they declared that they must do it again.

Many of the participants were known to Peter through his war-gaming activities. He had long complained that he disliked all the bother of having to move figures about on a sand table. 'What I'd like them to do,' he told Don Featherstone, 'is to move about on their own!' Shortly after the event at Edgehill he met Featherstone in a pub in Victoria and summoned him over by calling: 'Ah dear boy! Come over here and amuse me with your idle prattle!' Featherstone went to join him, conscious, as he did so, of the strange looks he was receiving. Before he could open his mouth Peter announced that he had solved the intractable problem of moving war-gaming figures.

'I am going to form my own army.'

When Featherstone asked what sort of army it would be he was told in no uncertain terms, 'The only one I could possibly have. The Royalist army of course.'

Chapter Nineteen

The Sealed Knot is Born

Peter later claimed that he had been persuaded – implying reluctance – to take the idea of a re-enactment society further following the success of that first meeting at Edgehill. Although the participants might have laboured under the delusion that they were inaugurating more of a debating society than a re-enactment society, Peter was already thinking rather in terms of war gaming than words. He must have given it considerable thought, for even a small group of people, scattered over the country, would require administrative support.

The launch of the book on Edgehill marked a watershed. The work was a great success and was used at Sandhurst as a text book. His quest to move out into the wider academic world had not prospered, but the decision to reduce the military history syllabus in the Commissioning Course had made his mind up for him – he resigned from the RMA in October 1968 and determined to write full time. The number of projects he had on hand convinced him that there was plenty of work out there, given his background, experience and reputation. Combined with his pension – much of which he had commuted when he left the Army – his income from writing should support them in the manner to which they had become accustomed.

In April 1968 he had achieved another literary step forward when he gave a paper to a meeting of the Sette of Odd Volumes, into which he was inducted under the soubriquet of Brother Amphibian, a nod to his Commando days. The subject of this exquisite presentation was 'Will Shakespeare: Top Military Expert'. His argument, beautifully expressed, begins with the premise that Shakespeare saw military service himself. Gordon Norwood published a slim volume in limited edition in 1972; what impresses about this short piece is not its cleverness – although it is delightfully clever – but its wit and charm, two characteristics which Peter had in abundance but which rarely obtrude in his other works.

A Lamb or a Costello could never have given us such portraits of generals as we have in Shakespeare's Henry V, his Othello, his Brutus or his Cassius. Indeed it was the quarrel scene between these last two that first brought home to me that where the military mind was concerned Shakespeare really knew his stuff. I had the play with me on the voyage to Sicily in 1943, a calm period after a long and generally frustrating spell of planning conferences with senior officers some of whom, with the arrogance of youth, I considered stupid and out of date and others of whom I thought did little but make difficulties. (Come to think of it, I still think they did.) And I still think as I did then, that the quarrel between Brutus and Cassius is unexampled as a picture of 'two second-rate general officers having a spiteful, touchy, nattering argument about seniority, nepotism, and various other causes of military discontents.'

Shortly after Peter retired he and Joan moved into a house in Windsor Forest, a pretty tile-hung property surrounded by woods called Lovel End. David Chandler bought Hindford from him. The two men were firm friends; and Peter had acted as father of the bride when Chandler married his wife, Gill, in Beverly Minster in 1960.

Peter was now working on a book called *Commando* which formed part of a successful series called the 'History of the Second World War', published by Purnell. Each book in the series was designed to encapsulate an aspect of the war using a pithy narrative accompanied by many photographs which would bring the subject to life, a new way to present material, using layout techniques hitherto confined to magazines and part-works. Peter's involvement in the project culminated in his being made editor-in-chief of Purnell's *History of the First World War* in 1970.

Meanwhile there was a meeting at the Mitre Hotel in Oxford on 28 February 1968 where the first decisions of the new re-enactment society were taken. The name was to be The Sealed Knot, after a secret society of Royalist sympathizers which had flourished during the Interregnum. As far as was practicable they decided to replicate the organizations and titles of the seventeenth century so Peter achieved his final military promotion, to Captain Generall – the rank enjoyed by King Charles I himself. He appointed an Inner Council,

227

which mirrored the King's circle of advisers, consisting of seven people, most of whom were at that meeting: David Chandler, David Fisher, Peter Morton, Edward Surén, Bernard Thorold, John Tucker and Peter Wenham.

The next step was to organize an event, a parade at Frimley Park on 21 July 1968. Peter consulted his address book and contacted anybody he thought might be willing to take part. He was, he admitted, surprised by the number of people his stunt attracted, but felt that his confidence had not been misplaced when he discovered Lieutenant Colonel J.B.R. Nicholson, lately a cavalry commander in the Indian Army and now editor of *Tradition* magazine, wearing a wig of shoulder-length grey hair – he was rarely seen in costume thereafter without it – jeans stuffed into wellington boots and an attempt at a lace collar, leaning against a tree and whittling a piece of wood with his penknife.

The assembled members were issued with some basic items of uniform – PVC buff coats, hats and baldricks – allocated units and given a rank; many of them had little or no previous military experience. Peter's address book was replete with names of his contacts in the war-gaming world, many of whom were modellers from whom he had previously bought figures – and, indeed, whole armies.

There was a further parade in September, this time at Blackdown Camp, the Depot of the Royal Army Ordnance Corps (RAOC), to prepare for their first major appearance in public, a muster at Edgehill on Sunday, 27 October. Here they began to come to grips with the intricacies of the drill manuals, confining themselves at this stage to the pike. A demonstration of simplified drill would be followed by a skill-at-arms competition and everyone present would be judged on their dress.

At this stage only the Captain Generall's Regiment was established, consisting of three Companies, Nos 1, 3 and 9. There were also some Dragoons and Reformadoes – officers without regiments. Nonetheless the society could already field some sixty people, making the parade an eye-catching event. They were watered but not fed; the order Peter issued advised the participants to 'bring the unconsumed portions of their day's rations if they hope to have any lunch'!

Peter had decided that the presence of artillery was a prerequisite for any re-enactment, and he had acquired two gun barrels from Old College at Sandhurst, unlimbered brass cannon dating from the nineteenth century. The terms upon which this equipment was secured were never satisfactorily spelled out. The barrels were delivered to

Peter Morton, an expert in artillery, and he had carriages built for them. As was the custom in the seventeenth century, they were given names, and became known to generations of Knotters as Sweet Lips and Magog.

The muster at Edgehill was a great success. The Dragoons, led by 'Lieutenant' Max Diamond, demonstrated some show-stopping manoeuvres; Diamond was a stuntman and had brought along several of his colleagues. Sweet Lips spoke for the first time and there were demonstrations of other martial arts, including sword fighting. The battle was described in detail as the participants demonstrated rather than fought it, making it more a lecture than a battle. Many items of uniform were from the recently released film *Cromwell*; the buff coats were plastic and the apostles on the bandoliers were fakes, but the overall effect was impressive. Peter welcomed non-fighting elements, adherents and camp followers, particularly if they were 'wenches'.

This first muster aroused great public interest – they had invited the press and TV companies to be present but had otherwise given out no publicity. The media were enthusiastic about this new venture – several television programmes were made about the Sealed Knot in its early years – and public reaction convinced the Inner Council that there was a market for their activities. What nobody had anticipated was that over 800 people would come to see the event. There was clearly a public appetite for something conceived as a war game but fought in a field instead of on a sand table.

The Captain Generall, conscious that his 'army' needed encouragement, had devised a system of rewards for valour and service: the Order of the Royal Oak and the Order of the Bear. (The first Order of the Bear was awarded for looking fierce in a press photograph.) Two further awards were also instituted but rarely conferred: the Forlorn Hope and the Order of the Bear Grand Chain.

The outcome of this muster was a flood of requests to join the society. By the following season close to a thousand people had been in touch to request more information; the June 1969 edition of 'Mercurius Militaris' (the Sealed Knot newsletter) announced that membership had doubled since Christmas and it became clear that there would have to be a charge to cover administration costs. This was initially £2 2s for the first year, which included a cost of 10/- for a badge and 2/6d for a certificate of membership. In subsequent years the cost was £1 11s 6d for members, £1 1s for Adherents (non-fighting members) and 10/- for those under twenty-one.

One of the new recruits was Peter Bloomfield who wrote to Peter asking to join and received a very cordial letter in return: 'You are most welcome to the Knot. I enclose an enlistment form. I have written to the Agitant-Generall to send you more information . . . The main thing is to get 'properly dressed' without delay so that you may enjoy some of the forthcoming musters.'

Bloomfield became a pikeman, went on to raise a company and ended his 'active service' as a tertio commander before joining the Yeomen of the Knot, a formation Peter founded in 1977 to honour long-serving members. This was a private army with a career structure.

Lessons were learnt during the 1969 'campaigning season'. At Basing House, in March, the Parliamentarians were represented by John Adair, garbed in sober black, who 'defended the house' with a few Sandhurst cadets. He was inevitably overpowered, captured and led away in chains. It was obvious that if 'battles' were to be fought there must be an enemy. Adair set about recruiting members with Parliamentarian sympathies. In June the battle at Marston Moor was largely fought between Sandhurst cadets and everybody else. The cadets – who included Mark Phillips, later to marry Princess Anne – took some hard knocks; the enemy were mostly local Camberley lads who enjoyed the opportunity to have a go at their normally un-attainable neighbours.

There were two further musters that year. At Leatherhead in July a respectable turnout included eighteen cavalry of the Captain Generall's Regiment, twenty-five infantry represented by four different units – the Captain Generall's Regiment of Foot, the Black Guard, Hinton's Greycoats and Nicholson's – and artillery which was commanded by 'Colonel' Duffy, who brought along a yellow mortar called Barbara. An embryonic Parliamentarian army was represented by 'Sergeant Major General' Adair's bodyguard, known as the Rusty Nails due to the colour of their uniforms. When the first Battle of Newbury was re-enacted at the end of September, Peter issued the warning order himself and wrote what can only be described as a seventeenth-century operations order to outline the detail of the battle. The ease with which he transformed this precise military document into a sort of theatrical aide-memoire demonstrated that he had a thorough grasp of what he was trying to achieve even at this early stage.

Peter's warning order for the Newbury muster also contained details of the first Sealed Knot banquet (cost £4). It was usual to invite the Captain Generall and his lady to these celebrations. Joan, who did not enjoy dressing up, would accompany Peter loyally as consort and driver.

The administration of the society required rapid adaptation to the unending stream of applicants. In July, Peter appointed a friend of his who had been an early recruit, Lieutenant Colonel Hastings Read, as Agitant Generall, although he continued to request that all application forms were sent to him so that he could enter the name of the recruit into the Great Roll of the Knot. Before long this practice ceased due to the numbers involved.

The names and titles of officers and units were carefully, indeed self-consciously, antiquated: Captain Generall, Agitant Generall, Trayne of Artillerie. The participants also wrote to each other in mock seventeenth-century language, which amused them although their attempts to replicate the style of the period were not completely successful. Peter's warning order for Marston Moor is a masterpiece of his early style:

Yett bee warned, One and All, ye Roundheads are stirringe. There is one Adair, an Anabaptist knave yet had fome command at Bafing, prater of the day he'll tumble both Crowne and Mitre (Forfoothe!). There is one Guard, more fanatic, if 'twere pofsible, even than the Man in Black, would raife horfe in ye Eafterne Counties and fmite ye Amalekites, by which fweete Malignants, he meaneth you and mee.

The Black Guard, which had made its debut at Leatherhead, was Peter's own bodyguard and he was rarely on the field without it. It included a number of his old wartime comrades, including Bob Christopher, whom he had persuaded to enlist in his army. Although well into middle age, they took to the field with gusto even if they found themselves putting their shoulders to the wheels of the artillery.

In 1972 former members of 3 Commando were shocked to hear of the death of John Durnford-Slater, who committed suicide. He had latterly kept a low profile and from time to time his former comrades had exchanged letters wondering how he was faring. It seemed that he could not adjust to life outside the army. He had had a succession of jobs but nothing seemed to lift him from the depression into which he fell. The men he had commanded mourned him sincerely – he had been an inspirational leader, never happier than when he was in battle himself.

The next few years saw the membership of the Sealed Knot explode. By the early 1970s it exceeded 2,000 and muster venues were scaled accordingly. Warwick Castle was popular and the Knot held two musters there at the beginning of the decade, one of which in 1972 was the subject of a television documentary. In 1971, the society was incorporated under the Companies Act and became The Sealed Knot Ltd – staging battles and handling considerable amounts of cash required an organization which could negotiate with promoters. It was also registered as an educational charitable trust recognized by the Charity Commission in 1974 – from the first the society had given all its profits to charity. The headed notepaper proclaimed Peter as Captain Generall, Hastings Read as Agitant Generall and George Stevenson as Chairman; there were thirteen directors. That year, however, some financial irregularities came to light and Hastings Read was removed as Agitant Generall which resulted in a lawsuit that dragged on for several years to nobody's ultimate satisfaction.

Peter now took to the battlefield on horseback which made him more visible to participants and public alike. From this elevated position he would wave languidly to the crowd as he passed. The decision to ride rather than walk was prompted by the return of an old injury which he had sustained on the hockey field as a boy; an ulcerated leg made walking difficult and he had begun riding after they moved to Lovel End. To begin with Joan had accompanied him, but after a bad fall she gave up and left him to it. Animals, in fact, took up an increasing amount of time – they had never been without an Alsatian since acquiring Tigla in Jordan. She had been succeeded by Jasmine and Honey, and they now had Ben who distinguished his early Knot career by eating a gauntlet at an early muster.

In 1971 they moved from Berkshire to Gloucestershire, acquiring a farmhouse in the village of Ripple with enough land to accommodate Peter's growing string of horses. He arrived with two: Roger (known as Splodge), an elderly chestnut, and Reuben, a roan pony with a pathological aversion to horse boxes. For a while he had on loan from Max Diamond a grey called Simon and he subsequently acquired several others, a dark bay called Edward who came on retirement from the Lifeguards in London, Heyday a rangy bay acquired from a riding school, as well as Solomon, Rock, Picasso and Whirligig, all of whom were old enough to look forward to a dignified retirement. He loved riding and he went out whenever he could spare the time, either for a hack down the local lanes or across the Worcestershire commons to a pub where Joan would meet him and his companions for lunch. He was enchanted to watch two hares boxing while he was out riding. 'A pretty sight,' he wrote. 'Dear things. They were so keen on their own affairs in a beet field that they ignored us, though we weren't a cricket pitch away!'

There had been a skirmish through Ripple and Uckinghall during the Civil War between Parliamentarian forces under Sir William Waller and Edward Massey, and Royalists under Prince Maurice. In 1971 Peter wrote a poem about the encounter which was published in the parish magazine. In part it reads:

> The Roundhead Waller, crafty fox,
> And Rupert's brother Maurice
> Exchanged a slash or two, and knocks,
> Near Uckinghall Post Office.
>
> Via Upton came the cavaliers,
> And soon they were detected
> By Massey's Bluecoat musketeers
> Just where they were expected.
>
> But Maurice was not quite as thick
> As some would have us think.
> He moved some horsemen, bloody quick,
> Right round by Severn's brink.
>
> Sir William stands at Ripple Bank:
> He hears a trumpet call:
> 'The Cavaliers are on my flank!
> Charging through Uckinghall.'

Mercurius Militaris had mutated into The Orders of the Daye which were issued every month during the campaigning season. The Captain Generall's improving thoughts always appeared on the first page: 'Given under my hand this day at Uckinghall'.

He loved life in Ripple and became well known in the neighbourhood, not only for his habit of riding around the local lanes (often in costume) but also for taking part in the life of the local community.

He was a regular churchgoer and took great delight in relating the local version of the General Confession. 'There was a farmer on one side who began "Almighty and most merciless Father," he claimed, 'and a little old lady on the other who went on, "We have erred and strayed from Thy ways like soft sheep."' He found these variations on the mighty King James Version most beguiling.

He moved beyond the merely military aspects of the period and began to gather an entire Court around him. Early recruits included an artist, Stephen Beck, and a musician, Ralph Willatt. Beck became Limner to the Captain Generall and Willatt became Master of the Captain Generall's Musick (they respectively commanded Nos 2 and 7 Company, King's Lifeguard of Foot). That he acquired the services of a Cupbearer showed Joan's subtle influence; she thought that if Peter did not pour the drinks he might imbibe less.

Beck, who joined the Knot in 1969 and was present at the first muster at Frimley Park, worked with Peter on several books; his charming line drawings were used in many of the Roundwood Press's publications. He also produced some fine battlefield maps in which Peter always featured in a prominent position. When Beck felt that he needed more practice in the difficult art of drawing horses Peter invited him up to Ripple for the day so that he could practice on his own animals.

Willatt, a music teacher by profession who war-gamed as a hobby, joined in 1970 and formed a group called the Captain Generall's Musick which performed at banquets and musters. In 1978 the group staged a masque, an entertainment much enjoyed at the Court of Charles I, which Peter attended, despite inclement weather. The piece was, optimistically, entitled 'The Triumph of Peace'.

From the beginning attention to drill and turnout were of the greatest importance. First pikemen, then musketeers were trained in the passage of arms and not permitted onto the battlefield until they had passed a test. This included performance of the postures as well as answering some basic questions about seventeenth-century warfare. What pleased and amazed the hierarchy was the number of people who not only had a keen interest in the period but an enthusiasm for research into every aspect of military life. In 1972 the first military handbook was published. Peter wrote the Foreword, and each chapter was written by a specialist in that subject. Thus, Lieutenant Colonel Nicholson (known as Colonel Nick), who happened to be an excellent artist and talented with a needle, wrote the chapter on military costume; Peter Morton, commander of the Great Trayne of Artillerie, wrote the chapter on Artillery. The book, competitively priced at £1.70, ran to three reprints.

There had been re-enactment societies before but none had prospered. The phenomenon of the Sealed Knot was hard to explain for, unlike its predecessors, it showed no sign of wilting and dying. Perhaps it was the inclusiveness which Peter cultivated – from the beginning it was advertised as something for the entire family. Women were welcome as camp followers and, in some units, combatants. Although uniform and turnout was important Peter understood the costs involved and allowed some leeway, although company commanders were often much stricter about appearance than he was; the era of the plastic buff coat and crimplene doublet did not last long.

Above all there was levity in proceedings; people did not take it too seriously. This was what Peter wanted: there was no real way to enforce conformity but the organization reflected his own vision through sheer force of personality, although it had developed rather differently from his original intention. By the mid 1970s he was heard to remark that if he had known what he was starting he might have thought twice about it; the tail, he thought, was now wagging the dog.

It was certainly a full-time job. He reckoned he wrote sixty letters a month on Sealed Knot business alone. He could not but note wryly that the Inner Council, so piquantly modelled on that of Charles I, soon began to replicate all the clashes of personality and thwarted ambition which history related of the original. He was constantly dealing with petitions from various parties to sort out disagreements – being head of the army also meant having to dispense summary justice.

Peter did not hold undisputed sway for there were others who felt they were capable of running the organization, and from an early stage he knew he had pretenders to his throne. One such was Nikolai Tolstoy whose flamboyant style made him a perfect 'Prince Rupert'. When it became clear that Peter was not going to tolerate him bucking his authority, Tolstoy began to recruit on his own account in the West Country. The organization he formed, the King's Army of the West, did not long survive; the Sealed Knot undertook one joint muster with it, in 1974, at Nunney Castle. It was not, from an organizational viewpoint, a great success. None of the palace coups caused Peter much concern; he was aware that most of the intrigue was more talk than action, having prudently ensured that his own adherents kept him well informed.

At the beginning of the campaigning season of 1973 Peter relinquished his infantry regiment, which became the King's Lifeguard of Foot, although he continued to take a keen interest in this formation, which maintained an impressively high number on its muster rolls. Numbers, in fact, were such an issue now that Peter found it necessary to divide the troops into tertios (brigades).

The two great musters which established the Sealed Knot as a professional outfit were the week-long festivities which the organization ran at the Tower of London in 1974, and the muster at Windsor to celebrate the Queen's Silver Jubilee in 1977. At the former a pageant and battle were run nightly in the moat just outside the main entrance at Byward Tower, which the public watched from the street. For the participants the opportunity to visit the Tower in costume was enhanced by the presence of the replica of the Golden Hind to which they were given free access. Undoubtedly, however, the highlight of that week was the march down The Mall, drums beating and colours flying, to present a loyal petition to Her Majesty. Peter led the parade on horseback; no squadron of Blues and Royals on Palace duties could have felt prouder than his troops as they left Admiralty Arch, undaunted by the damp weather. It was just this sort of theatrical gesture at which he excelled.

The Windsor muster was principally arranged by George Stevenson, who now styled himself Director General of the Sealed Knot. With Peter he negotiated a role in the celebrations far wider than just the battle which they planned. The Sealed Knot played a significant role, lining the route which the Royal Family took as they walked up to light the beacon which signalled the start of a nationwide blaze of celebration. As a bonus, and to Peter's delight, the horses were given permission to exercise on the Queen's Ride. One fine summer morning he led his cavalry on a gallop up to the famous statue of George III.

'I really believe,' he wrote to Alastair Bantock in November, '. . . that we have done a good job vice Nat. Service. How we have done so well with such a lack of the traditional officer corps is a mystery to me.' The machinations of the Inner Council were, however, starting to pall. 'I mean,' he wrote to Bantock in November 1977, 'to leave the Inner Council . . . AGMs are anathema to me also. At heart, I fear I am an autocratic old thing.' On 28 February 1978 he resigned from the Inner Council for although he wanted to remain titular head of the Sealed Knot, he was anxious to dispense with the day-to-day running of the organization. There were rumours that Bantock was trying to usurp him. Peter wrote to him in December that year: 'Yes, I had heard from some kind friends that you were moving heav'n and earth to be made C-G, but was content to suppose that you knew best! God knoweth I am very far from wishing to cling to office.' Thereafter, although he kept his finger on the pulse, he did not interfere with the workings of the Inner Council which had already existed far longer than its seventeenth-century counterpart.

He derived greatest pleasure from those campaigns and training weekends where there was no public and he could try out the paces of his soldiers. In 1974 the Captain Generall's Lifeguard of Horse was raised. Although nominally a Royalist unit, it fought on the Parliamentarian side where required, and ultimately became Waller's Horse. The new regiment embarked on a series of training exercises in which Peter enthusiastically took part. Chief among these were weekends spent on Exmoor where an exercise would be devised and the participants given objectives to achieve. Peter liked to end the day victorious on top of Dunkery Beacon. Such exercises served as a reminder to those volunteers who were used to performing to scripts that there was no substitute for training, vigilance and good leadership.

These evolutions were close to what he had originally had in mind – groups trained in the war gamer's art performing in the field what he had had to do with models and dice on a sand table. On only one occasion, at Ross-on-Wye, did he succeed in persuading the entire Sealed Knot to perform a war game. With umpires scattered across the field the armies set about each other, only to be sent back to the start line for performing manoeuvres unknown in the seventeenth century. It was torture for the troops, but the umpires had a wonderful time.

In the early years there were three major campaign re-enactments, which fell outside the period of the Civil War. Killiecrankie, originally fought in the Jacobite rising of 1689, was re-staged in the Scottish Highlands in 1974. Peter was on horseback throughout and rarely sober, trying to anaesthetize the pain of his ulcerated leg. It was a hilarious few days and on one occasion Peter, sitting on the parapet of a bridge resting, observed the approach of Marcus Hinton at the head of his Greycoats. Hinton, a dapper figure, asked which way they were meant to be going, whereupon Peter wickedly pointed back the way they had come. Solemnly, Hinton about-faced his troops and began his countermarch, to Peter's great amusement.

In 1975 the society staged a major pageant at Sedgemoor. Written and choreographed by David Chandler, this gorgeously accoutred display told the story of the whole Sedgemoor campaign of 1685, beginning with the skirmish at Norton St Philip. Although this event ranked as one of the best pageants the Sealed Knot ever staged it was less popular with the participants because it was so tightly scripted. It was, however, a huge success with the crowd.

In 1978 the exploits of the USS *Ranger* and its captain John Paul Jones were commemorated in a re-enactment of his landing at Whitehaven in 1778. For this event some members of the Sealed Knot worked on mid-eighteenth-century drill formations using Brown Bess muskets and borrowed uniforms from Stanley Kubrick's film *Barry Lyndon* – for which many of the costumes, thanks to David Chandler, were stored at RMA Sandhurst. For a season or so a small cadre of Knotters became the Seventeenth Foot (the Tigers) and practised by putting on small displays in the Midlands.

All these enterprises had Peter's full support. If his major interest was the Civil War he was also extremely knowledgeable about warfare up to the end of the Napoleonic period, and he war-gamed the whole era; his persona on the war-gaming table for the War of the Austrian Succession (1745), for instance, was Field Marshal Graf von Grunt.

When the Sealed Knot had been founded his friend and collaborator John Tucker had predicted that the organization would only last ten years, which is perhaps why Peter had given himself ten years at the head of the Inner Council. It was clear, by then, that Tucker's assessment had been pessimistic.

What Peter could not have predicted was that there would be so many people who wanted to be part of the Sealed Knot; what neither he nor they understood was how much the society reflected his own vision and leadership. Like the great actor he was, he revelled in the role of Captain Generall – his was a universally recognized figure, beloved and revered in equal measure – but the mechanics of keeping the organization going had become too serious.

He wanted to try to recapture the lightness of spirit that had informed the original venture. What, at the age of sixty-two, he no

238

longer craved was the concomitant responsibility of leadership – the background tasks that made the organization run smoothly. Henceforth he distanced himself from the quotidian problems of the Knot and left the mechanics to his younger, more energetic, followers.

Chapter Twenty

The Last Hurrah

When Peter left Sandhurst in 1968 he had embarked on a career as a self-employed military historian. He had a fine track record which covered a considerable spectrum – as author, lecturer and consultant he was in great demand from the moment he made it known that he was available. Anxious to ensure that he had a steady supply of projects to work on, he accepted any offer of work which interested him and soon discovered that he was finding it difficult to meet publishers' deadlines.

His agent, Bertie van Thal of London Management, an experienced mentor, deflected some of the pressure, but nonetheless by 1974 he was farming work out in order to get drafts completed on time. A glance at his output over these years is instructive: in 1970 *Cropredy Bridge 1644* (with Margaret Toynbee), *Marston Moor 1644* and *History of the British Army* (with Lieutenant Colonel J.P. Lawford); in 1972 *Washington's Army*; in 1973 *John Cruso, Militarie Instructions for the Cavall'rie* (with Lawford) and *Armies of the English Civil War, Blücher's Army, Wellington's Masterpiece* (with Lawford), *The War Game* (which he edited, but to which he was also a contributor) and *The Machinery of War*; in 1974 *The English Civil War* (with Richard Holmes), *Atlas of the Second World War, Strangers in Oxford* (with Toynbee), *The Cavalier Army* (with Wilfred Emberton); in 1977 *A Dictionary of Battles*, vols 1 and 2; in 1978 vol. 3 of the *Dictionary, Sieges of the Great Civil War* (with Emberton); in 1981 *Civil War England, D-Day, The Fighting Man.*

Between 1970 and 1974 he travelled regularly to London where he was editor for Purnell's *History of the First World War* and editor-in-chief for the Orbis part-work *World War II.*

The pressure was not eased by his decision to write a historical

240

novel, a potboiler, which remains unpublished. The project gave him much pleasure, however, since he indulged in his fantasy – to live in the seventeenth century and fight in the seminal battles of the Civil War. He had patently given some thought to the military mind of the period, as shown by this excerpt from a letter written in November 1973 about the Royalist march on York in 1644:

I guess the Army marched in Battle Order, Right Wing leading. When P[rince] R[upert] got to the holding position he left the R Wing of Horse to 'amuse' the enemy, giving them orders himself. Goring then took over as advanced guard, possibly overtaking Tillier to do so . . . Rupert would be with the leading cavalry and place the screen then push on, encouraging H[orse] and F[oot] as he passed. As his Adv. Gd. Reached Ure, Swale or Ouse he would be near to see how it went. That, at any rate, is how I would play it. Keep well up behind the leading troops; don't get committed, but be there to <u>push</u> them on, solve their problems; help them; watch them; weigh them up; stick for the laggards/carrots for the good. Get to know a newish army and see who's to be trusted. Useful summer days for a commander.

Fairfax was a lively commander. In his shoes I'd have said to my 2 i/c. Bring them back. I'm going ahead to see what's up. I'll keep you in the picture. I'm sure that was his form. He then went off with his Lifeguard leaving Lambert or some steady old file to turn his troops round and hurry after him . . .

The Screen having done its job would follow the rest of Rupert's Army – naturally. The Adv. Gd. Became the Rear Guard.

Here, as Wedgwood observed, is the perfect conjunction of his military experience and the historian; leadership does not change, only technology.

Ben the Alsatian developed epilepsy in 1975 and had to be put down. They had recently acquired a rescue dog of uncertain pedigree – Peter suspected that a setter and a whippet were involved – and this new addition to the household became a source of great joy. Peter called him Dobson because of his resemblance to the dogs in William Dobson's Civil War portraits. As time went by, Dobson acquired other names: Abelard because he had been neutered and Talbot because Peter thought he looked like the mythical beast on pub signs. Abelard Talbot Dobson became his boon companion, always at his heels at home or at musters. Peter claimed he had the same sense of humour as Buster Keaton because of his deadpan stare.

Joan's domestic burden increased during the 1970s when Marilyn's marriage foundered. Peter's contribution was to involve Marilyn's children in the Sealed Knot by dressing them up in uniform. He had always taken a detached view of Joan's previous marriage; if Bertie Rathbone had cause to telephone, Peter would summon Joan with the words: 'It's for you. It's yer 'usband!' He bore with equanimity Joan's occasional absences to help out during family crises – provided that his own needs were fully catered for before she left. Her tasks would include towing the caravan to a Sealed Knot muster and leaving it there, with sufficient provisions for Peter, for the weekend. Their frequent visitors enjoyed excellent hospitality: Earl Grey tea and hot-buttered crumpets were a signature dish, following which the Piesporter – Peter's favourite wine – appeared.

Despite the amount of work he had on hand, Peter's financial situation was causing concern. Whilst he had been employed, one way or another, by the Government, his salary was taxed at source and he thought no further about it. Once he became self-employed this was no longer the case but as soon as cheques arrived, they were spent. Nothing was set aside for the day when the tax man might call. By the mid 1970s the situation was parlous and Bank House had to be sold. For a while it looked as though they could do a deal with some Arab contacts, brokered by George Stevenson, which would have resulted in the purchase of Cuckfield Park, a large house with enough room to provide a home for Peter and Joan, and a headquarters for the Sealed Knot with a living history centre. In May 1977, however, the plan fell through.

They sold Bank House later that year and moved into a flat in Twyning Manor, not far from Ripple. It would be their last home. Peter had to sell half his books as well as other treasures but it was still, he said, like trying to fit a quart into a half pint pot.

As this personal crisis reached its height, Peter attended a Burma Star Association dinner in his honour on 22 May in Inverness. This involved Joan driving 1,029 miles in two days, but it was a significant occasion, reported in the local newspaper which published an interview with Peter:

Referring to the Burma Campaign, Young said that it had been the most important campaign of the war . . . the fighting in Burma was worse than he had seen anywhere else in the war.

242

Sir Philip Christison, who had written to apologise for being unable to attend, commended the way in which Peter and his men had tackled the battle at Kangaw, 'the fantastic, bitter, Beachwood, the manipulation of the Datang-born Chinese and the bloody repulse of the Kamikazi Jap attack on Hill 170'.

When this letter was read out to the assembled company, there was applause. Peter noted caustically to Bantock that he 'only touched one quaich of whisky! My strength of character,' he added bleakly, 'appals me.'

They took a nostalgic route back via Spean Bridge and Achnacarry, but the contemplation of his illustrious wartime career was cut short by the brutal reality of his circumstances and he spent most of the summer house-hunting, an occupation he detested all the more since it took him away from his writing.

Increasingly he suffered the minor aches and ailments of advancing age; a knee injury he had sustained during the battle at Windsor refused to mend and his leg continued to bother him. He was also going deaf in his right ear. These harbingers of old age were not welcome and when he rode at musters he continued to assuage the pain with alcohol which was unwise since horses and strong drink do not go well together, and on more than one occasion he came to grief.

Whatever the state of his health he continued to play a major role in the running of the Sealed Knot, often as a reluctant arbiter in the resolution of clashes and quarrels. He also corresponded energetically with many of his old soldiers and their reminiscent letters clearly brought back many memories of their valiant youth together – Christopher even did the football pools for him. In 1973 he wrote to Ted Piggott in response to a question from him:

> I was an ambitious soldier and I make no bones about it. Rank meant Power, and being a self-confident bastard (the words of one of my ex-girlfriends) I reckoned myself more fit to exercise command than most of the others I saw trying to do it, and for that reason strove to get on! It seems very brash looking back on it.

His old comrades were, like him, looking back affectionately on their wartime service; Ted McGovern wrote copiously to Peter even though his eyesight was failing. In 1985 he wrote:

I certainly wouldn't have missed my experiences with [6 Troop] for anything in the world. They were indeed very, very special and my admiration for all concerned is something that will remain with me for the rest of my natural life.

I wouldn't blame you if you were to call me a silly emotional Bugger, except for the fact that deep down inside you, your feelings are exactly the same.

They were your men, every one of them Peter, all of whom would have gone to the ends of the earth with you, and in fact many did, and never returned.

To his younger correspondents who had not known him during the War Peter's recollections of army life were wry:

I suppose that in a generation or so people will be writing novels featuring the Commando soldiers of WWII. I wonder what sort of lecherous rake-hell they will make of your C-G!! (in fact . . . I was extremely strait-laced in my youth! And always said what I thought, regarding tact as no virtue). I have changed my mind about THAT – with advancing years!

Of his medals he wrote in 1975:

I got my DSO at Dieppe as a Major; when I was a Lt-Colonel I was recommended (twice) for ye [sic] same (Normandy). But it got away. I expect I have often told you that I have three <u>MC</u>s – of which I am inordinately vaine [sic] – and I was recommended for one in 1940, wch also got away. I have also awarded myself the Forlorne Hope twice, and am v. Bolshy at being so undervalued. In fact I am not only a Gong-Hunter but a Gong SNOB. Why, I demand of myself, do people put up with me? How can I live with myself? I must be singularly insensitive. I suppose it is my warped sense of humour that permits me to survive with equanimity.

In 1979 he attended a dinner at the Mansion House and noted proudly that 'nobody present had as many gongs on his tail-coat as our modest hero.'

He was gratified to receive unexpectedly several Polish awards in recognition of his services to Poles during the Second World War which, literally, landed on his door mat during 1979, 1980 and 1981.

As he wrote when the first of them arrived:

> The President of the Republic of Poland (in Exile) has had the good taste to award me the CROSS OF FREEDOM AND INDEPENDANCE [sic] WITH SWORDS for participation in the fight for freedom of Poland during second world war 1939-1945. They have sent me the Diploma, but unfortunately 'The new consignment of these decorations is still at the factory'. I long to see my latest acquisition!

There is something disarming about the complete candour with which he confesses to a weakness which might otherwise seem rather tasteless.

It would be wrong to conclude, however, that there was no longer any fire in his belly. In 1979 he wrote to Piggott:

> Time takes its toll. I am not that fit – tho' I can still climb on to a horse! Smart – hardly. Fiery glint: I have delivered several good bollockings this summer – does the liver a World of good. Retired Schoolmaster: Not on your Nelly. Take a look at my Kindly Blue Eyes next time we meet! Inside I am still the same chap you knew, and though some of my teeth are false (!) I can still bite.

In August 1979, he was devastated when Lord Louis Mountbatten was murdered by the IRA. At the Bank Holiday muster in Oxford the Sealed Knot held a minute's silence in tribute to Mountbatten. He was gratified to be given a seat in Westminster Abbey for the funeral, in his capacity as a Vice-President of the Commando Association. 'It was,' he told Bantock, 'unforgettable.'

He continued to work hard for he was much in demand. He set the questions for Mastermind contestants twice. When he understandably interpreted *The English Civil War* as being about the military aspects of the conflict the contestant, who did not do well, complained that the questions had not encompassed the wider political issues that she had studied.

In 1980 negotiations began for a film being produced in Ireland called *The Year of the French* which concerned the uprising of 1798: a small French force had landed in Ireland with the intention of surprising the English garrison and fomenting rebellion among the Irish. Some of the soldiers were to be members of the Sealed Knot, and Peter was asked to be Military Consultant on the production. Accordingly, he went over to Ireland for the filming, accompanied by Alastair Bantock who had acted as his adjutant-cum-quartermaster throughout the preliminary negotiations. The filming was done, as far as possible, on the site of the original landings in Co Mayo and the two men therefore found a hotel in Ballina where they could stay in some comfort, for, as Peter said, 'I don't want to get involved in the day to day running of the camp, and transporting of the troops to the battlefield.'

It was hard work, leavened by some lively evenings in the bar. After Bantock had returned to England Peter remained behind and continued his adventures alone. On 25 August 1981 he wrote from the hotel to Bantock:

> There was a drama yesterday when I took it upon myself . . . to dismiss the British Horse and Foot, who had marched twice along a valley where the midges ate man and horse alive. They were incredible. Got in the throat – everywhere. (Footnote: When I got back to the car I rubbed BRANDY all over my visage, which put an effective end to my sufferings – rather to my surprise.) My horse was most docile – would walk calmly behind the drums. Ignored colours. Even[tually] he went crazy, and his saddle slipt [sic]. I held onto his mane and lowered myself over the port bow, escaping an almighty crash. Yes, I appeared as a redcoat, and on horseback. Mustache survived. Offered to take it off for £7.50 (sterling), but Niall declined this good offer . . . I expect to leave next Saturday, if I am not under close arrest!

In April 1977 Roy Plomley invited him on to his programme *Desert Island Discs*. The two men were friends and Plomley drew out from him a charming interview; Peter was in expansive and genial form, his ready laughter lurking in his voice throughout. His musical selections were at once eccentric and typical – his first choice, possibly unique in the history of the programme, was the mating call of the Hulot Gibbon with which he hoped to lure the local wildlife and forge some kind of contact, a leadership challenge of some magnitude! Amongst his more conventional musical choices were the 'Beggar's Opera', the 'Magic Flute', Handel's 'Water Music' and Ravel's 'Bolero'. For his luxury he chose a ton of treasure – doubloons, he specified, from about 1642, which he could pile up

246

and use to war-game with the monkeys; in the event that he was rescued he would be rich which, given his straitened circumstances doubtless weighed with him at the time.

He was in fact a frequent contributor to programmes on radio and television, and he travelled extensively lecturing both on the Second World War and the Civil War. One TV project was a series of programmes with the presenter Frank Delaney in which both men, in dinner jackets, pored over a sand table and re-fought battles from every period. Peter was not a great fan of the Romans, so the episode which examined the siege of Alesia in 52 BC, resulting in the capture of the Vercingetorix, showed him in fine debunking form. In 1983 he became involved in *By the Sword Divided*, a TV production set in the Civil War. Filmed at Rockingham Castle, it featured a number of battle scenes for which the Sealed Knot provided the soldiers. Peter was the historical consultant, a role he loved.

He also joined a group which was fighting the construction of a road across the southern part of the battlefield at Naseby. It was a long and bitter struggle which they ultimately lost – the A14 now runs through the rear of the Parliamentarian army's position and as a result some vital archaeology has been lost. The fight to preserve the battlefield at Naseby, undertaken by local landowners and supported by many eminent historians, had one notable result: the foundation of the Battlefields Trust. Coincidentally, at the time he was finishing his book on the Battle at Naseby, the last of his books on the great Civil War battles.

But by now he was undeniably slowing down. His health was becoming a cause for concern and in 1982 he spent some time in Cheltenham Hospital suffering from gout. While they were diagnosing his condition they also discovered that he had an enlarged heart and for both of these conditions he was prescribed pills, which he hated. Feeling that he lacked the energy to exercise his authority, he went to the Sealed Knot AGM, held at the August Bank Holiday muster at Cropredy Bridge, and announced his resignation as Captain Generall, wishing, he said, to revert to his substantive rank of Brigadier. 'I am sorry to say,' he wrote, 'that this was ill-supported.' Since he had by now sold the caravan even attending musters was becoming problematic – his 'private army' had outgrown him and had a life of its own.

It has been said that the creation of the Sealed Knot trivialized Peter's academic achievements as a military historian, but it is also true that the Knot as Peter envisaged it made history accessible and attractive to people who would not otherwise have had an opportunity to come to grips with this period of English history. That the organization grew so rapidly from its inception showed that he had struck a chord in the population at large; that the Sealed Knot continues to thrive and perform nearly forty years after it was founded proves that, whatever Peter's original intentions might have been, his private army fulfils a role for which there is a continuing public appetite.

Many of the present generation of Civil War historians have, at one time or another, been members of a re-enactment society – and most probably the Sealed Knot. They are the possessors of Peter's greatest legacy, his knowledge and enthusiasm. His own seminal works on the period have spawned others which build on his scholarship. There are other, lesser known, works which would not have seen the light of day without his generous sponsorship; books such as *Love Loyalty* by Wilf Emberton, published as a result of Peter's support, is a beautifully written account of the siege of Basing House. Many are the theses which benefited from Peter's wise counsel; he gave unstintingly of his time and research.

During the first decade of the Knot's existence, when Peter was still in full and joyful command of the organization, his ebullient presence was not only visible but audible. He had a vast repertoire of songs and he would stand outside his caravan on a sunny Saturday morning, before the commanders met to discuss the script for the coming battle, singing at the top of his not inconsiderable voice. Favourite tunes included 'I'm only a coster monger' which was an old music hall tune he had learnt in his childhood, most of the baritone canon of Gilbert and Sullivan, and *The Beggar's Opera* for which he had a particular fondness, identifying, he once confessed, with the rogue MacHeath in particular. He had first seen *The Beggar's Opera* before the war at the Lyric Theatre in Hammersmith and had been taken with both the honest way Gay treated the Hogarthian subject matter and the robust music, which portrayed the period more realistically than the 'folksier' approach which often characterised plays of that period. He particularly liked the two heroines, Polly Peachum and Lucy Lockett, and sang 'How happy could I be with either, if other dear charmer were away' with sincerity.

He loved talking to Knotters, finding out where they were from and why they had joined. If they had questions he was delighted to answer them. He took his army seriously, applying the same principles to this enterprise as he had to his wartime command, making sure that he met as many of his Knotting army as possible. Even after he ceased to have any formal function in the Sealed Knot his advice was still sought over certain promotions or decorations. He had always weighed up the people involved and his pronouncements were incisive and accurate.

In the early days he was not above taking credit for the weather at musters which rarely let them down. He prayed, he said, to War God, Sky Father and St Mary the Virgin of Ripple. This triumvirate covered the religious sensibilities of every possible atavistic warrior, which was doubtless why it was so effective.

One of his generals, Arthur Starkie, once likened him to Falstaff. 'Nonsense,' Peter retorted. 'Falstaff was a coward – I have never been afraid of anything in my life. Sir Toby Belch, now there's a character after my own heart.' If Peter had never been afraid of bullets, he certainly confessed to a fear of heights, and yet his sympathy with Belch's character might also be somewhat misleading – there is nothing in Shakespeare's character which compares with Peter's kindness and generosity of spirit.

His health continued in a gentle decline. A long battle with his weight and blood pressure was never quite successful, mostly because he refused to give up drinking. However, in 1984 he finally gave up whisky for Lent and found that he lost the taste for it, perhaps just as well since towards the end of that year he was diagnosed with diabetes and angina. He owed his continued periods of good health to Joan who, as he happily acknowledged, looked after him 'superlatively well'.

His wartime comrades continued to be solicitous of his well-being. When he had a bout of pneumonia in 1985 Piggott wrote: 'I am writing this to let you know that if there is any task I could do on your behalf – let me know – I will come "P.D.Q."!'

McGovern wrote: 'You can if you wish call me a sentimental old "Bugger" . . . my main concern is you, and I really would appreciate it if you could . . . keep me informed as to your improvement.'

Christopher merely commented that he was not surprised that Peter was ill because he was not there to look after him. Joan might have looked askance at such a statement, but would have understood the underlying affection which brought it forth.

Peter and Joan lived quietly and happily, going for walks on Bredon Hill when Peter's health allowed and attending those Sealed Knot musters which were within easy reach, where they were always accorded a great welcome. Peter was still a well-known presence even though he began to think that the newer generation of Knotters would not know who he was; on one occasion Arthur Starkie walked around with him and found, not greatly to his own surprise but to Peter's great pleasure, that everyone did indeed still recognize their erstwhile Captain Generall.

In 1986 Dobson fell ill and they feared that they would lose him, so much so that their neighbours dug him a grave. To Peter's relief, however, he recovered – he had been so upset at the thought of losing him that he had not been able to help with the grave and did not even know where it was. 'Wife,' he wrote to Ted Piggott, 'thinks he is deaf. More like obstinate I should say.' (He referred to Joan as 'Wife' and she retaliated by calling him 'Blind Pugh'.) In April 1988 Dobson did, finally, die at the age of fifteen. He had been Peter's familiar for the better part of thirteen years and he was sorely missed. They decided not to replace him; they occasionally entertained a house guest in the form of Marilyn's West Highland terrier, Mia, and that seemed enough for them.

In his seventy-fourth year, Peter was now too infirm to travel far; to his other woes he had added attacks of vertigo. At the end of August, however, he was feeling better, having recovered from a urinary infection and was able to catch up on his correspondence. When he heard from an old soldier who wanted to see a brief history of 3 Commando in print, he wrote to Ted Piggott: 'I have no intention of writing one!'

The end came suddenly. In mid-September Peter awoke in the night suffering stomach pains and was taken to the local cottage hospital. They were unable to do anything for him and he was moved to Cheltenham General hospital where he died on 13 September 1988. A post-mortem examination determined the cause of his death as a ruptured aneurism in his stomach.

There was an enormous sense of shock – within the Sealed Knot there had been a feeling that he would be there for ever. Three years earlier, on the occasion of his seventieth birthday, he had been presented with four engraved crystal goblets by the Chairman of the Inner Council, Dennis Spencer. Accepting them, Peter had said that the male side of the Young family was singularly misnamed since they suffered from acute longevity. The editor of the Orders of the Daye, Rory Kehoe, wrote: 'I think that when all around is in turmoil and a – movin' we, the Knot, are fortunate to have with us such a reliable and unmovable leader.' Coming to terms with the death of a man whom all the obituarists described as vital and exuberant was not easy. Peter Bentham Hill, then Agitant Generall of the Sealed Knot, expressed the feelings of the membership when he wrote: 'Peter acknowledged the Sealed Knot as a revolt against the times in which we live; he always emphasised the fun of it all and whilst we shall be sad for a while at his passing, we are the richer and grateful for having known him.'

Peter had always been a regular church-goer, his faith being lightly worn but deeply felt. An appropriate commemoration for his life seemed to be the dedication of a window in his beloved church in Ripple, and in 1990 this came to pass. Fittingly, both the great enterprises of his life are represented there. On one side there is the Commando insignia and on the other the arms of the Sealed Knot with its motto 'Fare fac reminiscere'. Taken in conjunction with the inscription on the Commando monument in Westminster Abbey, reiterated in the window at Ripple, there is no better encapsulation of his life: 'They performed whatsoever their King commanded'.

Bibliography

Much of the material for this book has come from unpublished sources. I have only included here published works which I have used for reference or which contain direct biographical information about Peter Young.

Dupuy, Ernest and Dupuy, Trevor, *The Encyclopedia of Military History*, Macdonald and Co., 1970.

Durnford-Slater, John, *Commando*, Greenhill Books, 2002.

Ford, Ken, and Gerrard, Howard, *D-Day 1944: Sword Beach and the British Airborne Landings*, Osprey Publishing, 2002.

Glubb, John Bagot, *A Soldier with the Arabs*, Hodder and Stoughton, 1957.

Young, Peter, *Bedouin Command*, William Kimber, 1956.

Young, Peter, *Storm from the Sea*, William Kimber, 1958.

Young, Peter, *Commando, Purnell's History of the Second World War No 7*, Macdonald and Co., 1969.

Young, Peter, *The Arab Legion*, Osprey Books, 1972.

Index

253